The Supreme Court and Social Science

UNIVERSITY OF ILLINOIS PRESS
Urbana Chicago London

THE
Supreme Court
AND
Social Science

Paul L. Rosen

In Memory of Martin Jay Rosen

Contents

Preface

In the landmark case of Brown v. Board of Education of Topeka,[1] decided in 1954, the U.S. Supreme Court ruled that racial segregation in public schools violated the equal-protection clause of the Fourteenth Amendment and was therefore unconstitutional. It was immediately apparent that the import of this case was truly epochal. For the Supreme Court after much hesitation had boldly confronted the endemic disease of racism, giving for the first time emphatic legal expression to the general principle, as stated by Alexander Bickel, "that it is wrong and ultimately evil to classify people invidiously by race."[2] While this principle ostensibly reflects one of the self-evident truths of American political thought, or at least embodies a truth that is not incompatible with a common-sense appreciation of political civility, needless to say, its legacy over the past eighteen years has been largely disputatious. A practical plan for eliminating *de facto* racial segregation in all public schools has yet to be devised. And although it is not surprising that a legal principle may be formulated more readily and easily than it can be implemented, a curious aspect of the Brown case today is that the wide-ranging controversy sparked by the Court's nomological statement that segregation was harmful still remains to be settled.

The root of this controversy derives from the fact that the Court's finding of segregation's harmfulness was not only a nomological statement but a sociological observation as well. In simple and eloquent language Chief Justice Earl Warren wrote

[1] Brown v. Board of Education of Topeka, 347 U.S. 483 (1954).
[2] Alexander M. Bickel, "Desegregation: Where Do We Go from Here?" *New Republic*, Feb. 7, 1970, p. 21.

on behalf of a unanimous Court that to separate children "from others of similar age and qualifications solely because of their race generates a feeling of inferiority as to their status in the community that may affect their hearts and minds in a way unlikely ever to be undone."[3] But this factual finding of harm was not based simply on an intuitive or common-sense understanding of the effects of racial segregation. Instead the Court's finding of fact was attributed to footnote eleven, referring to seven social science studies.

The troubled and sensitive nature of race relations in the United States, especially in the South, almost guaranteed that a desegregation decision would stir deep feelings of anxiety and hostility among those it touched most closely. As might be expected, many southerners were quick to berate the Brown decision as an unwarranted and illegitimate political intrusion by the federal judiciary into the internal affairs of the states. Not only did the substance of the Court's ruling draw adverse reactions, but the form of the chief justice's opinion was also bitterly criticized. The Court's use of modern social science was singled out as an unconventional and devious departure from constitutional law and was said to represent "a reasoning process which was heretofore unknown to jurisprudence. . . ."[4] For that matter, even some prominent northern liberal jurists who warmly applauded the decision made known their objections and reservations to the Court's conspicuous use of social science. No doubt the Court's reliance on social science findings exacerbated the legal and political misgivings engendered by the case, which would have been pronounced and strenuous enough even if the chief justice had contented himself with writing a pedestrian legal opinion.

Because the opinion foreshadowed a determined frontal assault upon the entire system of racial segregation, its detractors naturally looked for any ostensible legal irregularity or novelty to serve as an excuse for attacking the high bench. In this instance

---

[3] Brown v. Board of Education of Topeka, 347 U.S. 483, 494 (1954).

[4] Eugene Cook and William I. Potter, "The School Segregation Cases: Opposing the Opinion of the Supreme Court," in Hubert H. Humphrey, ed., *School Desegregation: Documents and Commentaries* (New York: Thomas Y. Crowell, 1964), p. 36.

modern social science provided critics with an opportune weapon. Yet the issues raised by the Court's use of social science, colored as they are by the strong emotions engendered by any discussion touching on the theme of race, deserve far more serious and extended thought than was generally afforded by the ensuing debate—much of it having been conducted in polemical and in some instances vituperative tones. Overlooked, so it seems, were the simple facts that the Supreme Court has never interpreted the Constitution solely in terms of strict legal criteria and that it has invariably made constitutional law on the basis of extralegal facts of one kind or another. Furthermore, while it is true that the Court's use of modern social science was in a sense a novel departure in the process of judicial interpretation, many observers failed to realize that it was the logical product of the slow but steady "factual" growth of American jurisprudence throughout the past half-century.

Indeed, the Brown case, as we shall see, was no fortuitous legal aberration but was instead the fruit of the collective hopes and efforts of a distinguished group of progressive jurists. Included in this group were such eminent figures as Roscoe Pound, Louis D. Brandeis, and Benjamin Cardozo, who were largely responsible for the development of the sociological school of jurisprudence, which stood for a more enlightened understanding of the nature and role of law in a rapidly changing democratic society. The impact of this school of legal thought and the early work of these men prepared the way for the Court's use of social science in 1954. Once this becomes evident, the groundwork will have been laid for an assessment of the significance of the Court's use of social science in this historic case. At the same time a perspective will be available for charting the problems and rich possibilities inherent in the relationship between constitutional law and social science. Some of the problems still remain to be clarified and solved, as the Court's modest use of social science after the Brown case presumably suggests. Yet none of these problems are insurmountable. And today it is vitally important that they be faced, for there are many critical and troublesome areas of constitutional law badly in need of the kind of factual illumination that can be provided by social science findings in the hands of a willing Court. There is good reason to believe that if the Supreme Court as an institution is able to transcend repeated attempts to humble and demean it, some issuing from the nation's highest political office, modern social science, instead of compounding the problems of judicial interpretation, will appreciably lighten the august judgmental burden the Court has on many past occasions carried so well.

I am happy to express my immeasurable indebtedness to the many scholars who have fashioned the vast and exciting body of literature dealing with law, social science, and the Court. I have drawn freely on their work. Several of my Carleton University colleagues patiently shared some of the trying moments that went into the writing of this book. Professors Claude Ake and Jon Alexander deserve a particular note of thanks for their gracious help. Professor Felicia J. Deyrup of the Graduate Faculty of the New School for Social Research carefully read the entire manuscript and offered a number of valuable suggestions. The good humor and wisdom of Ira Glasser, executive director of the New York Civil Liberties Union, was always there in the clutch. And finally my most profound debt is to my parents, who put up with my early eccentricities, and to Virginia, who puts up with them now.

It would be foolhardy and impossible to declare a moratorium on science as was proposed in the 1930's to cure the problems we then faced. It would be equally foolhardy and likewise impossible to declare a moratorium on emerging jurisprudence, as it struggles to meet the challenges of our time, which are so different from those of even our immediate ancestors and even of our youth.

EARL WARREN
"Science and the Law:
Change and the Constitution"

CHAPTER ONE

The Court, Judicial Interpretation, and Extralegal Facts

No other deliberative body has been as alive and receptive to the responsibilities of power and the spirit of idealism as the U.S. Supreme Court. In acting to defend and implement the highest ideals of the Constitution, the high bench has often spoken with fervor and gravity without in any way depreciating its effectiveness as a coordinate branch of the federal triumvirate. Indeed, the idealism of the Court accounts substantially for its remarkable authority and is the chief source of its greatness. Obviously the learned opinions of the Court are not idle speculation but are charged by the power of judicial review, with all the immediacy, relevance, and excitement that is characteristic of political action. By its exercise of the power of judicial review the Court has at times been vehemently criticized for being a "superlegislature," but to date it has displayed an uncanny facility for weathering the severest polemical attacks. The Court must always contemplate unfavorable or even hostile reactions to its decisions, because in reviewing the constitutionality of legislation, among other matters, it will sometimes pass judgment on legislative policy. It thereby substitutes its own notion of desirable policy for that of a legislative body whose mandate, unlike that of the Court, is derived directly from the people. Today, however, only disingenuous and shrill critics would argue that the Court could exercise judicial power without playing at least a modest political role in the affairs of the nation. It goes without saying that the Court can hardly interpret and administer the Constitution by doing less. For the Constitution is itself a declaration of national policy with broad guidelines that determine both the substance of policy and its procedural application.

It is ironic, however, that although the Court functions often as a broker between the dictates of political exigency and the lofty goals of the American political credo, it has long paid lip service to the notion that "political questions" are definitionally nonjusticiable and must be settled by some other branch of government. Thus, for example, very early in its history the Court ruled that it could not determine whether or not a treaty had been violated[1] and that the president without the aid of the judiciary must determine the existence of an emergency.[2] The Court has also held that where two state governments are vying for legitimacy, the discretionary action of the president in the dispute is beyond its power of review.[3] Even the question of whether the steps in the constitutional amending process have been satisfied, the Court has said, is none of its business.[4] More recently, the Court decided that the problem of equitable congressional districts was entwined in a "political thicket" and could not be adjudicated by a federal court.[5] But in the case of Baker v. Carr, decided in 1962, the Court suddenly found that the thicket of redistricting was not as thorny as it had previously supposed; it was indeed apparent that "[m]uch confusion results from the capacity of the 'political question' label to obscure the need for case-by-case inquiry."[6] Accordingly the Court reversed itself and held that inequitable representation surely did present a justiciable issue.

Clearly enough, the issues the Court has formally defined as political are those that it prefers not to adjudicate for fear that its decisions might be defied. Therefore, instead of being a workable formula that actually restricts the judicial power, it has long been recognized that "political questions" insofar "as they are questions

---

[1] Ware v. Hylton, 3 Dallas 199 (1796).
[2] Martin v. Mott, 12 Wheaton 19 (1827).
[3] Luther v. Borden, 7 Howard 1 (1849).
[4] Coleman v. Miller, 307 U.S. 433 (1939).
[5] Colegrove v. Green, 328 U.S. 549 (1946).
[6] Baker v. Carr, 369 U.S. 186, 210–11 (1962).

which have been adjudicated by the Supreme Court . . . are of necessity justiciable questions."[7] In brief, the "political question" has been an "open sesame word," as one observer put it, that relieves the Court of its responsibility for dealing with an issue and, for the time being, of its control over a problem.[8]

On the other hand, when the Court has decided to grapple with political problems and issues that the executive or legislative branches of government have chosen to ignore, it has, especially in the not too distant past, exercised the governmental initiative with relative vigor. But the Court's excursions into the political arena when it makes what are, in effect, sweeping rules of constitutional law must be delicately timed, because, aside from its moral authority, the Court lacks means for enforcing its decisions. Therefore, while the Court certainly is a political body, it is basically a passive one that needs to bear in mind Justice Harlan F. Stone's much-quoted admonition: "Courts are not the only agency of government that must be assumed to have capacity to govern."[9]

The limitations on the kinds of cases the Supreme Court may hear, as defined by the Constitution, the rules of appellate procedure, and indefinite and makeshift canons of judicial interpretation all contribute to the Court's passivity and reinforce its self-enunciated theme of restraint. Nevertheless, while the Court has often affirmed its reluctance to usurp the legislative function, the occasions are many when the exercise of judicial review did amount to judicial legislation.[10] Curiously, however, although the Supreme Court became consistently active in political matters toward the end of the nineteenth century, the traditional view of the judicial function, which held that the Court did not make but merely found law, persisted long after it had lost its credibility. For that matter, the development and expansion of the power of judicial review in the latter part of the nineteenth century, with its all-critical political implications, occurred almost surrep-

---

[7] Gregory and Charlotte A. Hankin, *Progress of the Law in the United States Supreme Court: 1930–1931* (New York: Macmillan, 1931), p. 413.

[8] Charles Gordon Post, *The Supreme Court and Political Questions* (Baltimore: Johns Hopkins Press, 1936), p. 11.

[9] United States v. Butler, 297 U.S. 1, 87 (1936) (dissenting opinion).

[10] See Fred V. Cahill, Jr., *Judicial Legislation* (New York: Ronald Press, 1952).

titiously. Even the perceptive political analyst Lord Bryce, writing in 1888 after the first momentous phase of the Court's application of judicial review in the defense of private property rights had begun, idealistically saw in this potent political instrument the mechanical scales of justice observed by passionless and impartial judges: "American judges have no will in the matter any more than has an English court when it interprets an Act of Parliament. The will that prevails is the will of the people, expressed in the Constitution which they have enacted. All that the judges have to do is to discover from the enactments before them what the will of the people is, and apply that will to the facts of a given case."[11] Bryce did concede that the broad and ambiguously worded language of the Constitution might complicate the task of judicial interpretation, but he noted that when the "generality of the words leaves open to the interpreting judges a far wider field than is afforded by ordinary statutes," all that is needed is "legal acumen," "judicial fairness," and "a comprehension of the nature and methods of government. . . ."[12]

Even though the Court, as it began to act as a permanent censor of social welfare legislation, was obviously making law, and not in the facile, impartial manner described by Bryce, popular recognition of the Court's political impact was slow in coming. This was so probably because the Court was and still remains, to a large extent, the American rendition of the English monarchy, by definition above the passions and vulgarities of politics. Public awareness of the creative lawmaking consequences of judicial review began to develop only after the emergence in the 1920s of the school of legal realism with its trenchant teachings. A better understanding of the judicial function was fostered by such realists as Karl N. Llewellyn, who favored stripping the law of barren rhetoric and remote usages and defining it as a set of flexible rules that have precise meaning only when prescribed for past acts, as opposed to acts that may be committed in the future. Law, wrote Llewellyn, is not merely a set of general propositions but is more concretely "what . . . officials (judges, sheriffs, clerks, jailers,

---

[11] James Bryce, *The American Commonwealth,* ed. Louis Hacker, 2 vols. (New York: G. P. Putnam's Sons, 1959), 1: 60.
[12] *Ibid.,* p. 61.

lawyers) do about disputes. . . ."[13] Of course, what the Court was doing about the constitutional disputes engendered by the passage of piecemeal social welfare legislation until 1937 was acting as if the Constitution spoke explicitly and exclusively about the sanctity of private property. Obviously, a Court that generally behaved as if the Constitution had designated it to be the vanguard of corporate interests was not likely to admit that in some ways it had become a superlegislature, and that its power to negate law for the purpose of perpetuating an outmoded system of laissez-faire economics was not very different from the express power to enact law.

After a lull in the policy-making output of the Court, brought on by World War II, the activism of the high bench that had for so long buttressed conservative political values was renewed. In the early fifties, however, liberal justices constituted a voting majority, and the Court began to display a special interest in the civil rights of the hopeless, the downtrodden, and the incarcerated. With the appointment of Earl Warren as chief justice in 1953, the Warren Court—as it was referred to thereafter, both in obliquity and admiration—rapidly became the most vigorous governmental guarantor of civil rights in American history. Thus the Court, by exercising the power of judicial review, was able to implement liberal political, social, and economic values as effectively as it had once implemented conservative ones.

The shifting concerns of the Court in the twentieth century— first, its long-standing preoccupation with property rights, then its preoccupation with civil rights under the leadership of Earl Warren, and presently its sounding of the ominous theme of "law and order" under Chief Justice Warren Burger—leave no doubt that the meaning of the Constitution changes or is clarified to a large extent in accord with the value preferences of the justices as they respond to the varied political, economic, and social moods and problems of the times. This is, of course, no novel discovery. Indeed, it is well known that the variegated meanings delivered

---

[13] Karl N. Llewellyn, *The Bramble Bush* (New York: Oceana Publications, 1960), p. 14. There are, however, severe shortcomings in Llewellyn's "realistic" definition, for its logical extension renders official murder, arson, rape, and robbery lawful. See Roscoe Pound, *Justice according to Law* (New Haven, Conn.: Yale University Press, 1951), p. 39.

from the Constitution have not sprung Minerva-like from the body of that document alone. Nor are Supreme Court justices simply the midwives of constitutional change. They are more properly the fathers of constitutional doctrines that are the law of the land. The latitude the justices enjoy in making law flows from the sweeping language of the Constitution, which easily lends itself to divergent interpretations. As Alexander Peckelis has written, "To say that compensation must be 'just,' the protection of the laws 'equal,' punishment neither 'cruel' nor 'unusual,' bails or fines not 'excessive,' searches and seizures not 'unreasonable,' deprivation of life, liberty or property not 'without due process,' is but to give a foundation to the law-making, nay constitution-making, activity of judges, left free to define what is cruel, reasonable, excessive, due, or for that matter, equal."[14]

Even a relatively narrow and tightly worded clause of the Constitution, such as the one dealing with contracts, may be treated as problematic enough to require judicial interpretation. Thus in 1819 Chief Justice John Marshall applied the contract clause to strike down a New York insolvency law, remarking that "the words of the Constitution . . . are express, and incapable of being misunderstood." The words of the contract clause, he added, "admit of no variety of construction, and are acknowledged to apply to that species of contract, an engagement between man and man for the payment of money, which has been entered into by these parties."[15] Nevertheless, Chief Justice Charles Evans Hughes, referring to the same clause in 1934 in the case of Home Building & Loan Association v. Blaisdell, announced, not without irony, that such "prohibition is not an absolute one and is not to be read with literal exactness like a mathematical formula."[16] Be that as it may, the Court has never answered satisfactorily the question of how the broad language of the Constitution or even the relatively more precise language of statutes should necessarily be read. Occasionally it has suggested that there are canons of judicial interpretation that can be utilized, but it seems certain that these are applied or ignored by

[14] Alexander Peckelis, "The Case for a Jurisprudence of Welfare," 11 *Social Research* 312, 315 (1944).

[15] Sturges v. Crowninshield, 4 Wheaton 122, 198 (1819).

[16] Home Building & Loan Association v. Blaisdell, 290 U.S. 398, 428 (1934).

the Court at will.[17] Therefore, particularly since the Constitution is devoid of legal technicalities and "was written to be understood by the voters," its words have been interpreted in a great variety of ways.[18] This should not be very surprising; as Justice Frankfurter has explained, all words "are symbols of meaning." And if "individual words are inexact symbols, with shifting variables, their configuration can hardly achieve invariant meaning or assure definiteness."[19] Moreover, since the words of the Constitution sketch only its bare outlines, it is easy to see why judicial interpretation is not merely a process of legal reasoning but is, above all, a critical political art.

The question remains, however, whether there is something more to the process of judicial interpretation than the flexible language of the Constitution and the input of the justices' value preferences. To be sure, the importance of a justice's political, economic, and social predilections should not be minimized in accounting for the reasons for his vote in a given instance. To date, a considerable body of research has confirmed the obvious: liberal and conservative justices, though such labels are crude at best, tend to vote in a predictable fashion on a wide range of issues, and the ideological balance of the Court dramatically affects its policy-making output. Thus it is obviously true, as Glendon Schubert has noted, that "the main reason for the Taft Court's conservative decisional policies . . . is, of course, that Taft himself and a solid majority of his colleagues were men with what were even for their day quite conservative value preferences. . . ."[20] Yet if one accepts the easy assumption that the justices simply vote their sympathies, then one must also be prepared to accept as adequate explanation that Taft uncharacteristically dissented in the Adkins case,[21] in which a federal minimum-wage law for women and children was invalidated, because he "had a soft spot

[17] See Harry W. Jones, "The Plain Meaning Rule and Extrinsic Aids in the Interpretation of Federal Statutes," 25 *Washington University Law Quarterly* 2 (1939).

[18] United States v. Sprague, 282 U.S. 716, 731 (1931).

[19] Felix Frankfurter, "Reflections on Reading Statutes," in Alan F. Westin, ed., *The Supreme Court: Views from Inside* (New York: W. W. Norton, 1961), p. 75.

[20] Glendon Schubert, *The Constitutional Polity* (Boston: Boston University Press, 1970), p. 91.

[21] Adkins v. Children's Hospital, 261 U.S. 525 (1923).

for women and children."[22] In the same vein, perhaps the conservative Justice James C. McReynolds voted to uphold the constitutionality of a federal bird-protection act, the effect of which enlarged the federal powers,[23] because he was "an inveterate duck hunter."[24] True enough, both Taft and McReynolds probably were voting their idiosyncratic sympathies. But in each instance, as Schubert makes clear, the justice was voting on an issue about which he had a larger personal fund of knowledge than he might have brought to bear on other issues—Taft having served as the chairman of the National War Labor Board and McReynolds having been an avid outdoorsman. This suggests, then, that although the value preferences of the justices do assuredly influence the process of judicial interpretation, another important variable that deserves consideration is the factual understanding or assumptions held by the justices about a given issue, as may be ascertained from the formal statement of facts set forth by the Court in its opinions.

In other words, each time the Supreme Court interprets the Constitution or makes constitutional law, technically it is applying a general legal principle or rule of law derived from the Constitution to a set of specific circumstances that it juridically defines as a fact situation. But constitutional adjudication is usually complicated by the relative ambiguity of general constitutional principles and the absolute uncertainty of all fact situations. Obviously, fact situations cannot be foreseen and determined in advance but require adjudication each time law is applied. More important, since constitutional principles are always applied to facts that cannot be known beforehand, these principles by their very nature cannot be fully known. Indeed, as Edward H. Levi has written, "in an important sense legal rules are never clear, and, if a rule had to be clear before it could be imposed, society would be impossible."[25] Thus the relative ambiguity of the Constitution is one of its virtues because it insures the necessary flexibility that allows the document to embrace unforeseen oc-

---

[22] Schubert, *The Constitutional Polity*, p. 84.
[23] Missouri v. Holland, 252 U.S. 416 (1920).
[24] Schubert, *The Constitutional Polity*, p. 96.
[25] Edward H. Levi, *An Introduction to Legal Reasoning* (Chicago: University of Chicago Press, 1968), p. 1.

currences. But fact situations are also flexible in the sense that their intrinsic uncertainty enables the Court to define them in alternative ways. Facts, contrary to common opinion, are not always objective and self-evident. Indeed, throughout its history the Court has exercised a great deal of discretion in defining basic fact situations. For the most part, they do not, as H. L. A. Hart has observed, "await us already marked off from each other, and labelled as instances of the general rule; nor can the rule itself step forward to claim its own instance."[26]

The general pattern of all legal reasoning, Levi suggests, is itself inseparable from the problem of fact-finding. This pattern, which he calls "reasoning by example," involves three steps: first, a similarity is noted between two cases; second, the rule of law in the first case is announced; and finally, the rule is applied to the second case.[27] Obviously, if the precise meaning of a general rule is to remain constant and unchanging, then the fact situations of two cases decided under the same rule have to be comparable. But since fact situations inevitably change to the point where they become noncomparable, the successful application of a given rule to noncomparable fact situations is itself an indication that the precise meaning of the general rule has changed. And since the precise meaning of a general rule can only be known in the context of specific fact situations, it is readily apparent that fact-finding is a crucial part of legal reasoning. Needless to say, then, a basic problem for the Supreme Court is not whether it will allow fact situations to influence its interpretation of the Constitution, but whether it will in adjudicating any given issue accept a statement of the relevant facts prepared by a lower court or instead set forth its own understanding of the facts.

Ostensibly, however, the primary task of an appellate tribunal is to ascertain whether or not the proper rule of law has been applied to a fact situation defined previously in a lower court. And since the Supreme Court's jurisdiction is mainly appellate, its primary concern would appear at first glance to be the interpretation of law rather than the finding of fact. It should be

[26] H. L. A. Hart, *The Concept of Law* (Oxford: Clarendon Press, 1963), p. 123.

[27] Levi, *Introduction to Legal Reasoning.* p. 2.

noted that the Constitution explicitly grants the Supreme Court appellate jurisdiction "both as to law and fact, with such exceptions and under such regulations as the Congress shall make." The finality of the Court's fact-finding authority is of critical importance because the traditional distinction that has been made between law and fact, the former being prescriptive and the latter descriptive, is largely chimerical. Therefore, while the process of judicial interpretation nominally involves the application of rules of law to fact situations, in practice questions of law and questions of fact impinge upon each other so directly that to prejudge one is to pre-decide the other. In other words, a candid appreciation of the relationship between questions of law and fact leads to the conclusion, as one observer has put it, that the "seemingly rigid dichotomy of law and fact is only a bit of legalistic mummery designed to conceal from the uninitiated the fact that the courts decide these questions about as they wish."[28] Moreover, since questions of law and fact are bound closely together, judicial interpretation may be viewed as a process through which the immediate and precise meaning of a general constitutional principle is derived dialectically from the Court's perception and delineation of the fact situation of a given case.

It follows that while constitutional disputes are necessarily settled within the general framework of law, factual questions arise that may be labeled as legal only if the term is stretched to its furthest limits. In other words, constitutional adjudication, more clearly than statutory adjudication or other kinds of litigation, requires the Court to pass judgment on factual questions that are remote from the field of law and that belong properly to the formal study of politics, sociology, economics, history, psychology, or for that matter to any discipline addressing itself to the manifold problems of human behavior.

To be sure, the high bench from its outset has often made constitutional law on the basis of factual judgments that were not inherently legal; for analytical purposes these will be defined paradigmatically as extralegal. As we shall see, the Court has

---

[28] Ray A. Brown, "Fact and Law in Judicial Review," 56 *Harvard Law Review* 899, 900 (1943).

assessed and defined fact situations in terms of hypotheses, assumptions, and social data that were regarded legally as facts even though they were derived from disciplines or sources plainly not internal to law. From the perspective of traditional American jurisprudence, with its stylistic reliance on mechanistic and syllogistic reasoning, these situations were thought to be beyond its province. Of course, insofar as the Court has used extralegal facts derived, for example, from the extralegal data of history, social Darwinism, or social science, such facts definitionally became legal simply because they were incorporated into law. In this sense the paradigm "extralegal" might be considered a legal misnomer or perhaps a tautology. Yet the paradigm takes this into account and is useful and revealing here because it easily conveys the idea that law cannot be circumscribed by a *cordon sanitaire,* that the borderline between the realms of the legal and nonlegal, especially as far as the Court is concerned, is as it should be—obscure and easily crossed.

Throughout the nineteenth century this border was crossed often and plainly enough when the Court used historical facts that were not a matter of legal record and were not easily associated with any category of legal knowledge. Nevertheless, mainly because history was endemic to constitutional law, its use by the Court attracted little notice.[29] Even to this day the Court's use of historical extralegal facts has never been regarded as an aberration in the normal pattern of constitutional adjudication. History could be taken for granted because the historical perspective was and still is part of the common-sense view of change, be it legal or political. Moreover, history was not apt to be recognized as an extralegal infusion into law because the common-law background of American legal institutions was itself a historical accretion rather than the offspring of any single court. Lawyers also were not likely to be concerned with history because most of them had little to do with constitutional law, and history was less relevant to other kinds of law. With legal training based primarily on the casebook method, an appreciation of law in its historical context was discouraged. Lawyers

[29] See Paul L. Murphy, "Time to Reclaim: The Current Challenge of American Constitutional History," 69 *American Historical Review* 64 (1963).

therefore tended to see the interpretation and consequent growth of constitutional law as a matter of the mechanical application of precedent. They remained, as did historians, oblivious of the Supreme Court's critical use of history, prompting Justice Frankfurter to remark, "Lawyers with rare exceptions, have failed to lay bare that the law of the Supreme Court is enmeshed in the country's history; historians no less have seemed to miss the fact that the country's history is enmeshed in the law of the Supreme Court."[30]

Courts, on the other hand, while paying lip service to the idea of a self-contained law, were finding and creating precedents often on the basis of extralegal facts derived from history. During the nineteenth century, a period of relative judicial quietude, the Constitution still underwent change at the hands of the Court as if it were the incidents of a mystical body of legal principles. Much in the fashion of priests, the justices failed to clarify the nature of their magical interpretive powers and characteristically chose to define their task as one of finding law rather than making it. The Court's use of history as extralegal facts was not controversial because history itself tended to be imperceptible. By regarding history as a record instead of an interpretation of the past, the Court could use history in order to "find" law without unnecessarily alerting anyone to the fact that law was actually being made.

In any event, there was little possibility that history would become a disconcerting element in the process of judicial interpretation, if not for the simple reason that students of constitutional history were in the first place largely conservative in their outlook. That is, for both the Supreme Court justice and the historian, the approach to historical reality was "one of philosophic-metaphysical analysis geared to establish the validity of political orthodoxy, or more crudely might merely be referred to as 'revealed' history to underwrite the virtue of established institutions."[31] Without doubt, nineteenth-century historiography was admirably suited to judicial interpretation

---

[30] Felix Frankfurter, *Mr. Justice Holmes and the Supreme Court* (Cambridge, Mass.: Belknap Press, 1961), p. 39.

[31] Murphy, "Time to Reclaim," p. 66.

oriented toward conservation rather than change. The Court's use of history in the celebrated Dred Scott case,[32] in which it attempted desperately to stave off the Civil War, illustrates how easily history can be blended into constitutional law for the purpose of upholding the status quo.

The Missouri Compromise of 1820, which forbade slavery north of the 36°30' line, excluding Missouri, was in 1857 only the second federal statute to be declared unconstitutional by the high bench. While this case provides a tragic example of how the Court can misgauge the effective limits of its power, more important, it also demonstrates that constitutional law is only nominally precedent-bound and that history actually facilitates the making of law. The main thrust of Chief Justice Roger Taney's argument was that Article IV, Section 2, of the Constitution—"The Congress shall have power to dispose of and make all needful rules and regulations respecting the territory or other property belonging to the United States . . ."— had no bearing on the slavery controversy because it was intended to apply only to those lands belonging to the United States in 1789, not to lands that might be acquired in the future.

Since the Constitution made no explicit reference to slavery and since the framers neglected to footnote their intentions, Taney was relatively free to elaborate a judicial version of history in order to explain his decision that the federal government had no constitutional authorization to forbid slavery in its territories. Taney thus used history to establish the extralegal fact that the status of the Negro at the time of the adoption of the Constitution was very low. He argued that it was clearly understood that the Negro was not a citizen but instead should be regarded as a chattel. Taney's conception of historical events conveniently clarified the meaning of the open-ended due-process clause of the Fifth Amendment. He reasoned that the Missouri Compromise, by forbidding slavery in the northern territories, violated basic property rights protected by the clause and was therefore unconstitutional.

Taney's convenient recourse to history did not go entirely

---

[32] Dred Scott v. Sandford, 19 Howard 393 (1857).

unnoticed. Abraham Lincoln, a bitter critic of the Dred Scott decision, was disturbed by the Court's easy use of history and decried the right of any man to "mislead others who have less access to history, and less leisure to study it. . . ."[33] Lincoln offered an alternative interpretation of historical events in his Cooper Institute address. He traced the careers of the thirty-nine constitutional signatories in order to demonstrate that despite the omission of an explicit constitutional prohibition against slavery in the territories, and in lieu of the indirect reference to slaves, through "contemporaneous history . . . this mode of alluding to slaves and slavery, instead of speaking of them, was employed on purpose to exclude from the Constitution the idea that there could be property in man."[34]

Even if it is granted that history was abused in the Dred Scott case and was used in a highly partisan manner on many other occasions, it does not necessarily follow that the liabilities of history negate any value it may have for the Court.[35] On the contrary, as Charles Miller has shown in his able work, history can serve many useful purposes.[36] The Court, for example, can use history to chart the past range of various meanings of legal terminology. It can also consult history to gain valuable insights into the origins of contemporary problems. In general, history can be used profitably by the Court to uncover and explain some of the permanent and shifting values that make constitutionalism worth preserving. Nevertheless, it must be said that history for many reasons can play only a limited or peripheral role in the process of judicial interpretation. To begin with, even if the Constitution could be considered a static instrument whose meaning did not change, a notion Justice David J. Brewer actually set forth—"That which it meant when [it was] adopted it means now"[37]—in searching the past for the buried

[33] Abraham Lincoln, "Address at Cooper Institute," in *The Life and Writings of Abraham Lincoln,* ed. Philip Van Doren Stern (New York: Modern Library, 1940), p. 579.

[34] *Ibid.,* p. 587.

[35] For a ringing indictment of the Court's use of history, see Alfred H. Kelly, "Clio and the Court: An Illicit Love Affair," in Philip B. Kurland, ed., *The Supreme Court Review* (Chicago: University of Chicago Press, 1965).

[36] Charles A. Miller, *The Supreme Court and the Uses of History* (Cambridge, Mass.: Belknap Press, 1969), p. 94.

[37] South Carolina v. United States, 199 U.S. 437, 448 (1905).

meaning of the Constitution, the Court would have to overcome the formidable problem of obtaining an objective record of history. And even if such a record were available, it obviously would be of little use to the Court in performing its basic function of adapting the Constitution to meet the perplexing and ever-changing issues of the present.

Putting the problems of historiography aside, the utility of history in the process of judicial interpretation is limited more fundamentally by the restricted terms of the kinds of legal questions history can specifically answer. In general, the basic historical question that the Court has often pondered relates to the intentions of the authors of a disputed law. This question, John G. Wofford has pointed out, can be refined further into three separate historical questions dealing with intent, meaning, and purpose.[38] To search for intent is to look for a "state of mind." The search for meaning looks for "something behind a word for which the word was said to stand as a sign." To search for purpose, however, is to look "for a state of facts, a series of events, a concrete problem" that law was "designed to remedy."[39] But in practice, Wofford writes, each of these separate historical questions blend into one another, and since "judges rarely distinguish between them," the basic historical question can be defined here as the search for both the explicit and implicit intentions of lawmakers.[40]

Needless to say, if the precise meaning of legal principles were determined simply by sounding the intentions of lawmakers, judicial interpretation would of necessity be a subjective and free-wheeling art. The Court would then necessarily possess a mandate to explore the subconscious levels of history. But the high bench has not been entirely unaware of the perils of historical mind reading, as can be gathered from Justice Frankfurter's remark: "We are not concerned with anything subjective. We do not delve into the minds of legislators or their draftsmen, or committee members . . . the purpose a court must effectuate is not that which Congress should have enacted, or

[38] John G. Wofford, "The Blinding Light: The Uses of History in Constitutional Interpretation," 31 *University of Chicago Law Review* 502 (1963–64).
[39] *Ibid.*, pp. 502–3.
[40] *Ibid.*, p. 502.

would have. It is that which it did enact. . . ."[41] Yet despite Frankfurter's insistence that the Court abjures subjective questions and that he himself has "avoided speaking of the 'legislative intent,' "[42] judicial interpretation, even when practiced by Frankfurter, has at times begged futilely the basic historical question of intention or has been reduced to an attempt at reading the minds of the legislators. In the case of Dennis v. United States, decided in 1951, Justice Frankfurter declared, "The language of the First Amendment is to be read not as barren words found in a dictionary but as symbols of historic experience illumined by the presuppositions of those who employed them. Not what words did Madison and Hamilton use, but what was it in their minds which they conveyed?"[43]

Intentions, of course, are not always clearly recorded for the sake of history and may even crystallize after the event in question. One of the most celebrated instances of disputed intentions arose when Roscoe Conkling in the case of San Mateo v. Southern Pacific Railway Co., decided in 1885,[44] argued before the high bench that the framers of the Fourteenth Amendment had intended to include corporations within its protective ambit.[45] Although Conkling made his argument sixteen years after the drafting committee had completed its work, and although persuasive historical evidence was lacking, the Supreme Court, a year after the San Mateo decision, afforded full recognition to Conkling's dubious idea of historical intent.[46]

To be sure, the search for intention remains a limited and inadequate approach to judicial interpretation. While constitutional principles have to be flexible, it is not possible at the same

[41] Frankfurter, "Reflections on Reading Statutes," p. 87.
[42] *Ibid.*, p. 86.
[43] Dennis v. United States, 341 U.S. 494, 523 (1951) (concurring opinion).
[44] San Mateo v. Southern Pacific Railway Co., 116 U.S. 138 (1885).
[45] See Andrew C. McLaughlin, "'The Court, the Corporation, and Conkling," 46 *American Historical Review* 45 (1940–41), and Howard J. Graham, "The 'Conspiracy Theory' of the Fourteenth Amendment," 47 *Yale Law Journal* 371 (1937) and 48 *Yale Law Journal* 171 (1938).
[46] Santa Clara County v. Southern Pacific Railroad Co., 118 U.S. 394 (1886). Justice Hugo Black, however, argued more than fifty years later that "neither the history nor the language of the Fourteenth Amendment justifies the belief that corporations are included within its protection," in Connecticut General Life Insurance Co. v. Johnson, 303 U.S. 77, 85–86 (1938) (dissenting opinion).

time to defend the notion that intentions, too, are flexible and will always be compatible with future exigencies. This is to demand too much of historical truth. For if history did provide the conclusive key to the meaning of the Constitution, each time the Court made new constitutional law, it would be faced with the Orwellian task of rewriting history. Obviously this would be no mean feat, especially when the Fourteenth Amendment, the most judicially distended section of the Constitution, is at stake. Thus it may be noted that in the very first test of the amendment, which took place in 1873, five years after its ratification when historical data were still fresh, Justice Samuel F. Miller set forth a highly restricted interpretation of its meaning. The "one pervading purpose," Miller wrote in the Slaughterhouse Cases, of the Thirteenth, Fourteenth, and Fifteenth Amendments, "lying at the foundation of each, and without which none of them would have been even suggested; [was] the freedom of the slave race, the security and firm establishment of that freedom, and the protection of the newly-made freeman and citizen from the oppressions of those who had formerly exercised unlimited dominion over him."[47] Yet despite this early historical understanding of the intentions of those who drafted and approved the amendment, its meaning was stretched to the point where the due-process clause is able to serve as a vehicle incorporating many of the sundry guarantees of the entire Bill of Rights.

In short, there are at least five reasons for the inadequacy of the basic historical question. First, as Wofford notes, it is never clear whose intentions are most relevant to the law in question. A law may be drafted by a few or by many people, but it is ultimately ratified by the legislature. Thus there are no clear grounds for determining whose intentions are most important. Moreover, this problem is particularly acute in the case of the Constitution, which "purports to be the expressed intent of a widely dispersed and numerically large sovereign electorate."[48] Second, it is the words, after all, and not intended interpreta-

[47] Slaughterhouse Cases, 16 Wallace 36, 71 (1873).
[48] Wofford, "The Blinding Light," p. 508.

tions, that are explicitly ratified. Third, intentions may not always be compatible with one another, as is suggested by the countless occasions when the Court has had to balance one constitutional right against another. Fourth, viable law is not static but of necessity acquires meaning that is independent of the intentions of lawmakers. Finally, and most important, the basic historical question falsely implies that the legislator can anticipate all the exigencies that law must inevitably treat and, to use the words of Julius Stone, that "he has been able to carry out so ambitious a scheme, though no codifier in history has ever succeeded in doing so."[49]

Insofar as history has never been a problem-solving discipline that could in the manner of a social science explain human behavior in causal terms, and bearing in mind the limited scope of the basic historical question, history was fated to become less important to the Court as soon as it became more deeply enmeshed in the adjudication of contemporary social problems. In the twentieth century the use and influence of history declined because the Court as a policy-making body could not function in an able way if it was tightly bound by historical strictures. Inevitably, it seems, the Court would have to turn to other kinds of extralegal data that would enable it to make informed policy judgments. And as Judge Charles E. Wyzanski has pointed out, history did begin to yield gradually "to social planning, to economic understanding, to avowed political policy."[50]

But before the Court actually turned this corner, for a long period the Constitution was interpreted on the basis of factual assumptions that were being drawn from social Darwinism and that added up to a distorted judicial picture of man and society. The jarring inconsistencies between the Court's perception of social reality and the growing fund of empirical insights into social behavior began to raise doubts about the rationality of the Court's decisions invalidating and undercutting social wel-

[49] Julius Stone, *Legal System and Lawyers' Reasonings* (Stanford, Calif.: Stanford University Press, 1964), p. 217.

[50] Charles E. Wyzanski, Jr., "History and Law," 26 *University of Chicago Law Review* 237, 238 (1958–59).

fare legislation. By no means, however, did the development of social science in the twentieth century result in an unimpeachable body of facts, nor did social science immediately throw the Court's more dubious factual assumptions into sharp relief. But the mounting concern with the methods used to study social facts shown by social scientists toward the end of the nineteenth century did mark the birth of a new and highly reputable body of social knowledge.[51] And as the various subdisciplines of social science developed more reliable methods of analysis and began to mature, higher cultural standards of objectivity and verification were established for society in general, and the nation's deeply rooted social prejudices, especially those concerning racial and economic issues, began slowly to erode.

Social scientists through the years have attempted to formulate empirical laws that explained the logical and causal relationships between human events. While they could not, of course, apply scientific method in a laboratory fashion, scientific method did color their thinking to the extent that it provided, as Ernest Nagel has put it, "the general logic . . . employed tacitly or explicitly, for assessing the merits of an inquiry."[52] The successful growth of science in the United States, especially natural science, resulted eventually in a new cultural standard of rationality that so conditioned the popular concept of truth that empiricism largely became the measure of all things. In retrospect, in view of the pervasive reverence for empiricism that developed in the United States, and because law is unquestionably culture-bound, it would seem to be only a matter of time before the Supreme Court granted formal recognition to modern social science and began to use its findings in place of the less convincing factual assumptions that had long influenced its interpretations of the Constitution. The Court, after all, has never been free to use facts loosely and to render decisions that offend public logic. To be sure, the Constitution has always reflected the values of its interpreters, but the justices were still

[51] See Emile Durkheim, *The Rules of Sociological Method,* tr. S. Solovay and J. Mueller, 8th ed. (New York: Free Press, 1966), p. lix.
[52] Ernest Nagel, "The Nature and Aim of Science," in Sidney Morgenbesser, ed., *The Philosophy of Science Today* (New York: Basic Books, 1967), p. 9.

compelled to write opinions that were compatible with the prevailing conception of rationality. Rationality in law is not easily defined, but Paul A. Freund has done well to suggest that rational thinking and action in law are generally "set off against nonrational modes like will, or power, or caprice, or emotion, against irrational modes like recklessness of means or ends or their relation, against rapacity or opacity. It is a warrant not so much of the soundness of a decision as of the course pursued— that the course of inquiry has been kept open and operating in appropriate ways and within appropriate termini."[53] The important point here is that in no small way the rationality of the Court's opinions and decisions has depended on the kinds of facts it has used, and these, it will soon be shown, invariably reflected the thinking and teachings of the times.

[53] Paul A. Freund, *On Law and Justice* (Cambridge, Mass.: Belknap Press, 1968), p. 64.

CHAPTER TWO

Social Darwinism
in the Law and the Rise
of Sociological Jurisprudence

Social Darwinism and Nineteenth-Century Social Science

The appearance in 1848 of Marx and Engels's *Communist Manifesto,* and eleven years later of Darwin's *The Origin of Species,* inaugurated two of the most influential ideologies of the nineteenth century. Contrary to the expectations of Marxism, American capitalism did not inspire its own destruction, but its rapid growth was abetted by Herbert Spencer's transliteration of Darwin's biological study into a "pseudo" social science. Spencer, an advocate of English liberalism, believed that the development of individual liberty decreased as state regulatory powers increased. He suggested that social problems resulting from laissez-faire governmental policies were not very disturbing because they would eventually solve themselves. While change was not to be deplored, Spencer argued, any artificial stimulation of change in human nature, which automatically adapts to the environment, would prove deleterious to the human species and would ultimately be fatal to society. Unbridled competition was in accord with nature: "Even a partial intrusion of the family regime into the regime of the State, will be slowly followed by fatal results. Society in its corporate capacity, cannot without immediate or remote disaster interfere with the play of these opposed principles under which every species has reached such fitness for its mode of life as it possesses, and under which it maintains that fitness."[1]

Spencer's popularization of social Darwinism after the Civil War affected all forms of social thought. The general impact of social Darwinism on anthropology, sociology, historiography, political theory, and economics was wide and deep. In particular, Spencer's influence on the founders of American sociology—Ward, Cooley, Giddings, Small, and Sumner—was especially significant.[2] Ostensibly, Spencer had successfully built a social science using the fundamental laws of natural science that had been revealed by Darwin, whose work was popularly regarded at the time as a major scientific discovery. Darwin's ideas were magnetically attractive. As Jacques Barzun has written:

> To scientist and layman alike, the appeal of natural selection was manifold. It had the persuasiveness of "small doses"; it was entirely automatic, doing away with both the religious will of a creator and the Lamarckian will of his creatures; it substituted a "true cause" for the "metaphysical" sort of explanation; lastly, natural selection was an exact parallel in nature to the kind of individual competition familiar to everyone in the social world of man. By joining the well-established notion of natural selection to the development theory which had been talked about for a hundred years, Darwin was felt to have solved the greatest problem of modern science. He had explained life, or almost. He had at any rate shown the primary animal basis of human progress and told "its law and cause."[3]

The striking success of social Darwinism in the United States is attested to by the fact that it became practically synonymous with social science. Most nineteenth-century social scientists adopted Darwinian biology as their paradigm for human behavior without considering that there might be a vital difference between the human and animal species that precluded sim-

[1] Herbert Spencer, *The Man versus the State* (Caldwell, Idaho: Caxton Printers, 1946), p. 106.
[2] Richard Hofstadter, *Social Darwinism in American Thought,* rev. ed. (Boston: Beacon Press, 1966), p. 33.
[3] Jacques Barzun, *Darwin, Marx, Wagner: Critique of a Heritage,* 2nd rev. ed. (Garden City, N.Y.: Doubleday Anchor Books, 1958), p. 57.

plified comparison. This was not the first time, of course, that natural science had inspired political and social thought. Thomas Hobbes's *Leviathan*, for example, was influenced by physics and was based on the comparable fallacy that animate and inanimate matter could be studied with the same method because both shared the common property of motion. Yet not every social scientist succumbed completely to the influence of social Darwinism. Lester Ward's *Dynamic Sociology*, for example, was a partial rejoinder to Spencer's *Social Statics*. Nonetheless, social Darwinism did set the tone of academic debate and, more important, served as a dramatic ideology for the proponents of a laissez-faire state. But it should be added, in all fairness, that social welfare legislation would probably have drawn the ire of business interests even if Darwin and Spencer had remained unknown.

Of special interest here, in view of the Court's use of the assumptions of social Darwinism as extralegal facts and its later use of modern social science, is the treatment of race by the nascent discipline of sociology. The publication of Count Arthur de Gobineau's *Essai sur l'inégalité des races humaines* in 1853, and its consequent influence upon the European discussion of race, did not presage an enlightened treatment of what was in the United States an increasingly perplexing political problem. Indeed, so sensitive and disturbing did the question of the Negro become during the Reconstruction era that all objective discussions of race were overshadowed by the emotion-laden political controversy to which it was tied. In this sense it cannot be said that race was in any way the subject of dispassionate scientific forums. Instead the social thought concerning race was highly prejudiced and thoroughly saturated and reinforced by biological concepts, including the Darwinian notions of universal competition, the survival of the fittest, and the adaptability of the species. They all conditioned and colored racial thinking.[4] In short, the ideas of the superiority of the white race and the danger of its possible pollution by the black race became matters

[4] E. B. Reuter, "Racial Theory," 50 *American Journal of Sociology* 452, 453–54 (1945).

of scientific plausibility. Madison Grant's *The Passing of the Great Race*, for example, which appeared in 1916, was a racial interpretation of history that warned of the impending inundation of the white race by the inferior black race. This work was one of the last major symptoms of nineteenth-century social science and marked the decline of this age of scientific ideas.

The Court and Social Darwinism

Undoubtedly the greatest practical triumph of social Darwinism and laissez-faire economics was achieved in the courts.[5] Though the Supreme Court was not actually in the vanguard of the march of social Darwinism, it did in due time begin to assert Darwinist precepts and assumptions with unflagging persistence, especially in due-process adjudication where the rights and privileges of property were at stake. Curiously enough, the two most important decisions regarding the early application of the due-process clause, the Slaughterhouse Cases and Munn v. Illinois,[6] suggested neither racism nor laissez-faire economics. On the contrary, the Court in the Slaughterhouse Cases ruled that the primary purpose of the Fourteenth Amendment was the protection of the civil rights of Negroes. And in the Munn case the Court approved state-imposed regulatory rates for grain elevators, despite the contention that the due-process clause precluded such action, a policy Herbert Spencer would surely have regarded as the first step down the road to slavery.

While the Supreme Court did not instigate the popular response to social Darwinism that took place in the 1870s, it subsequently served as an approving sponsor of these ideas. As the most articulate governmental organ, it translated them into what was, for all practical purposes, the policy of the national government. The rhetoric of social Darwinism won lay and juridical minds alike, even though the courts were distinguished

[5] Sidney Fine, *Laissez Faire and the General-Welfare State: A Study in Conflict in American Thought 1865–1901* (Ann Arbor: University of Michigan Press, 1967), p. 126.

[6] Slaughterhouse Cases, 16 Wallace 36 (1873); Munn v. Illinois, 94 U.S. 113 (1877).

as "the only trained and professional organs that we have [had] in our civil institutions" and therefore should have been more immune to polemical argumentation.[7] Ideally, the Court was not supposed to be concerned with the wisdom of social welfare legislation, and thus it should not have been deeply concerned with the threat that it posed to the conservative values of social Darwinism. At least it was not the Court's formal task to enact social Darwinism into constitutional law. However, not only was the Court receptive to the elitist and racist ideas of social Darwinism, but it appeared to be a most willing victim of a well-coordinated ideological crusade. As Benjamin Twiss has shown in his excellent study, *Lawyers and the Constitution*, social Darwinism and laissez-faire economics were deliberately foisted upon the Court primarily by a brilliant group of leading corporation lawyers.[8] Lawyers, Tocqueville has discerned, "do not, indeed, wish to overthrow the institutions of democracy, but they constantly endeavor to turn it away from its real direction by means that are foreign to its nature."[9] Thus, as Twiss has revealed, such legal works as Thomas M. Cooley's *A Treatise on the Constitutional Limitations Which Rest upon the Legislative Powers of the States of the American Union* (1868) and James Coolidge Carter's *Treatise on the Limitations on the Police Power* (1886) provided the Court with manuals that facilitated the transformation of the ideas of social Darwinism into legal doctrine. Moreover, such capable legal advocates of the period as Joseph H. Choate, Christopher G. Tiedeman, John Forrest Dillon, former Justice John A. Campbell, Solicitor General James M. Beck, and William M. Evarts prevailed upon and actually induced the Court to accept the tenets of social Darwinism.[10] But in the final analysis, it is not really surprising that the Court proved itself amenable to counsel's persuasive advocacy, since

[7] Ernst Freund, *The Standards of American Legislation* (Chicago: University of Chicago Press, 1917), p. 287.

[8] Benjamin R. Twiss, *Lawyers and the Constitution: How Laissez-Faire Came to the Supreme Court* (New York: Russell & Russell, 1962).

[9] Alexis de Tocqueville, *Democracy in America*, ed. Phillips Bradley, 2 vols. (New York: Vintage Books, 1961), 1: 286.

[10] Twiss, *Lawyers and the Constitution*.

outstanding legal talent was just as apt to be off the bench as on it.[11]

In general, social Darwinism was transformed into American law in much the same way that some other academic or quasi-academic writings have become institutionalized. A more recent example of this process is the rapidity with which Freud's technical psychoanalytic terminology has become part of the common language. American culture has held a ready ear to academic or technical argot, and such terminology, from "survival of the fittest" to "superego," "repression," and "alienation," has been absorbed quickly into common parlance. However, the popular understanding of these concepts is not always faithful to their original meaning. This is mainly true with respect to Charles Darwin, who was no social Darwinist. But even as sacred a subject as theology, as Max Weber has shown in his classic work, *The Protestant Ethic and the Spirit of Capitalism*, falsely served as the rationale during this time for a pure capitalist system.[12] The popularity of ideas, needless to say, has never been a function of their validity. In any event, the influence of social Darwinism became so pervasive that Oliver Wendell Holmes could say of Spencer in 1895, "I doubt if any writer of English except Darwin has done so much to affect our whole way of thinking about the universe."[13]

In view of the special efforts of lawyers and the general influence of social Darwinism, the justices did not even have to study Darwin and Spencer in order to learn their teachings. Indeed, Justice Holmes at one point admitted to Morris R. Cohen that he had never read Darwin or Spencer, "but as I say it was in the air."[14] To work against the "truths" of the Spencerian

[11] Several notable figures have refused to serve on the Supreme Court. Alexander Hamilton, for example, declined the chief justiceship. In 1874 such outstanding lawyers as Roscoe Conkling and Secretary of State Hamilton Fish declined appointments. See Allan Nevins, *Hamilton Fish* (New York: Dodd, Mead, 1937), p. 661.

[12] Max Weber, *The Protestant Ethic and the Spirit of Capitalism,* tr. Talcott Parsons (New York: Charles Scribner's Sons, 1958).

[13] Mark De Wolfe Howe, ed., *Holmes-Pollock Letters* (Cambridge, Mass.: Belknap Press, 1961), p. 58.

[14] Holmes quoted in Philip P. Wiener, *Evolution and the Founders of Pragmatism* (New York: Harper Torchbooks, 1965), p. 173.

social order was to commit legal heresy. This was made clear when Louis Brandeis put aside his lucrative corporate practice to fight for the legal acceptance of social reform. He was rewarded with the unconcealed enmity of the American bar. After President Wilson nominated Brandeis to a seat on the Supreme Court in 1916, seven past presidents of the American Bar Association, representing the elite opinion of their profession, registered strong and bitter protests. William Howard Taft, himself "a thoroughgoing Social Darwinist," typified the general reaction of the bar of Brandeis's appointment:[15] "It is one of the deepest wounds that I have had as an American and a lover of the Constitution and a believer in progressive conservatism, that such a man as Brandeis could be put in the Court. He is a muckraker, an emotionalist for his own purpose, a socialist. . . ."[16]

Plessy v. Ferguson and the Court's Implicit Use of Nineteenth-Century Social Science

The influence of nineteenth-century social science on constitutional law was clearly evident in the case of Plessy v. Ferguson,[17] decided in 1896. In the Plessy case, which became the constitutional foundation of racial segregation for fifty-eight years, the Court used extralegal facts implicitly derived from the current popularized understanding of social science. Although Justice Henry B. Brown may not have realized that he was using social science, his opinion nonetheless was based on several social science postulates that were interwoven in his definition of the fact situation of this landmark case.

Homer Plessy, an octoroon, had been convicted by a Louisiana court of violating a state statute enacted in 1890 that required the two races to use separate railway facilities. Plessy ultimately brought the case to the Supreme Court, charging that the statute violated his rights as guaranteed by the Thirteenth and Four-

[15] Alpheus Thomas Mason, *William Howard Taft: Chief Justice* (New York: Simon and Schuster, 1965), p. 16.
[16] Taft quoted in Alpheus Thomas Mason, *Brandeis: A Free Man's Life* (New York: Viking Press, 1946), p. 470.
[17] Plessy v. Ferguson, 163 U.S. 537 (1896).

teenth Amendments. But Justice Brown on behalf of the Court reasoned instead that the Louisiana statute did not deprive Plessy of his rights. Specifically, Brown reasoned that the statute did not violate the equal-protection clause of the Fourteenth Amendment, because a statute that merely established a "legal distinction" between the two races had no tendency to undermine their equality. Moreover, Brown made a point of denying that the law could create feelings of racial inferiority. He did this by stressing the extralegal fact that the overt differences between the two races were explainable in biological instead of social terms. Ironically, however, Brown also went along with the environmental perspective that would later characterize modern social science. He suggested that if Negroes considered themselves to be inferior, it was no fault of the statute but was due instead to a false interpretation they had put on it: "Laws permitting, and even requiring . . . separation . . . do not necessarily imply the inferiority of either race to the other." If "the enforced separation of the two races stamps the colored race with a badge of inferiority . . . it is not by reason of anything found in the act, but solely because the colored race chooses to put that construction upon it."[18] Brown's opinion was therefore illogical because he had unintentionally conceded the point that the "misconstrued" act was responsible for the inferiority feelings suffered by Negroes. And clearly enough, while Brown disputed the cause of these feelings, he never bothered to question their existence. Most important, there can be no doubt that Brown not only believed that Negroes were different but also accepted as a matter of fact their biological inferiority—the underlying rationale of racial segregation.

The statute was in no way arbitrary, Brown continued, but was surely a "reasonable regulation." While he conceded that the definition of what was reasonable did involve a large measure of discretion on the part of the legislature, the reasonableness of legislative action could be determined with reference to the "established usages, customs, and traditions of the people, and with a view to the promotion of their comfort, and the preservation of the public peace and good order."[19] These customs and

[18] *Ibid.*, pp. 544, 551.
[19] *Ibid.*, p. 550.

traditions, Brown intimated, should not be treated lightly by courts or legislatures. For even if custom only reflects "social prejudices," they cannot be eliminated by legislation. Yet there was little in Brown's opinion to suggest that he believed the statute in question was simply the by-product of southern prejudices. On the contrary, Brown strongly implied that the statute was a reflection of indelible biological characteristics that distinguished and separated the two races. Because of these crucial characteristics, Brown believed that racial customs could not and should not be disturbed. Racial customs were perceived by the Court as the species's payment of social deference to unalterable biological laws. "Legislation," Brown concluded, "is powerless to eradicate racial instincts or to abolish distinctions based upon physical differences, and the attempt to do so can only result in accentuating the difficulties of the present situation."[20]

There is little doubt, as Barton J. Bernstein has observed, that "sociological and psychological theories controlled the court's decision," even though these theories were not formally presented to the high bench and were not given formal recognition.[21] "At least four questionable factual allegations or dubious legal and scientific theories" used by Brown were implicitly tied to nineteenth-century social science. Brown maintained first that the Louisiana statute was enacted in "good faith" and was not designed as an "annoyance or oppression"; second, that racial segregation was a custom or tradition in the South; third, that law which followed custom was reasonable, while law which conflicted with custom was unreasonable; and finally, that law was incapable of restructuring racial instincts.[22]

Justice Brown's contention that the act was the work of a benevolent legislature was reminiscent of the ancient Greek argument that the institution of slavery was designed primarily for the good of the slave. But Justice John M. Harlan, dissenting sharply, made short shrift of this claim and undermined in general the credibility of the majority opinion.

[20] *Ibid.*, p. 551.
[21] Barton J. Bernstein, "Plessy v. Ferguson: Conservative Sociological Jurisprudence," 48 *Journal of Negro History* 196, 198 (1963).
[22] *Ibid.*, pp. 199–200.

Every one knows that the statute in question had its origin in the purpose, not so much to exclude white persons from railroad cars occupied by blacks, as to exclude colored people from coaches occupied by or assigned to white persons. . . . The thing to accomplish was, under the guise of giving equal accommodations for whites and blacks, to compel the latter to keep to themselves while travelling in railroad passenger coaches. No one would be so wanting in candor as to assert the contrary. . . .

The arbitrary separation of citizens, on the basis of race, while they are on a public highway, is a badge of servitude wholly inconsistent with the civil freedom and the equality before the law established by the Constitution. . . .

We boast of the freedom enjoyed by our people above all other peoples. But it is difficult to reconcile that boast with a state of law which, practically, puts the brand of servitude and degradation upon a large class of our fellow-citizens, our equals before the law. The thin disguise of "equal" accommodations for passengers in railroad coaches will not mislead anyone, nor atone for the wrong this day done.[23]

But the majority of the justices were not inclined to admit that the statute was oppressive, because they believed firmly that racial segregation simply implemented and confirmed the natural inequality of the two races. Laissez-faire policies, given the tenets of social Darwinism, complemented natural processes that ultimately worked toward the improvement of the human species. Conversely, legislation that artificially interfered with the natural order, as Herbert Spencer had argued, posed a real threat to society and was to be regarded as oppressive and arbitrary. The statute did not stamp "the colored race with a badge of inferiority." Any such interpretation was false, because the Court simply did not feel that human behavior could be explained in the context of socialization processes or more generally in terms of environmental influences. Instead the Court reasoned in terms of the leading teachings of the day: "racial instincts" were controlling, and racial inferiority was caused by these instincts, not by legislation.

Historical research suggests that the legal basis of racial segre-

[23] Plessy v. Ferguson, 163 U.S. 537, 557, 562 (1896) (dissenting opinion).

gation was virtually nonexistent in the nineteenth century and that the only segregation law adopted by a majority of southern states was of the very type contested in the Plessy case.[24] Undoubtedly there was a southern predisposition to deny the Negro the usual amenities of social life, but the domestic service sector of the economy certainly revealed racial commingling. And although frequency curves are unavailable, it is apparent that southern white gentlemen long commingled in bed with Negro females.[25] Therefore, it remains open to question whether the Court's decision was based on custom and tradition or if, in fact, the Plessy decision actually prompted the growth of new social patterns. In any event, the disruptive effects of the Civil War and the subsequent development of industrialism were hardly signs of stability; they suggest instead that southern society was passing through a transitional stage. Be that as it may, Justice Brown's assertion that racial segregation existed in the South by virtue of tradition and custom meant that the Plessy decision was in reality dictated by the law of nature. Brown's opinion, then, was wholly consistent with social Darwinism. As William Graham Sumner, Spencer's leading apostle, later wrote, "Constitutional institutions are the great reliance for rights and justice and the great ground of hope and confidence in the future. Nevertheless, constitutional government can never overcome the mores."[26]

Brown's argument that law is reasonable if it follows custom was not itself legally unsound. As Justice Holmes later remarked, "Tradition and the habits of the community count for more than logic."[27] But it does not follow from this principle that all customs must be enacted into laws, for if customs are to be understood as an effective means of informal social control, their

[24] C. Vann Woodward, *The Strange Career of Jim Crow*, 2nd rev. ed. (New York: Oxford University Press, 1966), p. 97.

[25] John Dollard, *Caste and Class in a Southern Town*, 3rd ed. (Garden City, N.Y.: Doubleday Anchor Books, 1957), pp. 139–40. See also Allison Davis et al., *Deep South: A Social Anthropological Study of Caste and Class*, 2nd ed. (Chicago: University of Chicago Press, 1965), pp. 31–37.

[26] William Graham Sumner, "The Mores of the Present and the Future," in *Essays*, ed. Albert G. Keller and Maurice R. Davie, 2 vols. (New Haven, Conn.: Yale University Press, 1934), 1: 87.

[27] Laurel Hill Cemetery v. San Francisco, 216 U.S. 358, 366 (1910).

strength is by definition independent of law. If, on the other hand, the Court had invalidated the Louisiana statute, this action would not necessarily have violated custom, since such a decision would not have compelled the mixing of the races on railroad cars. If segregation was customary, as the Court maintained, it would have prevailed in any event. A negative ruling by the Court would only have denied express legal approval of such practices.[28]

The Court's most important extralegal factual assertion, that "racial instincts" could not be altered by legislation, was central to the Darwinian view of human nature. Darwin had emphasized that "it will be universally admitted that instincts are as important as corporeal structures for the welfare of each species, under its present conditions of life."[29] But any modification of instincts, Darwin explained, was due to natural selection, and no Darwinist would have attributed any such change to legislation. While Darwin's ideas were abused and in this sense were a spur to racism, it is interesting to note that the cardinal ideas of both Gobineau and Spencer had been formed before either had become familiar with Darwin. Likewise scientific racism in the United States was not coeval with Darwin; in fact, the academic discussion of anthropology before 1859 actually helped set the stage for Darwin's appearance.[30] American historians in particular welcomed Darwin's theories, for they saw in them dramatic confirmation of the ethnic, political, and cultural superiority of the Anglo-Saxon race.[31] However, the belief that instinct was a cause of human behavior gained wide acceptance, not because the existence of racial instincts had been verified by scientific method but because the idea of racial instinct complemented the reigning social and political ideology. Nineteenth-century social science was itself an important part of that ideology. Academic psychology, for example, was at the time in a biological stage. The belief in instinct as the cause of

[28] Bernstein, "Plessy v. Ferguson: Conservative Sociological Jurisprudence," p. 201.

[29] Charles Darwin, *The Origin of Species* (London: Dent & Sons, 1963), p. 231.

[30] William Stanton, *The Leopard's Spots: Scientific Attitudes toward Race in America, 1815–1859* (Chicago: University of Chicago Press, 1960), p. 196.

[31] Louis L. Snyder, *Race: A History of Modern Ethnic Theories* (New York: Longmans, Green, 1939), p. 231.

human behavior subsided later, but very slowly. The well-known psychologist William McDougal as late as 1923 claimed that instincts remained a crucial determinative factor in human behavior. McDougal scientifically enumerated at least thirteen vital instincts and was driven to look for more, because "the number is notoriously unlucky, [and therefore] I should like to add to it."[32]

In short, Justice Brown's affirmation of the factual existence of racial instincts was unmistakably grounded in popular thought and seemed eminently plausible in the context of current science. Brown's linkage of the concepts of tradition and instinct, in particular, paralleled the theories of William Graham Sumner, which appeared in his monumental *Folkways*, begun in 1899. This work recapitulated the lectures Sumner had delivered at Yale University for the past fifteen years. Folkways, Sumner maintained, were a societal force and developed along with instincts.[33] While law could rationalize folkways, they existed independently of law. And even if laws and tribunals should fail, Sumner contended, mores or customs conducive to welfare would operate in their place. But behind folkways is the struggle for existence, which is the all-important factor in the development of social organization.[34] Therefore, since instincts were ostensibly revealed in the law of nature, it would have been a futile gesture for the Supreme Court to have invalidated the Louisiana statute, which as far as anyone could see plainly stood in accord with that higher law.

By upholding racial segregation, the Supreme Court introduced a new element of inequality into constitutional law. The Court's implicit use of contemporary social science marked the beginning of a new constitutional era in the area of civil rights. In following the most prominent strain of thought in social science, the Court established as legal precedent the "separate but equal" principle in the Massachusetts case of Roberts v.

[32] William McDougal, *Outline of Psychology* (New York: Charles Scribner's Sons, 1923), pp. 163–64.
[33] William Graham Sumner, *Folkways* (Boston: Ginn and Co., 1940), p. 2.
[34] *Ibid.*, p. 16.

City of Boston,[35] decided in 1849. Under this principle separate facilities from railway cars to schools, indeed, the entire system of racial segregation, was condoned and put on a legal footing by the Court. Given the extralegal facts of social Darwinism, racial segregation was easily found to be compatible with the equal-protection clause of the Fourteenth Amendment. Thereafter, separate facilities for the two races would be considered constitutional as long as they were nominally equal. The Court thus helped perpetuate the fiction that a wide variety of separate facilities could actually be equal. Throughout the South such separate facilities as schools were rarely equal. But as long as the Negro was considered biologically inferior to the white man, or as an unfit competitor in the perpetual struggle of the species for survival, it made no sense to grant him equal and hence artificial recognition in law.

The New Social Science

The influence of social Darwinism lingered on into the twentieth century. Even the learned and enlightened Justice Holmes, although he had pointedly remarked that the "Fourteenth Amendment does not enact Mr. Herbert Spencer's Social Statics,"[36] reasoned in terms that reflected social Darwinism. In the case of Buck v. Bell,[37] decided in 1927, Holmes on behalf of the Court sustained the compulsory sterilization of a retarded patient interned in a state mental institution. Holmes, a wounded veteran of the Civil War, reasoned that if society could call on its elite members to make great sacrifices, it could also call on those who "already sap the strength of the State for these lesser sacrifices . . . in order to prevent our being swamped with incompetence." Furthermore, Holmes stated, "it is better for all the world, if instead of waiting to execute degenerate offspring for crime, or to let them starve for their imbecility, society can prevent those who are manifestly unfit from continuing their kind. The principle that sustains compulsory vaccination

---

[35] Roberts v. City of Boston, 59 Mass. 198 (1849).
[36] Lochner v. New York, 198 U.S. 45, 75 (1905).
[37] Buck v. Bell, 274 U.S. 200 (1927).

is broad enough to cover cutting the Fallopian tubes. . . .
Three generations of imbeciles are enough."[38]

Nineteenth-century social science not only enabled the Court
to restrict civil rights but was ideologically compatible with the
growing excesses of industrialism. It is therefore somewhat ironic
that twentieth-century social science was later used to support
the legal efforts of Negroes to achieve civil rights and the programs of federal and state governments oriented toward amel-
iorating the rigors of societal competition. But before this could
occur, social science had to abandon its biological model and its
Hobbesian and Darwinian laws of nature. Instead of regarding
nature as a deterministic force that encouraged and abetted
inevitable human inequality, social scientific thought in the
twentieth century gradually came to hold that man was a pro-
ducer of his environment as well as a product. When social
scientists began to affirm that the individual "self" was a product
of society and was maintained through the dialectical relationship of the individual with society, then different political
implications could be drawn from social science. Only then did
social science suggest that the willful political control of society
was possible; in many academic quarters the opinion arose that
such control was a necessity.[39]

The most significant contributions to American social science
that inspired its reaction against social Darwinism were made
by Charles Horton Cooley and George Herbert Mead. Cooley
received his Ph.D. from Michigan in 1894, where he remained
until his death in 1929. His most notable concept, the "looking-
glass self," suggested that individuality or man's awareness or
perception of himself mirrored the estimation of him by the
group.[40] Mead, a social psychologist, graduated from Oberlin
College in 1879. After further study at Harvard and Berlin,
Mead taught for three years at Michigan, where he befriended
Cooley. Thereafter Mead remained at the University of Chicago
until his death in 1931. Mead's most important work, *Mind, Self*

[38] *Ibid.*, p. 207.
[39] See, for example, John Dewey, *Liberalism and Social Action* and *Freedom
and Culture* (New York: Capricorn Books, 1963).
[40] Charles Horton Cooley, *Human Nature and the Social Order* (New York:
Charles Scribner's Sons, 1902), p. 152.

and Society, published in 1934 by his students from their lecture notes, provided social scientists with seminal insight into the socialization process.[41] Mead's concept of "the generalized other" signified the process by which social structure was internalized by the individual into psychic structure, an event concurrent with the emergence of "self." Subdivisions of self, such as "I" and "me," depended on society for their definition or substance.

The subsequent development in the 1920s of the "Chicago school of sociology," as it was called, revolutionized the social sciences. In general, biogenetic determinism was replaced by environmental determinism. The works of Robert E. Park, E. Franklin Frazier, Charles S. Johnson, and Louis Wirth were examples of studies of the urban Negro that were based on an environmental rather than the once-dominant biological perspective. Charles Horton Cooley was one of the first social scientists to challenge the old scientific notions of racial inequality.[42] As a result of the work of the Chicago school, a new social science took form. With the growing acceptability of "role theory," perhaps the only uniquely American contribution to sociological theory, the Court's contention that racial segregation did not impose a stigma on the Negro lost all credence and support from the mainstream of social scientific thought.

Social Science and the Emergence of Sociological Jurisprudence

Before the late nineteenth century there had been little legislation in the United States that aimed at the protection of life and limb. Industrialism introduced the machine, which helped alleviate the physical tedium of labor but also exposed man to a new maiming force. On the positive side, science developed new techniques to combat human misery. The machine and science provided the immediate background to the surge of social welfare legislation. The growth of such legislation revealed

[41] George Herbert Mead, *Mind, Self and Society,* ed. C. W. Morris (Chicago: University of Chicago Press, 1934).

[42] Robert E. L. Faris, *Chicago Sociology: 1920–1932* (San Francisco: Chandler Publishing Co., 1967), p. 69.

two inclinations in social and political thought: an increasing concern for the value of the individual human personality and a gradual change in priorities. Such a change was signified by the idea of the public good, from the security and stability of the state and an obsession with the rights of the individual to the immediate social needs of the people.[43] Yet the humanism of social welfare legislation was not itself directly attributable to natural science or social science. Many welfare measures, curiously enough, were carried out over the protests of professional economists, and many public health laws were based on theories of disease that were later rejected.[44] Thus, while science may have beneficially influenced legislation, the public utility of science was not necessarily related to its validity. And while many American political thinkers have commonly described science as a liberating force or as a vehicle of liberalism,[45] Frederick Winslow Taylor, the proponent of scientific management, honored an equally important implication of scientific thought when he wrote in 1911: "In the past the man has been first; in the future the system must be first."[46] Indeed, as we have already seen, the prevailing ideologies of nineteenth-century social science—social Darwinism and laissez-faire economics—had served to reinforce the conservative tendency of law to block beneficial social change.

Social science was itself a product of the nineteenth century, although many political and sociological theories were rooted in antiquity. Auguste Comte had provided the discipline of sociology with its name in 1837. At about the same time jurisprudence also began to be treated as an independent science. Previously, jurisprudence was viewed along with ethics and politics as a part of theology. After Grotius separated law from theology in 1625, jurisprudence had been combined with politics

[43] Freund, *Standards of American Legislation*, pp. 20–22.

[44] *Ibid.*, p. 249.

[45] Cf. Gerard Piel, *Science in the Cause of Man* (New York: Alfred A. Knopf, 1961), p. 81, and Louis Hartz, *The Liberal Tradition in America: An Interpretation of American Political Thought since the Revolution* (New York: Harcourt, Brace and World, 1955), p. 180.

[46] Frederick Winslow Taylor, *The Principles of Scientific Management* (New York: W. W. Norton, 1967), p. 7.

and international law and was studied under the heading of the "law of nature and nations."[47] By the nineteenth century jurisprudence was regarded as a distinct discipline.

Although the term "sociology" was coined in the nineteenth century, modern sociology could trace many of its ideas and concepts to Montesquieu's *Spirit of the Laws*, completed in 1748. Therefore, it was not surprising that such eminent sociologists as Durkheim, Duguit, and Weber, concerned basically with the problem of social control, should turn their attention to the institution of law. The sociology of law, like most sociological theory, was of European origin. However, both sociologists and jurists were suspicious of the sociology of law, as Georges Gurvitch has noted. The former feared that the study of law would bring the covert introduction of value judgments into sociology, and the latter were sensitive to the possibility that sociology, which purported to be "value free," would undercut the normative basis of law.[48] Actually the sociology of law had no direct relationship to jurisprudence, since sociologists treated law as only one of a number of agencies of social control, with no greater normative significance than other social institutions. As Gurvitch has pointed out, "The task of the sociology of law is not at all to define categories or jural values. The so-called 'sociological theory of law' is merely the positivistic interpretation of the philosophy of law."[49]

Sociological jurisprudence, which should be distinguished from the sociology of law, developed primarily as a reaction to the analytical and historical schools of jurisprudence. Sociological jurisprudence was ostensibly a by-product of the development of sociology, which Comte believed was the outcome of the passage of social thought through three stages—theological, metaphysical, and positivistic. In effect, sociological jurisprudence was an attempt to infuse the sociological perspective into the study of law. The proponents of sociological jurisprudence

---

[47] Roscoe Pound, "Sociology and Law," in William F. Ogburn and Alexander Goldenweiser, eds., *The Social Sciences and Their Interrelations* (Boston: Houghton Mifflin, 1927), p. 319.

[48] Georges Gurvitch, *Sociology of Law* (New York: Philosophical Library, 1942), p. 2.

[49] *Ibid.*, p. 67.

believed that this approach to law was necessary because traditional jurisprudence had immunized the Court to an awareness of the social needs of the nation. Although sociology was not a normative discipline and could be considered simply as the comparative analysis of society, sociological jurisprudence borrowed from sociology its vision of group dynamics and social action, adding this nominally value-free analysis to a jurisprudential and hence normative account of law.

According to Roscoe Pound, an eminent and prolific authority, sociological jurisprudence had its immediate origin in what Comte termed the positivistic stage of social thought. Similarly, wrote Pound, sociological jurisprudence also passed through three distinct stages—mechanical, biological, and psychological—before it matured. The mechanical stage, which occurred in the first half of the nineteenth century, was contemporaneous with the identification of scientific thought with the mechanical processes of the physical universe. Science was an attempt to describe the laws of the natural universe and to translate them into mathematical symbols. This tendency of scientific thought appeared in the first stage of sociological jurisprudence. In the last third of the nineteenth century jurists began to conceive of law in biological terms. The Darwinian ideas of natural selection and the struggle for existence strongly influenced jurisprudential concepts. Finally, the psychological stage, which partially overlapped the biological stage, was moulded by the incorporation of such ideas as "group personality," "group will," "psychic forces," and psychological and sociological laws of "imitation." These three stages, then, were amalgamated or unified at the end of the nineteenth century into sociological jurisprudence.

While sociological jurisprudence was at once a combination of all three stages of its growth, it differed, Pound wrote, from any single stage in at least five ways. First, sociological jurisprudence was more concerned with the working of law rather than abstract content. Second, instead of being conceived as abstract concepts, law was treated as a social institution and, more important, one that was amenable to progress. Third, sociological jurisprudence emphasized the social objectives of law rather than penalties and sanctions. Fourth, legal rules and precepts were regarded as flexible guidelines instead of rigid strictures that would lead to "socially just" results. Finally, sociological jurisprudence was regarded as a means of achieving the various purposes of law. Sociological jurisprudence, Pound contended, was able to attract jurists of diverse philosophical persuasions who might disagree on the general principles of law but would happily agree on the methods for solving concrete problems.[50]

The teachings of sociological jurisprudence were used to support the general charge that the Court was guilty of applying a "jurisprudence of conceptions" or abstract and mechanical rules of law that denied, especially in the case of the workingman, meaningful justice. An example of this failing of justice was the Court's unrealistic interpretation of the due-process clause, much to the detriment of labor, "under the belief that every man, being a free moral agent, could freely contract for himself and was not in need of special assistance against the powerful and crafty more favorably situated than he. . . ."[51] Sociological jurisprudence was seen as the proper replacement for the "decadent" analytical, historical, and philosophical schools of jurisprudence and was regarded as the champion of the individual as opposed to the corporation.[52]

Sociological jurisprudence, according to one of its early advocates, Joseph H. Drake, was simply a reflection of the question of "hermeneutics," or how the principles of a legal document could be preserved and yet adapted to changing conditions.[53] Insofar as this problem was coeval with law, Drake pointed out that there was nothing unusual about the development of sociological jurisprudence. Indeed, he argued, "sociological interpretation" was inevitable in any legal system administered by professional experts:

[50] Roscoe Pound, "The Scope and Purpose of Sociological Jurisprudence," 25 *Harvard Law Review* 489 (1912).

[51] E. F. Albertsworth, "Program of Sociological Jurisprudence," 8 *American Bar Association Journal* 393, 394 (1922).

[52] *Ibid.*

[53] Joseph H. Drake, "The Sociological Interpretation of Law," 16 *Michigan Law Review* 599, 604 (1918).

A juridical process that has been endorsed and adopted by Gaius and Justinian, by Bartolus and the Humanists, by English Justices of the King's Bench and Chancellors in Equity, by Continental jurists and American legalists and finally by Justice HOLMES, Justice BREWER and the United States Supreme Bench can hardly be waived aside as the academic vaporings of professorial theorists. It would seem rather to be a part of the much lauded "Natural Law" or of what is called in modern phraseology, philosophic justice.[54]

However, sociological jurisprudence was rarely distinguished from the sociology of law, and its proponents seemed to eschew precision. Drake, for example, was very flexible in categorizing his favored mode of analysis—if "we are frightened because of the likeness of the term sociological to socialistic, we may well call it a rational and not a sociological jurisprudence."[55] This was not the kind of thinking that led to rigorous discriminations; it encouraged instead the general confusion between sociological jurisprudence and the sociology of law.

Sociological jurisprudence was not always best served even by those most closely associated with it. Such distinguished American legal thinkers as Holmes, Brandeis, Pound, and Cardozo, who wished to reform moribund nineteenth-century law, often approached sociological jurisprudence in an undisciplined manner and confused it with the sociology of law. Benjamin Cardozo, for example, clearly failed to distinguish sociology from sociological jurisprudence when he stated in 1921, with some exaggeration, "The method of sociology . . . puts its emphasis on the social welfare."[56] In addition, the progress of sociological jurisprudence was made uncertain by the prevalence of what Morris Cohen has called "scholastic constitutionalism," or a general reluctance on the part of legal thinkers to extend their analysis of law beyond the confines of

[54] *Ibid.*, p. 616.
[55] *Ibid.*, p. 615.
[56] Benjamin N. Cardozo, *The Nature of the Judicial Process* (New Haven, Conn.: Yale University Press, 1961), p. 71. On the contrary, sociologists have stressed that sociology has little to do with social work. See Peter Berger, *Invitation to Sociology: A Humanistic Perspective* (Garden City, N.Y.: Doubleday Anchor Books, 1963), pp. 1–24.

the legal textbook.[57] Thus, even after mid-century, sociological jurisprudence was still characterized as a tentative legal science.[58]

Although the new, environmentally oriented social science had encouraged the development of sociological jurisprudence, there was no logical reason to suppose that sociology would provide American jurisprudence with techniques that would prompt the Court to protect the interest of the downtrodden individual as well as that of the prosperous corporation. Sociology was not, as we have seen, synonymous with modern-day liberalism, nor did sociology automatically cleanse its practitioners of anti-egalitarian biases. Indeed, Ludwig Gumplowicz, a nineteenth-century Austrian sociologist, had argued that law was ideally the perpetuator of political, social, and economic inequality. According to Gumplowicz, law was a form of social life arising from the competition of diverse groups of unequal strength and served to maintain established inequality.[59] There was, of course, nothing new in this Thrasymachean notion. Karl Marx also emphasized the exploitative character of bourgeois law. But even though Marx, one of the founders of social science, did "unmask" the state as the tool of vested class interests, it is clear that both nineteenth-century social science and its newer form gave no indication that modern social science would eventually be used as a vehicle of liberal reform within American constitutional law.

Since sociological jurisprudence was a normative enterprise, it should have been carefully distinguished from the sociology of law, which did not intrinsically profess any social values. Because the value-free nature of scientific method was not clearly understood, jurists tended to treat sociological jurisprudence and the sociology of law as one and the same subject.[60] Thus, while nineteenth-century social science had reinforced the conservative inclinations of law, the new social science came to be seen as

[57] Morris R. Cohen, *American Thought: A Critical Sketch,* ed. Felix Cohen (Glencoe, Ill.: Free Press, 1954), p. 178.

[58] Roscoe Pound, "Jurisprudence," in Edwin R. A. Seligman, ed., *The Encyclopaedia of the Social Sciences,* 7 (New York: Macmillan, 1957): 483.

[59] Edgar Bodenheimer, *Jurisprudence: The Philosophy and Method of the Law* (Cambridge, Mass.: Harvard University Press, 1962), p. 104.

[60] Gurvitch, *Sociology of Law,* pp. 122–35.

a liberal value system. Gradually the new social science began to seep into constitutional law; it received express recognition from the Court in 1908 in the case of Muller v. Oregon.[61] And since legal procedure was especially designed to insulate courts from uncorroborated or extralegal data, the Supreme Court's formal announcement in the Muller case that it was interested in "all matters of general knowledge" was hailed as an important milestone in American jurisprudence.[62] This advance must be understood first in terms of the Court's interpretation of the due-process clauses of the Fifth and Fourteenth Amendments and consequently in terms of the unhurried and piecemeal success of social welfare legislation.

[61] Muller v. Oregon, 208 U.S. 412 (1908).
[62] *Ibid.*, p. 421.

CHAPTER THREE

Toward a More
Factual Jurisprudence

The Development of Substantive Due Process

American constitutional law, as we have seen, was never the simple interpretive labor of justices working in a solitary courtroom sealed off from the draft of ideas circulating through the outside world. On the contrary, the Supreme Court during the nineteenth century had used extralegal facts in the form of history and social Darwinism in some of its most important opinions. Indeed, the Court could hardly interpret the Constitution without making some factual assumptions, whether they were correct or not, about man and society. Preferably, however, if the Court was going to serve the common good, its factual assumptions would have to be consistent with social realities. As Charles Evans Hughes put it in 1928, two years before he became chief justice, "The protection both of the rights of the individual and of those of society rests not so often on formulas . . . but on a correct appreciation of social conditions and a true appraisal of the actual effect of conduct."[1]

Individual rights, societal rights, and certainly corporate rights in this century have rested largely on the Supreme Court's interpretation and elaboration of the due-process requirements of the Fifth and Fourteenth Amendments. As might be expected, the

---

[1] Charles Evans Hughes, *The Supreme Court of the United States: Its Foundation, Methods and Achievements: An Interpretation* (New York: Columbia University Press, 1928), pp. 165–66.

Court's finding of extralegal facts forms a significant theme in the development of the modern conception of substantive due process, which formally began around 1890. Whether the extralegal facts found by the Court at this time provided a valid description of "effects" and "social conditions" is another matter.

A due-process clause was originally included in the Fifth Amendment, which was ratified as part of the Bill of Rights in 1791. The pertinent phrase of the amendment reads: ". . . nor [shall any person] be deprived of life, liberty, or property, without due process of law. . . ." However, the first ten amendments were intended to restrict the federal government alone, and while there were suggestions that they might be applied to the states, Chief Justice Marshall had explicitly rejected this idea in 1833.[2] Although the principle of due process had never been comprehensively defined in a detailed fashion, it was generally assumed to provide what are called procedural safeguards; examples are the right to a trial by an impartial jury and the right to counsel. But as early as 1856 a New York court decided a case that suggested that due process could embrace substantive as well as procedural rights. The court in this instance ruled that a state law regulating the manufacture of liquor was invalid because it interfered with the right to private property, which was protected by the due-process clause of the state constitution.[3] This decision, like that of Dred Scott, was portentous, because the principle of due process was later construed by the Supreme Court to include substantive restrictions as well and was used primarily to invalidate many social welfare programs.

When the Fourteenth Amendment was adopted in 1868, the principle of due process became applicable to the states. The amendment reads in part: ". . . nor shall any State deprive any person of life, liberty, or property, without due process of law. . . ." The idea behind this legal principle, which was soon used by the Court essentially to protect private property, and much later to defend civil liberties, long pre-dated the Constitution. The idea of due process seems to be as old as Magna Carta; the thirty-ninth article states, "No free man shall be seized

[2] Barron v. Baltimore, 7 Peters 243 (1833).
[3] Wynehamer v. New York, 13 N.Y. 378 (1856).

or imprisoned, or stripped of his rights or possessions, or outlawed or exiled . . . , nor will we proceed with force against him . . . except by the lawful judgement of his equals or by the law of the land." But the idea of due process did not lie dormant before the adoption of the Constitution, nor was its transformation from procedure to substance as sudden as it appeared. Actually, according to Howard Jay Graham, the idea of due process was very much evident in colonial ethics, religion, and political theory, and by the eighteenth century its substantive connotation became "an element in a constitutional trinity."[4] Thus the formal substantive enlargement of the principle of due process in the late nineteenth century was "in reality so deeply enrooted in our national consciousness that its judicial achievement was quite as much a result as a cause of widespread popular usage."[5]

The formal foundation for the substantive expansion of the due-process clause was laid in 1886, when the Court held that corporations were persons and were therefore entitled to the protection of the Fourteenth Amendment.[6] The Court thus transcended its earlier restricted interpretation of the amendment as applying chiefly to the emancipated Negro.[7] The scope of the clause was vastly increased in 1890 when the Court signaled the opening of a new constitutional era. It held for the first time that a state statute regulating railroad rates violated the due-process clause of the Fourteenth Amendment and was therefore void.[8] Seven years later, in Allgeyer v. Louisiana,[9] the Court upset a state statute on the ground that it violated the individual's freedom to contract, which the Court asserted was protected by the due-process clause of the Fourteenth Amendment. Justice Rufus W. Peckham, speaking for the Court, sounded an ominous note:

> The liberty mentioned in that Amendment, means not only the right of the citizen to be free from the mere physical restraint of

[4] Howard Jay Graham, "Procedure to Substance: Extra-Judicial Rise of Due Process, 1830–1860," 40 *California Law Review*, 483, 489 (1952–53).

[5] *Ibid.*, p. 500.

[6] Santa Clara County v. Southern Pacific Railroad Co., 118 U.S. 394 (1886).

[7] Slaughterhouse Cases, 16 Wallace 36 (1873).

[8] Chicago, Milwaukee & St. Paul R.R. v. Minn., 134 U.S. 418 (1890).

[9] Allgeyer v. Louisiana, 165 U.S. 578 (1897).

his person, as by incarceration, but the term is deemed to embrace the right of the citizen to be free in the enjoyment of all his faculties; to be free to use them in all lawful ways; to live and work where he will; to earn his livelihood by any lawful calling; to pursue any livelihood or avocation, and for that purpose to enter into all contracts which may be proper, necessary and essential to his carrying out to a successful conclusion the purposes above mentioned.[10]

The due-process clause and the legal formula or subprinciple of liberty to contract consequently became significant constitutional limitations upon the state police power. From 1890 to 1937 the due-process clause was used in a great number of cases to invalidate federal and state statutes. During this period a total of 55 federal and 228 state statutes were held unconstitutional, many of them on due-process grounds.[11]

Interestingly enough, the development of substantive due process was not incompatible with the more traditional principle of procedural due process, nor did it represent in terms of legal theory an artificial line of growth in constitutional law. Instead substantive due process was a logical offspring of procedural due process for the obvious reason that arbitrary and unreasonable legislation could easily be enacted without necessarily implying the violation of legal procedure.[12] Be that as it may, the establishment of the substantive character of the due-process clauses enabled the Court for almost fifty years to manifest an intense concern with legislative policy matters. In other words, the realization of the principle of substantive due process allowed the Court, in spite of its denials, to become deeply involved in politics as a judicial legislature. As Arthur Miller has written, substantive due process "changed judicial review from a seldom used, innocuous power to one of the most (outwardly) awesome powers of government."[13] The Court's sustained in-

[10] *Ibid.*, p. 589.

[11] Edward S. Corwin, ed., *The Constitution of the United States: Analysis and Interpretation* (Washington, D.C.: U.S. Government Printing Office, 1953), pp. 1243–54.

[12] Bernard Schwartz, *A Commentary on the Constitution of the United States*, vol. 2, *The Rights of Property* (New York: Macmillan, 1965), pp. 26–27.

[13] Arthur Selwyn Miller, *The Supreme Court and American Capitalism* (New York: Free Press, 1968), p. 56.

volvement in politics, in turn, marked two interrelated inno-
vations in American jurisprudence: the modification of the
traditional principle of presumptive constitutionality and the
formal acknowledgment and endorsement of the relevance of
extralegal data to constitutional law.

Presumptive Unconstitutionality

According to the traditional principle of presumptive constitutionality, ostensibly a basic axiom of constitutional law, all
legislation is presumed to be constitutional unless proven otherwise. However, presumptive constitutionality was frequently
eclipsed in due-process adjudication that primarily involved
social welfare legislation.[14] What seems like the predestined unconstitutional fate of many social welfare statutes suggests, in
effect, that the Court frequently applied a polar principle that
can be called the principle of presumptive unconstitutionality.
While the Court never formally acknowledged this principle, it
was still applied in practice to legislation that regulated terms of
employment through the establishment of minimum-wage and
minimum-hour standards. The principle of presumptive unconstitutionality was operative, for example, in the case of Adkins v.
Children's Hospital,[15] decided in 1923; there, as noted earlier,
the Court invalidated a federal minimum-wage act. Justice
George Sutherland gave expression to the principle of presumptive unconstitutionality when he announced, "Freedom of contract is . . . the general rule and restraint the exception; and the

[14] Presumptive constitutionality has also been eclipsed in later cases that
dealt with basic freedoms. The so-called preferred-status test has been applied
by the Court to several basic freedoms protected by the First Amendment, such
as religion, speech, and press. The judicial notion that basic freedoms should
receive preferred treatment was first announced in a footnote in the case of United
States v. Carolene Products Co., 304 U.S. 144 (1938). Justice Stone gave clear
indication that the principle of presumptive constitutionality was not to be regarded as inflexible judicial dogma. Stone wrote, "There may be narrower scope
for operation of the presumption of constitutionality when legislation appears on
its face to be within a specfic prohibition of the Constitution, such as those of
the first ten amendments, which are deemed equally specific when held to be em-
braced within the Fourteenth" (p. 152, n. 4). See also Murdock v. Pennsylvania,
319 U.S. 105 (1943), and Thomas v. Collins, 323 U.S. 516 (1945).
[15] Adkins v. Children's Hospital, 261 U.S. 525 (1923).

exercise of legislative authority to abridge it can be justified only by the existence of exceptional circumstances."[16]

Sutherland's dictum was subsequently reiterated on several occasions,[17] substantiating the Court's negative attitude toward social welfare legislation and its frequent application of the principle of presumptive unconstitutionality. Obviously this principle could not be formally enunciated. Prudence suggested that the Court could not announce simply that most social welfare legislation was *prima facie* unconstitutional. For that matter, not only did the Court refuse to acknowledge its role as a superlegislature or a social welfare censor, but it even denied the existence of a substantive judicial power to review social welfare legislation. Thus Justice Sutherland remarked in the Adkins case, "This is not the exercise of a substantive power to review and nullify acts of Congress, for no such substantive power exists."[18]

Substantive due process not only marked the development of the principle of presumptive unconstitutionality; it also committed the Court to a course that, as Edward S. Corwin has pointed out, "was bound to lead, however gradually and easily, beyond the precincts of judicial power, in the sense of the power to ascertain the law, into that of legislative power which determines policies on the basis of facts and desires."[19] In other words, the development of substantive due process meant that the Court had to be prepared to test the "reasonableness" of legislative policies.[20] There then occurred "a concomitant change of view on the part of the Court as to the sort of facts of which it could take 'judicial cognizance' in deciding constitutional cases."[21] The Court's heightened awareness of the critical legal

[16] *Ibid.*, p. 546.

[17] Chief Justice Taft wrote, "Freedom is the general rule, and restraint the exception. The legislative authority to abridge can be justified only by exceptional circumstances." See Wolff Packing House Co. v. Court of Industrial Relations, 262 U.S. 522, 534 (1923). See also Morehead v. New York ex rel. Tipaldo, 298 U.S. 587, 611 (1936).

[18] Adkins v. Children's Hospital, 261 U.S. 525, 544 (1923).

[19] Edward S. Corwin, "The Supreme Court and the Fourteenth Amendment," in *American Constitutional History: Essays by Edward S. Corwin,* ed. Alpheus Thomas Mason and Gerald Garvey (New York: Harper Torchbooks, 1964), p. 96.

[20] See Robert H. Jackson, *The Struggle for Judicial Supremacy: A Study of a Crisis in American Power Politics* (New York: Vintage Books, 1941), p. 290.

[21] Corwin, "The Supreme Court and the Fourteenth Amendment," p. 91.

import of its definition of fact situations meant that it would be attaching a greater significance to extralegal facts. More important, it raised the possibility that the legal relevance of extralegal data might be formally confirmed. The Court had all along been using extralegal facts in the form of history and social Darwinism. One should keep in mind the new concern manifested by social scientists about scientific method at the end of the nineteenth century and the subsequent growth of more reliable standards for measuring the validity of factual assumptions expressed by the Court. It then stands to reason that once the Court became conscious of the critical importance of the role of facts in the process of judicial interpretation or directed the attention of the public to its use of facts, it would have to exercise, sooner or later, greater care and caution to insure that when extralegal facts were used, they depicted realities and not fictions.

Legislative and Adjudicative Facts

The Court claimed broad powers of judicial review during the first three-quarters of the nineteenth century, but in practice it rarely exercised them. The largely agrarian character of the United States gave little impetus to legislatures to exercise their powers and consequently provided few occasions for the application of the power of judicial review. However, toward the end of the century the Court was faced with an expanding volume of state regulatory legislation passed under the police power. By 1885 the police power was construed with wide latitude and subsequently became an important constitutional concept. It was defined in that year by Justice Stephen J. Field as the power "to prescribe regulations to promote the health, peace, morals, education, and good order of the people, and to legislate so as to increase the industries of the State, develop its resources, and add to its wealth and prosperity."[22]

Given the broad nature of the constitutional mandates authorizing the federal powers, and the all-embracing nature of the state police power, legislatures exercised extensive powers to enact a wide range of regulatory statutes. Since most reform

[22] Barbier v. Connolly, 113 U.S. 27, 31 (1885).

legislation that regulated diverse enterprises—from employment agencies to cemeteries—could plausibly be enacted under the police power, the Court began to inquire into the legislative facts that purportedly justified such legislation.[23] If the Court had simply assumed that all legislation enacted under the aegis of the police power was constitutional, the power of judicial review would have been rendered meaningless. Unless the Court was willing to take issue with legislative facts offered in support of a contested statute, the mere existence of legislative facts would have served as the test of constitutionality. Similarly, judicial review would have been a moot power. Thus, when the Court struck down social welfare legislation, it did so by disputing legislative facts.

There are basically two legal categories of facts within constitutional law: adjudicative facts and legislative facts. The Supreme Court had always been concerned with facts, but primarily with adjudicative facts. Adjudicative facts describe what has happened in a particular case, and they are usually established by a jury. In other words, adjudicative facts link litigant to statute and are therefore central to all legal controversies. For example, whether an individual ran an employment agency without applying for a license, as required by law, poses a question of adjudicative fact. On the other hand, the question of whether a statute that requires such a license is a reasonable exercise of the police power is one of legislative fact. Legislative facts therefore relate legislative policy to the purported constitutional authorization of a statute.[24] Insofar as legislative facts demonstrate an ostensible social need or salutary effect of a given statute, they are characteristically extralegal; such judgments cannot be based wholly on materials internal to the law. Since legislative facts are in effect a legal synonym for sociological analysis, it would seem inevitable that the legislature that formulated them, or the court that reviewed them, would take note of the social sciences.

[23] See H. W. Bickle, "Judicial Determination of Questions of Fact Affecting the Constitutional Validity of Legislative Action," 38 *Harvard Law Review* 6 (1924–25).

[24] Cf. Francis D. Wormuth, "The Impact of Economic Legislation upon the Supreme Court," 6 *Journal of Public Law* 296, 304 (1957), and Paul A. Freund, "Review of Facts in Constitutional Cases," in Edmond Cahn, ed., *Supreme Court and Supreme Law* (Bloomington: Indiana University Press, 1954), pp. 47–54.

Once the Court seriously began to review legislative facts, especially with respect to social welfare legislation, it was faced with two alternatives. First, the Court could note the existence of legislative facts, thereby confirming the reasonableness and constitutionality of the statute in question; second, it could dispute the validity of legislative facts, thereby denying the reasonableness and constitutionality of the statute. The second course of action was the one usually pursued by the Court in reviewing social welfare legislation. Thus the Court's growing inclination to test legislative facts was related concurrently to the emergence of the new principle of presumptive unconstitutionality. On the other hand, when the traditional principle of presumptive constitutionality was operative, its force varied inversely with the extent of the Court's knowledge in favor of the statute. When legislative facts were not convincing enough to justify a contested statute, the Court in sustaining the statute would rely on the traditional principle of presumptive constitutionality and, if necessary, hypothesize on what the legislative facts might have been.[25] To be sure, substantive due-process adjudication plunged the Court into a maelstrom of factual problems. Once the Court began to traffic in legislative facts, it called into question not only its construction of the Constitution but also its construction of social reality.

Adjudicating Legislative Facts

Before the Court chose to construe the due-process clause as a substantive limitation on the police power of the states, in the case of Munn v. Illinois,[26] decided in 1877, it sustained an Illinois statute that fixed rates for grain elevators. Significantly in the Munn case the Court refused to raise the question whether a state of facts actually existed that justified the exercise of the police power. Instead the Court relied on the traditional principle of presumptive constitutionality, stating that such power had long been justified by Anglo-American history. Chief Justice Morrison

[25] Note, "The Presumption of Constitutionality Reconsidered," 36 *Columbia Law Review* 283 (1936).

[26] Munn v. Illinois, 94 U.S. 113 (1877).

R. Waite did assume that something must have happened to prompt the legislature to enact rate regulations, although he gave no indication of what that exigency might have been. Instead Waite accepted the description of the available grain market facilities presented by the plaintiffs in error, but this description did not persuasively demonstrate the need for the Illinois statute. The principle of presumptive constitutionality, Waite argued, made it unnecessary for the Court to press the question of legislative fact: "For our purposes we must assume that, if a state of facts could exist that would justify such legislation, it actually did exist when the statute now under consideration was passed. . . . If no state of circumstances could exist to justify such a statute, then we may declare this one void, because in excess of the legislative power of the State. But if it could, we must presume it did."[27]

Waite thus held that "when private property is 'affected with a public interest, it ceases to be *juris privati* only.'" This constitutional rule had been announced "by Lord Chief Justice Hale more than two hundred years ago, in his treatise *De Portibus Maris* . . . and has been accepted without objection as an essential element in the law of property ever since." Therefore, Waite emphasized, when "one devotes his property to a use in which the public has an interest, he, in effect, grants to the public an interest in that use, and must submit to be controlled by the public for the common good, to the extent of the interest he has thus created."[28] Curiously enough, he also argued that this legal conception of property was based on a "long known and well-established principle of social science."[29] However, Waite did not bother to explain or clarify this principle of social science. In any event, the social science Waite had in mind bore no resemblance to the economics of Adam Smith or David Ricardo, and it certainly was unrelated to the Darwinistic social science that prevailed in the nineteenth century.

Today it is commonly agreed that a free market that benefits everyone cannot be preserved without economic regulations. Like-

---

[27] *Ibid.*, p. 132.
[28] *Ibid.*, p. 126.
[29] *Ibid.*, p. 133.

wise, in the Munn case, the Court acknowledged that it approved the Illinois rate regulations because they were designed to curb monopolistic practices. Now it is also a common assumption that the police power should be exercised in order to promote the general welfare of the community. However, this has not always been the case. On occasion the police power was used to promote vested interests, as was true in the case of Powell v. Pennsylvania,[30] decided in 1888. In this instance the Court upheld a statute forbidding the manufacture or sale of oleomargarine. As in the Munn case, the Court also accepted without question the legislative determination that the police power had been reasonably employed. Specifically, the Court accepted the legislative fact that oleomargarine was dangerous to the public health and unfit for consumption. A lower court had rejected counsel's offer to provide contrary evidence—that oleomargarine was a wholesome and nutritious article of food. The Supreme Court rejected a similar offer and relied instead on the legislature's judgment. On behalf of the Court Justice Harlan refused counsel's offer of an alternate statement of facts, commenting, "It is entirely consistent with that offer that many, indeed, that most kinds of oleomargarine butter in the market contain ingredients that are or may become injurious to health. The Court cannot say, from anything of which it may take judicial cognizance, that such is not the fact." The determination of potential danger, Harlan argued, was the special job of the legislature, and he announced that there were no apparent facts (as there could hardly be if the Court refused to look at them) showing that rights protected by fundamental law had been violated.[31]

Since Harlan's opinion was written only three years before the Court signaled its readiness to find substantive restrictions in the due-process clause, it is important to note here the Court's conception of its fact-finding mandate. Harlan accordingly emphasized that courts should not enter into a discussion of legislative facts: "It is not a part of their functions to conduct investigations of facts entering into questions of public policy merely, and to sustain or frustrate the legislative will, embodied in stat-

[30] Powell v. Pennsylvania, 127 U.S. 678 (1888).
[31] *Ibid.*, p. 684.

utes. . . ."[32] The responsibility for such investigations, Harlan pointed out, is political and belongs to the legislature. The Pennsylvania legislature, "upon the fullest investigation, as we must conclusively presume," has determined that the prohibition of the sale of oleomargarine promotes the public health. If this legislation were merely unwise, appeal must be had to the ballot box and not the judiciary.[33]

Since the Court did not evaluate legislative facts for itself but only "presumed" that they were valid, the high bench was manifestly employing the traditional principle of presumptive constitutionality in defense of the police power. However, it is noteworthy that Harlan concluded by suggesting that the Court would not always assume every exercise of the police power to be constitutional. What is more, Harlan paradoxically indicated that in the future the Court would not be reluctant to conduct its own factual investigation. The judiciary department, Harlan wrote,

is bound not to give effect to statutory enactments that are plainly forbidden by the Constitution. This duty, the Court has said, is always one of extreme delicacy; for . . . it is often difficult to determine whether such enactments are within the powers granted to or possessed by the Legislature. Nevertheless, if the incompatibility of the Constitution and the statute is clear or palpable, the courts must give effect to the former. And such would be the duty of the court if the State Legislature, under the pretence of guarding the public health, the public morals, or the public safety, should invade the rights, life, liberty, or property, or other rights, secured by the supreme law of the land.[34]

It is apparent from Justice Field's dissenting opinion that the Court knew that the real purpose of the Pennsylvania statute was to protect dairy farmers from competition. But by applying the traditional principle of presumptive constitutionality, and by assuming the existence of valid legislative facts, the Court found it unnecessary to question whether the Pennsylvania statute violated any rights of due process.

[32] *Ibid.,* p. 685.
[33] *Ibid.,* p. 686.
[34] *Ibid.,* pp. 686–87.

The Powell case, as we have noted, brought the Court to the threshold of the substantive due-process era. Although the Court emphatically disavowed the task of examining legislative facts, it nevertheless indicated that it stood ready to invalidate any abuse of the police power. If the traditional principle of presumption continued to operate, and if the Court continued to assume and not question the validity of legislative facts, it would be difficult for the high bench to negate any exercise of the police power. Had Harlan's dictum that courts should not "conduct investigations of facts entering into questions of public policy" actually prevailed on the Court, how could the high bench determine when an exercise of the police power violated constitutional guarantees? Certainly, in order to hold open all the options of judicial review, questions of legislative facts would have to be considered as questions of law.

Undoubtedly the Powell decision brought the Court closer to a substantive interpretation of the due-process clause. Another case decided in the same year also portended the rapidly developing kinship between substantive due process and private property. The Kansas legislature in 1881 had passed a statute forbidding the manufacture of intoxicating beverages except those used for medical and scientific purposes. The Court sustained this act in Mugler v. Kansas[35] on grounds similar to those used in the Powell case—that the legislature could lawfully exercise the police powers for the protection of public morals, health, and safety. Yet Justice Harlan warned again that not all exercise of the police power would be presumed constitutional: "It does not at all follow that every statute enacted ostensibly for the promotion of these ends, is to be accepted as a legitimate exertion of the police powers of the State. There are, of necessity, limits beyond which legislation cannot rightfully go."[36] More significantly, Harlan suggested that the Court was not bound by an abstract jurisprudence. Indeed, he intimated that the Court was developing a new attitude toward legislative facts: "The courts are not bound by mere forms, nor are they to be mislead by mere pretenses. They are at liberty—indeed, are under a solemn duty

[35] Mugler v. Kansas, 123 U.S. 623 (1887).
[36] *Ibid.*, p. 661.

—to look at the substance of things whenever they enter upon the inquiry whether the legislature has transcended the limits of its authority."[37] If the Court was going to seriously question the "substance of things," it would also have to seriously examine legislative facts. The Court would shortly do just that when oleomargarine again became a contested product.

In the case of Schollenberger v. Pennsylvania,[38] decided in 1898, the Court retreated from the Powell decision, striking down a Pennsylvania statute that forbade the importation of oleomargarine into the state. Although the Court now found that oleomargarine was a wholesome commodity, thus reversing its previous appraisal of legislative fact, Justice Peckham declared that his decision was not "inconsistent" with the Powell case. On the contrary, Peckham argued, the two cases could be differentiated because the exercise of the police power in the Powell case did not affect interstate commerce. Thus, while the Powell case primarily posed an issue of due process, the Schollenberger case was different because it required adjudication under the commerce clause. Therefore, Peckham argued, Pennsylvania could prohibit the manufacture and sale of oleomargarine because such action did not affect interstate commerce. But the state could not prohibit the importation of oleomargarine because such action would interfere with interstate commerce.

In state due-process adjudication the Court can uphold legislation, as it did in the Powell case, regardless of its own appraisal of legislative facts. Or, if the Court so chooses, it can make its own finding of legislative facts and rule in accord with them. But in adjudication under the commerce clause the factual problem is somewhat different. Because the commerce clause grants the federal government broad powers, the Court acts, in effect, like an umpire of the federal system when interpreting the clause. Therefore, in this kind of adjudication the Court is more likely to find legislative facts for itself. In the Schollenberger case the Court did find its own legislative facts, but in doing so the high bench disregarded its previous assumption that oleomargarine was dangerous. The Court now

[37] *Ibid.*
[38] Schollenberger v. Pennsylvania, 171 U.S. 1 (1898).

found that oleomargarine was a pure food product and consequently ruled that any state restriction on its importation would conflict with the federal government's power to control interstate commerce.

In order to demonstrate that oleomargarine was wholesome, the Court used extralegal facts. What was not known about oleomargarine in the Powell case had suddenly become, in the Schollenberger case, universally apparent. According to Justice Peckham, oleomargarine was obviously wholesome, and "every intelligent man knows its general nature, and that it is prepared as an element of food, and is dealt in as such to a large extent throughout this country and in Europe."[39] Peckham quoted the *Encyclopaedia Britannica* to this effect and referred to the reports of the Commissioner of Agriculture. These extralegal facts, he said, persuasively demonstrated that oleomargarine was a proper subject of commerce among the states.[40] However, Justice Horace Gray in a dissenting opinion argued that the two cases were inconsistent. In one instance, Gray pointed out, the Court ignored extralegal data that might have had an important bearing upon the outcome of the case; in the other the Court had relied upon extralegal facts. Gray insisted that the Powell decision had "establish[ed] that the courts cannot take judicial cognizance, without proof, either that oleomargarine is wholesome, or that it is unwholesome; and we are unable to perceive how judicial cognizance of such a fact can be acquired by referring to the various opinions which have found expression in scientific publications, or in testimony given in cases before other courts and between other parties."[41]

The Schollenberger case divided the Court on the propriety and consistency of its use of extralegal facts. Thus far the Court's policy on the use of extralegal facts seemed to be underscored with ambivalence. It can be said in general that the process of judicial interpretation at this time did not so much begin with a premise that led the Court to a conclusion but, to use Jerome

[39] *Ibid.*, p. 10.
[40] *Ibid.*
[41] *Ibid.*, p. 27 (dissenting opinion).

Frank's words, appeared to start "with a conclusion more or less vaguely formed. . . ."[42]

Affirming the Fact-Finding Prerogative

"The general experience of mankind,"[43] Justice Brown had indicated in 1898, would help guide the Court in its decision-making process. In the new century due-process adjudication, given the Court's negative approach to social welfare legislation, transformed the Court's somewhat ambivalent attitude toward legislative facts into one of intense concern. American constitutional jurisprudence had clearly entered a new phase. The law, Woodrow Wilson wrote optimistically, would follow the facts, and not precede, predict, or invent them.[44] While this prediction was not entirely accurate, extralegal facts did become increasingly conspicuous in Supreme Court opinions. More important, the Court's consistent use of extralegal facts in due-process cases actually marked the beginning of a long trend in judicial interpretation that eventually led to the Court's use of modern social science and to the making of a more objective and realistic constitutional law.

To be sure, although the Court had clearly warned that it would be looking at "the substance of things"—would be defining fact situations in a more diligent and exacting manner—still the justices did not rush to discard their conservative biases and value preferences. If the "paternal theory of government," which Justice Brewer was frank enough to call "odious,"[45] was only half as repugnant to the rest of the Court, it was not likely that facts would serve as an immediate and effective remedy for such a

[42] Jerome Frank, *Law and the Modern Mind* (Garden City, N.Y.: Doubleday Anchor Books, 1963), p. 108.

[43] Holden v. Hardy, 169 U.S. 366, 396 (1898). Here the Court sustained a Utah statute restricting the hours of work in underground mines on the basis of the "general experience of mankind" that more than eight hours of such toil is dangerous. Justice Brown's opinion, however, was not free from the suggestion that comparable legislation for other industries would be unconstitutional.

[44] Woodrow Wilson, "The Law and the Facts," 5 *American Political Science Review* 1, 2 (1911).

[45] Budd v. New York, 143 U.S. 517, 551 (1892) (Justice Brewer's dissenting opinion).

strong prejudice. However, once the Court did emphasize its fact-finding prerogative and evinced a formal interest in extra-legal data, it would be more difficult for it to make constitutional law by using abstract legal fictions. With the Court prepared to examine various factual questions for itself, the theoretical distinctions between law and fact and between adjudicative and legislative facts, always tenuous enough, became in practice even more ambiguous, in effect losing their significance altogether. The Court's new attitude toward fact-finding meant an expansion of the appellate function, because, as noted previously, appellate courts traditionally did not find facts but more often than not merely took cognizance of them. In view of the complex social and economic questions the Supreme Court was called upon to decide, and given the abundant and by no means consistent technical evidence the Court would have to sift, taking cognizance of facts became analogous to finding them.

While the Supreme Court was demonstrating a pronounced interest in facts,[46] there was no clear indication of what kind of facts the Court would accept on other authority and what kind it might want to establish for itself. But it is apparent that the Court was particularly inclined to find facts in cases involving disputed property rights. When, for example, the Court affirmed the constitutionality of a Texas act of 1897 that had been challenged as a violation of the contract clause,[47] it explicitly stated that regardless of any ruling by a state court, it nonetheless possessed "paramount authority to determine for itself the existence or the non-existence of the contract set up, and whether its obligation has been impaired by the state enactment."[48] When the Court sustained a Virginia seizure of land over a challenge that the taking was not for public uses, it noted that although there had been no specific finding of fact that Virginia's power of eminent domain had been exercised for a public use, it was willing to presume that this was the case. However, the Court saw fit to warn that the principle of presumptive constitutionality was not inviolable and would not inhibit it from making its own

[46] See Elwell v. Fosdick, 134 U.S. 500, 513 (1890).
[47] Wilson v. Standefer, 184 U.S. 399 (1902).
[48] *Ibid.*, pp. 411–12.

finding of facts. Justice William H. Moody accordingly wrote, "No case is recalled where this court has condemned as a violation of the Fourteenth Amendment a taking upheld by the state court as a taking for public uses in conformity with its laws. . . . We must not be understood as saying that cases may not arise where this court would decline to follow the state courts in their determination of the uses for which land could be taken by the right of eminent domain."[49] Doubtless, then, the issues in question rather than any logical and coherent legal theory were shaping the Court's new attitude toward facts.

Be that as it may, extralegal facts and common beliefs were cited by the Court to sustain a compulsory vaccination law in the case of Jacobson v. Massachusetts,[50] decided in 1905. The Court referred to "high medical authority" to substantiate the common belief that vaccinations tended to halt the spread of disease. However, the Court in this instance had to choose between conflicting medical statements. In effect, then, the Court had to make the ultimate finding of legislative fact, demonstrating that the formal distinction between law and fact was primarily a matter of academic concern. Whether the statute actually contributed to the public health constituted a question of legislative fact. Whether the facts justified the legislature's exercise of the police power posed a question of law. But since the Court had to answer both questions, and whereas the factual finding obviously dictated the legal answer, clearly "the borderline between law and fact" was indeed "hazy enough to make differentiation extremely difficult."[51]

The Court again confirmed its new concern for legislative facts in the case of Laurel Hill Cemetery v. San Francisco,[52] decided in 1910, where it upheld a municipal ordinance prohibiting burials within city limits. In emphasizing the Court's willingness to find legislative facts for itself, Justice Holmes wrote, "Where the finding of fact is merely a premise to laying down a rule of law . . . this Court has power to form its own judgment without the

---

[49] Hairston v. Danville & Western Railway Co., 208 U.S. 598, 607 (1908).
[50] Jacobson v. Massachusetts, 197 U.S. 11 (1905).
[51] Note, "The Presentation of Facts Underlying the Constitutionality of Statutes," 49 *Harvard Law Review* 631, 632 (1936).
[52] Laurel Hill Cemetery v. San Francisco, 216 U.S. 358, 365 (1910).

aid of a jury."[53] However, Holmes also indicated that for the time being the Court would not be unduly influenced by scientific authority. Accordingly the Court rejected the plaintiff's contention, which was based on scientific authority, that city burials did not pose any danger to the public health. While the Court noted that the "opinions of scientific men" regarded as mere superstition the fear that such burials caused disease, and even though Holmes was personally receptive to these opinions, he reasoned that "tradition and the habits of the community" provided a more important basis for judgment.[54]

Nevertheless, there can be no doubt the Court had declared itself free both to scrutinize and to establish crucial legislative facts. Speaking for the Court in 1924, Holmes again stressed the point he had made in the Laurel Hill case: the Court stood ready to establish any fact relevant to the decisional process. The Court, he wrote, "may ascertain as it sees fit any fact that is merely a ground for laying down a rule of law. . . ."[55] Even the proliferation in later years of regulatory agencies, with their special role of finding facts and making administrative rules, did not prompt the Court to limit its ultimate fact-finding authority in the field of administrative law.[56]

The Court's reiteration of its freedom to adjudicate legislative facts did not mean that the high bench would only entertain narrowly drawn factual questions raised by isolated legal controversies. On the contrary, since constitutional cases by definition involve not only individual litigants but general categories of potential litigants, and since constitutional issues usually reflect architectonic political problems, the Court's professed interest in legislative facts meant that the courtroom would be a forum for speculation on broad social problems. The Court, needless to say, would be making factual pronouncements on theoretical issues that concerned the social sciences.

As Kenneth Karst has written, "Every constitutional issue contains important factual elements which control the decision

[53] *Ibid.*
[54] *Ibid.*, p. 366.
[55] Chastleton Corp. v. Sinclair, 264 U.S. 543, 548 (1924).
[56] See Louis L. Jaffe, "Judicial Review: Question of Fact," 69 *Harvard Law Review* 1020 (1956).

whether they are expressly considered or remain buried in the mental equipment which the judge brings to the decisional process."[57] This means that questions of legislative fact are inevitably answered by the judge whether he is aware of it or not. In general, Karst has pointed out, legislative facts must be determined when two basic questions concerning a statute are raised. First, with respect to the objective or the purpose of the statute:

1. How much will this regulation advance the chosen governmental objective? . . .
a) If the regulation is completely successful, how much more safe, or healthy, or moral will the community be?
b) What is the chance of complete success for the regulation? Of partial success?
2. How much more will this regulation advance the objective than some other regulation which might interfere less with constitutionally protected interests?

Second, with respect to the effect or impact of the statute:

1. How much will freedom (of speech, of commerce, etc.) be restricted by this regulation? . . .
a) If the regulation operates with its maximum restrictive effect, how, and how much, will freedom be restricted?
b) What is the chance that the regulation will have its maximum restrictive effect? A partial effect?
2. How much more restrictive is this regulation than some other regulation which might achieve the same objective?[58]

Although early substantive due-process adjudication did pose complex factual questions of the kind delineated by Karst, the Court was not necessarily interested in valid answers. That is, the Court was generally not prepared to debate the quality or validity of legislative facts. What did concern the Court at first was whether a body of legislative facts existed on the basis of which the legislature could claim that its enactments were reasonable. This would not always remain, even in a legal sense,

[57] Kenneth L. Karst, "Legislative Facts in Constitutional Litigation," in Philip B. Kurland, ed., *The Supreme Court Review* (Chicago: University of Chicago Press, 1960), p. 84.
[58] *Ibid.*

the Court's only concern with extralegal facts. For the time being, however, when the Court did use extralegal facts, this did not mean that it had confirmed the scientific validity of these facts. In any event, the Supreme Court's firm expression of interest in legislative facts did suggest that a relatively more factual jurisprudence was beginning to develop. With the Court busily engaged in striking down social welfare legislation, impetus was added to the factual development of American constitutional law when progressive jurists, shortly after the turn of the century, began to call for a greater exposure of the law to the new social science. However, the first problem to be surmounted was that of bringing the lessons of nascent social science to the attention of the high bench. For though the Supreme Court was functioning as a superlegislature, it remained, after all, a court of law. Therefore, the Court's social science education would have to conform with legal usage.

CHAPTER FOUR

Extralegal Facts
and the Court's Defense
of Property Rights

Facts as Judicial Therapy

In substantive due-process adjudication between 1908 and 1937, the Court demonstrated a keen interest in legislative facts. Yet the Court's pronounced interest in fact-finding did not mean that fact situations would necessarily be defined in an accurate and realistic way just because it was using extralegal facts. Indeed, the Court's generally negative approach to social welfare legislation suggested that it lacked a valid factual appreciation of many of the critical issues and problems of the day. Louis D. Brandeis saw no hope for a progressive and enlightened jurisprudence unless the Court could gain a better command of the facts. Constitutional law, Brandeis noted, had a tendency to lag behind the facts of life and had not adjusted to emerging political, economic, and social ideals. "No law, written or unwritten," he insisted, "can be understood without a full knowledge of the facts out of which it arises, and to which it is to be applied."[1] Brandeis therefore concluded that greater judicial scrutiny of social facts was sure to make the Court more sympathetic to social needs. Other liberal jurists agreed and, with Brandeis, suggested that facts might serve as a therapeutic treatment for a Court that

[1] Louis D. Brandeis, "The Living Law," 10 *Illinois Law Review* 461, 467 (1916).

stubbornly resisted social welfare legislation because, from its high perch on Mount Olympus, it was unable and perhaps unwilling to see industrial conditions and the vital needs of the people.

Thus Benjamin Cardozo stated that courts and legislatures were operating in "proud and silent isolation."[2] Cardozo suggested that if judges and social scientists would begin to communicate, a mediation between court and legislature would follow. To achieve this end, Cardozo proposed that a ministry of justice be established that would operate as a board to consolidate all facts germane to the judicial decision-making process. This board "would enlighten itself constantly through all available sources of guidance and instruction; through consultation with scholars; through study of the law reviews, the journals of social science, the publications of the learned generally; and through investigation of remedies and methods in other jurisdictions, foreign and domestic."[3] While such a board would only have the power of recommendation, the subsequent creation of lines of communication would mean that the "spaces between the planets will at least be bridged."[4]

Likewise, Edward S. Corwin, reporting to the National Conference on the Science of Politics in 1924, saw the need for the development of a scientific technique and methodology so that the various fields of political science might formulate their inquiries on a factual rather than a judgmental basis. Corwin conceded the usefulness of a statistical methodology and an applied psychology for several facets of public administration, but he was not certain how any of these methods could be applied to the problems of public law. Nevertheless he did call attention to gaps in the mechanism of judicial review having to do with the Court's "ability to take cognizance of the facts alleged in support of legislation, especially in the broad field in which the question of constitutionality of statutes pivots on the question of their 'reasonableness.' "[5] To fill this gap, Corwin urged that an agency

[2] Benjamin N. Cardozo, "A Ministry of Justice," 35 *Harvard Law Review* 113, 114 (1921).
[3] *Ibid.*, p. 124.
[4] *Ibid.*, p. 125.
[5] Edward S. Corwin, "Reports of the National Conference on the Science of Politics," 18 *American Political Science Review* 148, 153 (1924).

similar to Cardozo's ministry of justice be created that would offer factual advice to the Court. However, neither Cardozo nor Corwin explained how extralegal data could be effectively brought to the attention of the Court through nonjudicial channels without compromising the Court's independence.

The Court's Sources of Information

Though the Supreme Court obviously did not possess proper facilities for finding facts or for reappraising the fact-finding task the legislature presumably had already performed, social welfare legislation was often found unconstitutional on the basis of the Court's own finding of facts.[6] Theoretically, appellate courts were not intended to be original triers of facts. However, substantive due-process adjudication left the Court with little choice but to perform the functions of a legislative research committee. Accordingly the Court has relied on at least five sources for finding or corroborating its facts.

First, by applying the traditional principle of presumptive constitutionality, the Court could simply accept the legislature's statement of fact that conditions existed which made the statute in question reasonable. Needless to say, the Court's invalidation of social welfare legislation signified that it had rejected the legislature's statement of fact. But when the Court was prepared to agree with the legislature's judgment, this acquiescence pointed to a source of judicial information. Second, the Court could question legislative findings by requiring that the justification for legislation be established by evidence tendered in ordinary litigation. Thus, for example, when the New York milk control law of 1933 was contested, which had permitted dealers without well-advertised trade names to sell their produce one cent cheaper than other producers, the Supreme Court returned the case to a district court, stating, "With the notable expansion of the scope of governmental regulation, and the consequent assertion of violation of constitutional rights, it is increasingly important that when it becomes necessary for the Court to deal

[6] See Ernst Freund, *The Standards of American Legislation* (Chicago: University of Chicago Press, 1917), p. 96.

with the facts relating to particular commercial or industrial conditions, they should be presented concretely with appropriate determinations upon evidence, so that conclusions shall not be reached without adequate factual support."[7] Third, legislation was often drafted in such a way as to contain the reasons for its enactment; the Court could then use the legislative draft itself as a source of judicial information.[8] Fourth, the Court could find facts by citing "common knowledge," as in Jacobson v. Massachusetts,[9] or by referring to reference books, as in Schollenberger v. Pennsylvania.[10] The Court technically received information this way through the device of judicial notice. Fifth, the Court could draw its information from the brief of counsel or, as it became popularly known, a Brandeis brief.[11]

Although none of these five sources of information was ideal, according to Felix Frankfurter, it was the responsibility of the Supreme Court to insist at least on the adequacy of the data presented to it. But, as Frankfurter noted, the data should have been "already explored and sifted by trial and intermediate tribunals."[12] Even when this was done, the Supreme Court set forth its own definition of fact situations by relying for the most part on judicial notice and the Brandeis brief.[13]

[7] Borden's Co. v. Baldwin, 293 U.S. 194, 210 (1934).

[8] See, for example, Lindsley v. Natural Carbonic Gas Co., 220 U.S. 61 (1911).

[9] Jacobson v. Massachusetts, 197 U.S. 11 (1905).

[10] Schollenberger v. Pennsylvania, 171 U.S. 1 (1898).

[11] Felix Frankfurter and James M. Landis, *The Business of the Supreme Court* (New York: Macmillan, 1927), pp. 312–15.

[12] Felix Frankfurter and Henry Hart, "The Business of the Supreme Court at October Term, 1934," 49 *Harvard Law Review* 68, 96 (1934).

[13] It should be noted that the Court does not normally treat questions of ordinary facts, although exceptions to the rule are sometimes made. For example, the Court honored this rule in the breach in the case of Dick v. New York Life Insurance Co., 359 U.S. 437 (1959). The case involved the narrowly drawn issue of whether an insuree had died as a result of suicide or accident. The state law presumed in the given circumstances that the death was accidental and placed the burden of proof upon the insurer to prove otherwise. A jury found that the death was accidental, and the district court ruled in favor of the beneficiary. But the court of appeals overturned the decision, ruling that the evidence did not justify the submission of the issue to a jury. The Supreme Court, after reviewing the evidence on this constitutionally remote issue, held that the evidence was sufficient to raise a jury question. But Justice Frankfurter, in a spirited dissent, found it necessary to remind the Court that "questions of fact have traditionally been deemed to be the kind of questions which ought not to be recanvassed here unless they are entangled in the proper determination of constitutional or other important legal issues" (p. 454).

Judicial Notice

Judicial notice is the act by which a court, on its own, establishes facts without the formal submission of evidence. These facts are not properly the subject of testimony and are regarded instead as having been established by common knowledge. The Court has recognized a wide range of facts: "that there has been a depression, and that a decline of market values is one of its concomitants . . . that Confederate money depreciated in value during the war between the states";[14] that "unparalleled demands for relief arose during the recent period of depression";[15] and that "air carriage has brought Hawaii closer to the continent."[16] Judicial notice allows the Court to give legal expression to what is taken to be common knowledge; as Justice Harlan has stated, "What everybody knows the court must know. . . ." Thus common beliefs, like common knowledge, do not have to be backed by evidence in order to sustain the action of either legislatures or courts.[17] As Justice Joseph McKenna has observed, the Court "should not shut its eyes to the facts of the world and assume not to know what everybody else knows."[18]

However, common knowledge is not always compatible with scientific knowledge. Nor is there any guarantee that the Court's definition of common knowledge might not constitute a subjective judgment. Therefore, when the Court did take notice of common knowledge, at the beginning of the century, it did not necessarily have a full knowledge of the facts, nor did common knowledge constitute a sound basis for the determination of what was a reasonable exercise of the police power.

This was clearly evident in the celebrated case of Lochner v. New York,[19] decided in 1905, in which a New York statute making it unlawful for an employee in a bakery to work more than ten hours a day or sixty hours a week was struck down. In holding the act unconstitutional, the Court contended that there

---

[14] Ohio Bell Telephone Co. v. Commission, 301 U.S. 292, 301 (1937).

[15] West Coast Hotel Co. v. Parrish, 300 U.S. 379, 399 (1937).

[16] Stainback v. Mo Hock Ke Lok Po, 336 U.S. 368, 375 (1949).

[17] Jacobson v. Massachusetts, 197 U.S. 11, 30, 35 (1905).

[18] Caminetti v. United States, 242 U.S. 470, 502 (1917) (dissenting opinion).

[19] Lochner v. New York, 198 U.S. 45 (1905).

was no reasonable relationship between the hours prescribed by the statute and the purity of bread or the health of a baker. Though Justice Peckham admitted that statistics suggested that the trade of baking was not as healthy as some other occupations, he could find no grounds for the legislature to restrict the baker's "right to enter into a contract of his own choosing." Inasmuch as an individual's right to buy or sell labor was part of the liberty protected by the Fourteenth Amendment, the exercise of the police power, Peckham emphasized, necessarily raised vital questions the Court must answer. Therefore, in each instance the Court must ask, "Is this a fair, reasonable and appropriate exercise of the police power of the State, or is it an unreasonable, unnecessary and arbitrary interference with the right of the individual to his personal liberty or to enter into those contracts in relation to labor which may seem to him appropriate or necessary for the support of himself and his family?"[20] This was not a question, Peckham hastened to add, "of substituting the judgment of the court for that of the legislature."[21] But it was the judgment of the Court that "there can be no fair doubt that the trade of a baker, in and of itself, is not an unhealthy one to that degree which would authorize the legislature to interfere with the right to labor. . . ."[22] Peckham's critical statement of fact was based not on an investigation of the facts but, rather, on "the common understanding that the trade of a baker has never been regarded as an unhealthy one."[23] Common knowledge, Peckham reasoned, suggested that the New York statute violated the due-process clause of the Fourteenth Amendment.

As the Lochner case indicates, not only does the Court exercise complete discretion about what it will judicially notice, but such notice did not mean that the Court was necessarily bound by a fact situation it had voluntarily recognized. That is, even when the Court did take notice of common knowledge to the effect that a legislature had exercised the police power in an arbitrary fashion, it could still decide not to invalidate the contested statute. When,

---

[20] *Ibid.*, p. 56.
[21] *Ibid.*, pp. 56–57.
[22] *Ibid.*, p. 59.
[23] *Ibid.*

for example, a Montana statute was enacted requiring a license for all persons employed in hand laundry work, except for those employed in the steam laundry business and women in places where not more than two persons were employed, the Supreme Court refused to invalidate the statute, even though it was aware that the statute discriminated against Chinese. Justice Holmes, speaking for the Court, emphasized that the statute was the business of the state, even though "it is a matter of common observation that hand laundry work is a widespread occupation of Chinamen in this country while on the other hand it is so rare to see men of our race engaged in it that many of us would be unable to say that they ever had observed a case."[24] However, while Holmes clearly intimated that the statute was unconstitutional as a violation of the equal-protection clause, the Court nevertheless chose to uphold it on the grounds that the bench had not been formally informed of what it obviously already knew.

Common knowledge could be cited in support of legislation or it could be willfully ignored. It is clear that the Court was not bound by common knowledge but remained free to promulgate its own conception of social reality. For example, in the case of Coppage v. Kansas,[25] decided in 1915, the Court reversed a statute designed to insure that employers did not coerce or restrain employees from joining or remaining members of labor unions. The Court's reasoning closely followed the Lochner case: the right of personal liberty, guaranteed by the due-process clause, included the broad right to make a contract for the acquisition of property. The Court's protection of this right certainly amounted to a profitable grant of freedom to employers, but the Court also insisted, unrealistically, that employees benefited equally from this freedom. As Justice Mahlon Pitney remarked, "The right is as essential to the laborer as to the capitalist, to the poor as to the rich. . . ."[26] This hollow dictum was compounded by the Court's ironic insistence that constitutionality did not depend on the mere form of the law or its declared

[24] Quong Wing v. Kirkendall, 223 U.S. 59, 63 (1912).
[25] Coppage v. Kansas, 236 U.S. 1 (1915).
[26] *Ibid.*, p. 14.

purpose but, rather, on its actual operation and effect upon concerned parties.[27] It is certain that the statute strengthened the bargaining position of laborers who previously were unable to negotiate with employers on an equal basis. Indeed, this truth was difficult to deny, as the Court itself almost admitted: "It is said by the Kansas Supreme Court to be a matter of common knowledge that 'employees as a rule, are not fundamentally able to be as independent in making contracts of purchase thereof.'" But in view of this common knowledge, "no doubt, wherever the right of private property exists, there must and will be inequalities of fortune . . . it is self-evident that, unless all things are held in common, some persons must have more property than others. . . ."[28] Although Pitney had confirmed the factual findings of the Kansas Supreme Court, he refused to acknowledge the existence of a reasonable relationship between the statute and health, safety, morals, or general welfare. However, the Court adduced no factual reason for its position.

The Coppage case indicates that the existence of common knowledge did not compel the Court to either sustain or invalidate legislation enacted under the police power. In the following year the Court upheld a Washington statute that imposed license taxes on the privilege of using profit-sharing coupons and trading stamps. In applying the traditional principle of presumptive constitutionality, Justice McKenna remarked on behalf of the Court, "As to what extent legislation should interfere in affairs political philosophers have disputed and always will dispute. It is not in our province to engage on either side, nor to pronounce anticipatory judgments." If the statute was enacted upon a nonarbitrary belief in present evils, the Court was not prepared to match its estimates against that of the legislature.[29] In this instance experience was germane. For, McKenna stated, "if it may be said to be a judgment from experience as against a judgment from speculation, certainly, from its generality, it [the act] cannot be declared to be made in mere wantonness."[30]

[27] *Ibid.*, p. 15.
[28] *Ibid.*, p. 17.
[29] Tanner v. Little, 240 U.S. 369, 385 (1916).
[30] *Ibid.*, p. 386.

Obviously, then, the Court has exercised wide discretion in recognizing, through the device of judicial notice, facts that normally are established under the rules of evidence. This leaves the Court free from the ordinary restrictions of legal procedure to utilize extralegal facts. In the widest possible view of judicial notice, it has been used to refer to any method by which a court receives information apart from the normal legal procedures.[31] It is plain, however, that judicial notice was at best a makeshift device enabling the Court to cite extralegal facts in an arbitrary fashion. Formally, judicial notice permits the Court to recognize common knowledge or extralegal facts of common notoriety. But in performing the delicate task of deciding the permissible extent of the police power, the Court was grappling not with things everybody knew but, rather, with complex economic and social data that made even expert analysis difficult. What the Court actually required was a channel through which it could obtain independent and impartial information.[32] Because the Court lacked such a channel, it was not always as well informed as it might have been. In short, as Jerome Frank has suggested, facts acquired through judicial notice are not necessarily reliable, and such information often amounts to nothing more than "cocktail-hour knowledge."[33]

The Brandeis Brief and "More Authoritative Extra-Legal Data"

Writing in 1909, Roscoe Pound observed that the Supreme Court was unable to obtain the critical facts necessary for the making of informed judgments: "In the ordinary case involving constitutionality, the court has no machinery for getting at the facts. It must decide on the basis of matters of general knowledge and on accepted principles of uniform application."[34] With specific regard for due-process adjudication involving social welfare legis-

---

[31] Howard L. Korn, "Law, Fact, and Science in the Courts," 66 *Columbia Law Review* 1080, 1089 (1966).

[32] See Note, "Social and Economic Facts: Appraisal of Suggested Techniques for Presenting Them to the Courts," 61 *Harvard Law Review* 692 (1948).

[33] Jerome Frank *et al.*, "The Lawyer's Role in Modern Society: A Round Table," 4 *Journal of Public Law* 1, 16 (1955).

[34] Roscoe Pound, "Liberty of Contract," 18 *Yale Law Journal* 454, 469 (1909).

lation, Pound suggested that the American legal system had decayed because of its exclusive concern for "technicality." As a result, a paramount characteristic of the Court's "mechanical jurisprudence" was "the rigorous logical deduction from predetermined conceptions in disregard of and often in the teeth of the actual facts. . . ."[35] To be sure, the Court's application of laissez-faire principles of law to a growing industrial society indicated that the legal conception of reality was antithetical to the reality of industrialism.

As Calvin Woodard has emphasized, reality "in an industrial society is decidedly at odds with the laissez-faire standard."[36] At least two principles forming this standard were implicit in the Court's negative approach to social welfare legislation. First, the Court's reasoning usually suggested that a moral or thinly veiled biological factor was the actual determinant of economic success. Second, economic inequality, more specifically, economic deprivation and poverty, was considered by the Court to be inevitable.[37] As Julius Stone has put it, the root of the Court's false and unrealistic laissez-faire standard lay in its basic factual "assumption that economic relations [did] not affect political and moral relations." This judicial conception of reality could possibly be defended if it could be shown that employers and employees came to the bargaining table with equal resources or with equal "waiting power" and, more important, "if economic relations left the environment and the distribution of social power unaltered."[38] It is obvious, however, that these two propositions were patently false.

The Court's tenuous and false conception of social reality, as previously indicated, was cultivated as it began to wield the power of judicial review in a negative fashion. From 1790 to 1880 the Court had declared only 123 federal, state, and municipal enactments unconstitutional. In contrast, in the thirty-year period from 1880 to 1910, the Court invalidated 150

---

[35] *Ibid.*, p. 462.

[36] Calvin Woodard, "Reality and Social Reform: The Transition from Laissez-Faire to the Welfare State," 72 *Yale Law Journal* 286, 305 (1962).

[37] *Ibid.*

[38] Julius Stone, *Human Law and Human Justice* (Stanford, Calif.: Stanford University Press, 1965), p. 95.

enactments.[39] Not all of these acts were social welfare measures. But the scope and total effect of the Court's power to block social welfare legislation cannot be calculated simply on the basis of the number of acts that were struck down. As Benjamin Cardozo pointed out, "[T]he utility of an external power restraining the legislative judgment is not to be measured by counting the occasions of its exercise."[40] For example, when the Court reversed a Kansas statute that prohibited yellow-dog contracts in the Coppage case,[41] similar statutes were nullified in twelve other states at the same time.[42]

As we have already suggested, the negative use of the power of judicial review in substantive due-process adjudication of social welfare measures meant that the Court had abandoned the traditional principle of presumptive constitutionality. In practice, then, the Court replaced the traditional principle with the new principle of presumptive unconstitutionality. This informal substitution suggested that the burden of proof no longer rested with the party that challenged the constitutionality of a statute enacted under the police power, but rested instead with the legislature. These were the days, Louis Jaffe has remarked, when "economic regulation was fighting for its life. Statutes regulating economic matters, for example, prices and working conditions, were doomed. . . ."[43] Judicial interpretation under the laissez-faire standard had, "in effect, created rights against the public," Charles Fairman has put it, which was "one of the most striking aspects of American public law."[44]

In 1905 Curt Muller, the proprietor of the Grand Laundry in Portland, Oregon, was convicted of violating a state statute specifying in part "that no female be employed in a mechanical establishment, or factory, or laundry more than ten hours during

[39] Blaine F. Moore, *The Supreme Court and Unconstitutional Legislation* (New York: Longmans, Green, 1913), p. 139.

[40] Benjamin N. Cardozo, *The Nature of the Judicial Process* (New Haven, Conn.: Yale University Press, 1961), p. 92.

[41] Coppage v. Kansas, 236 U.S. 1 (1915).

[42] John R. Schmidhauser, *The Supreme Court as Final Arbiter in Federal-State Relations* (Chapel Hill: University of North Carolina Press, 1958), p. 122.

[43] Louis L. Jaffe, "Was Brandeis an Activist? The Search for Intermediate Premises," 80 *Harvard Law Review* 986, 991 (1967).

[44] Charles Fairman, *Mr. Justice Miller and the Supreme Court* (New York: Russell & Russell, 1966), p. 234.

any one day." Muller eventually brought his case to the Supreme Court in expectation that his "rights against the public" would be sustained. But Muller had drawn a formidable opponent: representing the state of Oregon was "the people's attorney," Louis D. Brandeis.

Brandeis recognized the inadequacy of the traditional technique of advocacy based on precedents and abstract legal logic. He understood that radical social welfare measures required an equally radical defense before the Court. If the Supreme Court could be advised of the actual facts, or could be made to see the new social reality, then perhaps it would abandon nineteenth-century judicial rhetoric along with the economics of Adam Smith. Brandeis therefore asked his sister-in-law, Josephine Goldmark, chairman of the Committee on Legislation of the National Consumers' League, to gather the "*facts,* published by anyone with expert knowledge of industry in its relation to women's hours of labor. . . ." A research staff of ten under the direction of Miss Goldmark was formed, and this group, along with a medical student who independently studied the hygiene of occupations, provided Brandeis with the factual material he had requested.[45]

In order to redress the Court's unfavorable attitude toward social welfare legislation, or the unstated principle of presumptive unconstitutionality, Brandeis in the case of Muller v. Oregon,[46] decided in 1908, marshaled his facts in a novel brief. This brief was recognized immediately as an innovation in American advocacy. Traditional advocacy, or legal syllogism based on precedents, was conspicuously absent in the Brandeis brief. Indeed, only two of the brief's 113 pages resembled the traditional form of advocacy. The most salient characteristic of the brief was the numerous extracts of reports by physicians, economists, such critics as Beatrice Webb, factory inspectors, various industrial committees, and sundry bureaus of statistics. These reports provided the Court with detailed descriptions of

[45] Alpheus Thomas Mason, "The Case of the Overworked Laundress," in John A. Garraty, ed., *Quarrels That Have Shaped the Constitution* (New York: Harper and Row, 1964), p. 181.
[46] Muller v. Oregon, 208 U.S. 412 (1908).

industrial conditions and, in particular, of their physical and moral effect on women. Brandeis's unique collection of facts surely represented "the first brief ever based upon authoritative extra-legal data."[47]

Brandeis's use of traditional advocacy was short, simple, and concise. He cited only three cases. Brandeis quoted Justice Peckham in Lochner v. New York[48] to prove that the liberty to sell one's labor, although protected by the Fourteenth Amendment, could be restricted by a "reasonable" use of the police power. Referring to Jacobson v. Massachusetts,[49] he reiterated the Court's argument that the "mere assertion" of a relationship between the restriction and the public health, safety, morality, and general welfare was insufficient and that a "real and substantial relation" had to be demonstrated. Finally, Brandeis cited Holden v. Hardy[50] to the effect that the Court could take notice of extralegal data or "common knowledge." The thrust of Brandeis's formal legal argument was that extralegal data demonstrated the reasonableness of the Oregon statute.

The formal legal argument did not by itself demonstrate the constitutionality of the statute. Brandeis used traditional legal logic for the purpose of convincing the Court that his massive collection of facts was relevant to the process of judicial interpretation. In other words, Brandeis was attempting to establish formally the legal relevance of extralegal data. He relied on extralegal data to substantiate his hypothesis that it was harmful for women to work more than ten hours a day. In effect, Brandeis's case was largely based on extralegal data. Accordingly he argued, "The facts of common knowledge of which the Court may take judicial notice . . . establish, we submit, conclusively, that there is reasonable ground for holding that to permit women in Oregon to work in a 'mechanical establishment, or factory, or laundry' more than ten hours in one day is dangerous to the public health, safety, morals, or welfare."[51]

---

[47] Alpheus Thomas Mason, *Brandeis: Lawyer and Judge in the Modern State* (Princeton, N.J.: Princeton University Press, 1933), p. 107.
[48] Lochner v. New York, 198 U.S. 45 (1905).
[49] Jacobson v. Massachusetts, 197 U.S. 11 (1905).
[50] Holden v. Hardy, 169 U.S. 366 (1898).
[51] Brief for defendant in error, Muller v. Oregon, p. 10.

Actually, the Brandeis brief can be divided into three sections. The first, as we have seen, consisted of a formal legal argument. The second section was a survey of existing domestic and foreign legislation comparable to the statute in question. Finally, the largest section, the one peculiar to the Brandeis brief, consisted of a compendium of the "world's experience upon which the legislation . . . [was] based."[52] This experience was gleaned from more than a hundred sources. Various domestic and foreign medical reports were cited; Dr. Edward Jarvis's *Report of the Massachusetts State Board of Health* (1873) and the *Hygiene of Occupations* by the Swiss physician Theodore Weyl are examples. Also included were such economic reports as *Hours and Wages in Relation to Production* by Luigi Brentano and Professor Etienne Baver's *Travail de nuit des femmes dans l'industrie*. A work by the distinguished psychologist Havelock Ellis, *Man and Women*, and *The Case for the Factory Act* by Beatrice Webb were quoted. The brief also contained many reports by factory inspectors, such as the *Report of the British Chief Inspector of Factories and Workshops* (1901) and the *Report of the German Imperial Factory Inspectors* (1898). Reports from the U.S. Industrial Commission, the French Labor Office, and such meetings as the industrial conference of the National Civic Federation appeared in the brief. In addition, Brandeis produced extracts from reports of many bureaus of statistics representing California, Colorado, Connecticut, Maine, Massachusetts, Nebraska, New Jersey, New York, Pennsylvania, and Wisconsin. Finally, the brief included reports from such diverse bodies as the British Houses of Commons and Lords, the French Senate, the British Association for the Advancement of Science, and the U.S. Senate. Not overlooked was President Roosevelt's State of the Union message delivered to the Fifty-ninth Congress.

Extralegal data from these and other sources were used by Brandeis to substantiate five specific hypotheses. (1) Women are physiologically different from men and are more susceptible to injury resulting from unregulated industrial conditions. (2)

[52] *Ibid.*

Excessive hours of labor generally endanger the health, safety, and morals of women. In particular, the effects of childbirth are disastrous and consequently affect the welfare of the nation. (3) Short workdays foster individual health and improve homelife. The nation in general prospers. (4) Short workdays produce economic benefits. Efficiency and the quality of production are increased. Regularity of employment is stabilized, customers readily yield to the requirements of a fixed working day, the production of inventions is stimulated, and the sphere of female labor increases. (5) The aforementioned benefits result only from uniform restrictions on the workday.

To be sure, Brandeis's objective in advancing these five hypotheses was somewhat paradoxical. While he had obviously filled his brief with a persuasive array of facts, he never insisted that his facts were incontestable. Instead Brandeis simply concluded that in view of the facts presented, "it cannot be said that the Legislature of Oregon had no reasonable ground for believing that the public health, safety, or welfare did not require a legal limitation on women's work in manufacturing and mechanical establishments and laundries to ten hours in one day."[53] This argument was not made for reasons of temporary legal expediency. Brandeis consistently advanced this argument even from the bench, as can be seen from his dissenting opinion in the case of Adams v. Tanner: "These enquiries are entered upon, not for the purpose of determining whether the remedy adopted was wise or even for the purpose of determining what the facts actually were. . . . The sole purpose of the enquiries is to enable this court to decide, whether in view of the facts, actual or possible, the action of the State of Washington was so clearly arbitrary or so unreasonable, that it could not be taken 'by a free government without a violation of fundamental rights.' "[54]

In general, Brandeis stopped short of arguing that facts presented in support of contested legislation were necessarily valid because he did not believe that it was the function of the Court

---

[53] *Ibid.*, p. 113.
[54] Adams v. Tanner, 244 U.S. 590, 600 (1917) (dissenting opinion). Cf. New State Ice Co. v. Liebmann, 285 U.S. 262, 286–87 (1932).

to judge the wisdom of legislation. In his view the Court had merely to discern whether a statute was unreasonable or arbitrary. If extralegal data could be presented in support of a statute, or in support of the reasons for which a statute had been enacted, then the data were *prima facie* proof that the legislature had acted in good faith or had reasonable grounds for believing that its action was necessary. In other words, as long as the Court did not formally profess any interest in the wisdom of legislation, and no Court had, Brandeis could logically argue that the mere existence of extralegal data constituted grounds for accepting the statute in question as a reasonable exercise of the police power.

Justice Brewer's opinion in the Muller case was tersely worded. Speaking for a unanimous Court, Brewer announced that the principle formulated in Lochner v. New York was still binding— legislation that inhibited an individual from contracting freely to work as long as he chose was an "unreasonable, unnecessary and arbitrary interference" with rights and liberties guaranteed by the Constitution. "But this assumes," Brewer added, "that the the difference between the sexes does not justify a different rule respecting a restriction of the hours of labor."[55]

On the contrary, Brewer reasoned, "it may not be amiss, in the present case, before examining the constitutional question, to notice the course of legislation as well as expressions of opinions *from other than judicial sources.*"[56] Having thus extended formal recognition to Brandeis's presentation of extralegal data, Justice Brewer took the unusual step of referring to counsel by name: "In the brief filed by Mr. Louis D. Brandeis, for the defendant in error, is a very copious collection of all these matters, an epitome of which is found in the margin."[57] These extralegal data, Brewer emphasized, "may not be, technically speaking, [legal] authorities, and in them is little or no discussion of the constitutional question presented to us for determination, yet they are significant of a widespread belief that woman's physical structure, and the functions she performs in consequence thereof,

[55] Muller v. Oregon, 208 U.S. 412, 419 (1908).
[56] *Ibid.*, p. 412. Emphasis supplied.
[57] *Ibid.*, p. 419.

justify special legislation restricting or qualifying the conditions under which she should be permitted to toil."[58] Brewer did point out that the Constitution provides "unchanging form limitations upon legislative action." But he also stated, with great significance, "At the same time, when a question of fact is debated and debatable, and the extent to which a special constitutional limitation goes is affected by the truth in respect to that fact, a widespread and long continued belief concerning it is worthy of consideration. We take judicial cognizance of all matters of general knowledge."[59]

The Court had explicitly granted formal approval to the Brandeis brief. Justice Brewer, armed with Brandeis's extralegal data, then emphasized the extralegal fact: "That woman's physical structure and the performance of maternal functions place her at a disadvantage in the struggle for subsistence is obvious." Driving home the point, Brewer stated, "By abundant testimony of the medical fraternity continuance for a long time on her feet at work, repeating this from day to day, tends to injurious effects upon the body, and as healthy mothers are essential to vigorous offspring, the physical well-being of women becomes an object of public interest and care in order to preserve the strength and vigor of the race."[60] Having established that there were legally relevant differences between men and women, the Court ruled that the female "is properly placed in a class by herself and legislation designed for her protection may be sustained, even when the legislation is not necessary for men and could not be sustained."[61] Brewer's opinion was clearly based on extralegal facts showing that the Oregon statute was reasonable and had been enacted for the express purpose of protecting the female "from the greed as well as the passion of man."[62] In passing, he noted that the Court was not questioning the Lochner ruling. However, there could be no doubt that in the course of formally

---

[58] *Ibid.,* p. 420.
[59] *Ibid.,* pp. 420–21.
[60] *Ibid.,* p. 421.
[61] *Ibid.,* p. 422. It may be noted that many women today would find such a special "class" to be an invidious and insufferable legal category and would certainly spurn the special protection of the law that was offered here by a chivalrous Justice Brewer.
[62] *Ibid.*

recognizing the utility of extralegal facts, the Court had judiciously maneuvered around the Lochner decision.

The Brandeis Brief and Nascent Social Science

Although Brandeis had argued that the sole purpose of his novel brief was to demonstrate to the Court the existence of a reputable body of knowledge that would confirm the reasonableness of legislative action, his larger purpose was to provide the Court with the pertinent "facts" of industrial society. Brandeis formally argued that the existence, not the validity, of facts was conclusive. But it is open to question whether the distinction between existence and validity was nothing more than a tenuous advocative fiction. To be sure, Brandeis never suggested that mere uninformed or dubious opinions would substantiate the reasonableness of the Oregon statute. He argued emphatically, after all, that the facts of the matter proved that the statute was reasonable. Therefore, while Brandeis insisted that he was simply calling the Court's attention to the existence of facts, and not to their validity, presumably he intended to leave the impression that his facts were valid. In other words, Brandeis's argument implicitly begged the question of validity because it is a matter of common agreement that a fact, by definition, cannot be invalid.

Unless this underlying premise of validity is recognized as a logically implicit part of Brandeis's explanation of the function of his factual brief, it might seem that false data had a proper place in the brief. However, Brandeis never claimed that any collection of extralegal data or false data would demonstrate the reasonableness of a statute. Brandeis argued that the Court did not have to question the validity of his facts because he was also contending that the traditional principle of presumptive constitutionality should operate in his favor. Yet, as we have seen, the antithetical principle was usually applied by the Court to social welfare legislation. Had the traditional principle actually been operative, there would have been little reason for Brandeis to compose his innovative brief in the first place. However, since the Oregon statute, like most social welfare legislation, represented an unprecedented extension of the legislative power, there were few persuasive precedents Brandeis could base his argument on. Indeed, one of the four cases Brandeis cited was Lochner v. New York, in which a comparable enactment was struck down. In order to defend the Oregon statute, he was pushed by the force of circumstances beyond the law, to rely on nascent social science instead of precedent.

As we have already seen, Brandeis presented the Court with five extensively documented nascent social science hypotheses. Justice Brewer conspicuously employed three of these hypotheses regarding the physiological uniqueness of the female and her special role in society. In view of our present understanding of scientific method, Brandeis's hypotheses were not scientifically verified, for it appears that most of his data was collected at random. In addition, he made no attempt to control any of the multiple variables that conditioned his problem. Most important, there is no indication that Brandeis actually tested any of his hypotheses. In short, although he had demonstrated a plausible relationship between hypotheses and data, it is more than doubtful whether he had scientifically proved a logical and empirical relationship between the two.

However, it is important to note that at the turn of the century social science was still in an embryonic stage of development. Sociology was "more of a yearning than a substantial body of knowledge, a fixed point of view, or a rigorous method of research."[63] In other words, the methodology employed in the Brandeis brief was compatible with the canons of science as it was then understood. For as the distinguished social scientist Lester Ward wrote at the time, "Science itself, insofar as it is distinguishable from knowledge in a general sense, consists in a co-ordination and subordination of the different kinds of knowledge; in a word, the essential of all science is the classification of knowledge."[64] Clearly, then, Brandeis's emphasis on observable facts instead of abstract legal logic—in particular, his collection

[63] Albion W. Small quoted in Robert E. L. Faris, *Chicago Sociology: 1920–1932* (San Francisco: Chandler Publishing Co., 1967), p. 3.
[64] Lester F. Ward, *Dynamic Sociology: Or Applied Social Science*, 1 (New York: D. Appleton & Co., 1913): 2.

and classification of social data—made him for all practical purposes a social scientist. But in terms of our contemporary understanding of scientific method, Brandeis's hypotheses can only be described as nascent social science at best.

Although Brandeis was committed to scientific explanation, his role as a social scientist was subordinate to the requirements of advocacy. Quite obviously, no social scientist would argue formally that the existence and not the validity of data was the primary question at stake. But this did not mean that Brandeis was unconcerned with the validity of social science. Indeed, he was too much the meticulous master of detail to be that crass. Nevertheless, Brandeis was both a skeptic and an optimist regarding the progress of the social sciences. In his words, "The economic and social sciences are largely uncharted seas. We have been none too successful in the model essays in economic control already entered upon. . . ." But he was quick to add, ". . . yet the advances in the exact sciences and achievements in inventions remind us that the seemingly impossible sometimes happens."[65]

Brandeis therefore used nascent social science in the service of a sociological jurisprudence in order to implement democratic values. Nascent social science constituted, in effect, a *prima facie* argument for the constitutionality of legislative experiments designed to further the common good. Curiously, however, Brandeis's belief in democracy at the same time made him suspicious of all expert claims. He once said, "When I began to practice law I thought it awkward, stupid, and vulgar that a jury of twelve inexpert men should have the power to decide. I had the greatest respect for the Judge. I trusted only expert opinion. Experience of life has made me democratic. I began to see that many things sanctioned by expert opinion and denounced by popular opinion were wrong."[66] Nevertheless, as a democrat Brandeis was open to change and experimentation and therefore was inextricably attracted to the ethos of science.

It followed in law that the Brandeis brief could be legally relevant without necessarily being scientifically valid. Brandeis

[65] New State Ice Co. v. Liebmann, 285 U.S. 262, 310 (1932) (dissenting opinion).
[66] Louis D. Brandeis, *The Curse of Bigness: Miscellaneous Papers,* ed. Osmond K. Fraenkel (Port Washington, N.Y.: Kennikat Press, 1965), p. 41.

deliberately made no pretentious claim for the scientific character of his brief. Since his primary purpose was legal reform, he saw no inconsistency in using nascent social science without evincing a similar concern for the methodological problems of social science.

The Legacy of the Brandeis Brief

The Muller decision was unquestionably a measured victory for legal reform. Moreover, the Court's formal approval of the Brandeis brief constituted a major advance toward a more realistic jurisprudence. The Court had definitely acknowledged that it was receptive to extralegal data, but this did not mean that it had accepted the responsibility of keeping informed of the findings of social science. Indeed, three years later, in the case of Quong Wing v. Kirkendall,[67] discussed earlier, Justice Holmes asserted that it was primarily the task of counsel to provide courts with sociological insight into the consequences of a statute, insofar as it could be shown that rights guaranteed by the Constitution had been violated. Holmes was effectively endorsing the Brandeis brief when he wrote, "There are many things that courts would notice if brought before them that beforehand they do not know. It rests with counsel to take the proper steps, and if they deliberatively omit them, we do not feel called upon to institute inquiries on our own account."[68]

On the other hand, when property rights were threatened by legislation, the Court's attitude toward facts was somewhat different. For example, when a New York statute was enacted to prevent the waste of mineral waters and gas drawn from a common supply, the Court applied the traditional principle of presumptive constitutionality and accepted without further question the legislature's declaration of fact. The New York Mineral Springs Act was based on the assumption that porous rock lay beneath the lands of several proprietors. The existence of such rock was precisely the factual question upon which the constitutionality of the statute rested. Yet Justice Willis Van

---

[67] Quong Wing v. Kirkendall, 223 U.S. 59 (1912).
[68] *Ibid.*, p. 64.

Devanter saw no need to entertain this factual question. In his words, "3. When the classification in such a law is called in question, if any state of facts reasonably can be conceived that would sustain it, the existence of that state of facts at the time the law was enacted must be assumed. 4. One who assails the classification in such a law must carry the burden of showing that it does not rest upon any reasonable basis, but is essentially arbitrary."[69] Furthermore, Van Devanter stated, each state has the power to prescribe rules of evidence operative in its courts, even to the extent of providing that a particular fact or group of facts may be *prima facie* evidence of another fact.[70]

Although the Court was more inclined to presume the existence of facts that supported the defense of property rights, nevertheless, in several instances the use of Brandeis briefs led to the confirmation of enactments similar to the one upheld in the Muller case.[71] The Court consequently became accustomed to using extralegal facts in support of select social welfare measures. For example, in the case of Bosley v. McLaughlin,[72] decided in 1915, the Court cited extralegal facts to show that "there is plainly no ground for saying that a restriction of the hours of labor of student nurses is palpably arbitrary."[73]

In the case of Bunting v. Oregon,[74] decided in 1917, Brandeis continued his factual fight for social welfare legislation. In this instance a Brandeis brief, actually completed and presented by Felix Frankfurter after Brandeis was called to the high bench, was used in support of a statute that limited to ten hours the labor of all industrial workers, with certain exceptions. Frankfurter's brief consisted of 1,021 pages in which only eight precedents were cited. His facts ranged from a description of the "contractions of a frog's gastroenemius muscle" to a Senate document entitled "Why the Victor Talking Machine Co. Changed to the Eight-Hour Day"![75]

---

[69] Lindsley v. Natural Carbonic Gas Co., 220 U.S. 61, 78–79 (1911).

[70] *Ibid.*, p. 81.

[71] See Hawley v. Walker, 232 U.S. 718 (1914).

[72] Bosley v. McLaughlin, 236 U.S. 385 (1915).

[73] *Ibid.*, p. 394.

[74] Bunting v. Oregon, 243 U.S. 426 (1917).

[75] Felix Frankfurter and Josephine Goldmark, Brief for defendant in error, Bunting v. Oregon, reprinted in *The Case for the Shorter Work Day*, 2 vols. (New York: National Consumers' League, 1915), pp. 297, 937.

In defending the statute, Frankfurter pointed out, "It is now clear that 'common understanding' is a treacherous criterion both as to the assumptions on which such understanding [of the act] is based, and as to the evil consequences, if they are allowed to govern. Particularly in the last decade science has been giving us the basis for judgment to which, when furnished, judgment by speculation must yield."[76] The statute was upheld by the Court, and in doing so Justice McKenna cited extralegal facts describing legislation and working conditions in thirteen other countries in order to demonstrate that the act was related to the public health. With respect to Frankfurter's charge that "experience . . . must be allowed to challenge the assumptions of theory and disprove its prophecies,"[77] McKenna responded that the Court could not know all the conditions that gave rise to the law. "But," he added, "we need not cast about for reasons for the legislative judgment. We are not required to be sure of the precise reasons for its exercise or be convinced of the wisdom of its exercise."[78]

It appeared for the time being that the Court had accepted Brandeis's argument that the legislative exercise of the police power could be sustained simply on the basis of the existence of facts in support of contested legislation. In the case of Stettler v. O'Hara,[79] also decided in 1917, Brandeis presented another factual brief, this time in support of an Oregon statute that fixed minimum wages for women. In this instance Brandeis argued that while facts were controlling, the Court could uphold the statute without taking into consideration all the facts of the matter and without questioning the validity of those facts that had been brought to its attention. In anticipation of criticism of his factual material, Brandeis argued:

> In answer to the question, whether this brief contains also all the data opposed to minimum-wage law, I want to say this: I conceive it to be absolutely immaterial what may be said against such laws. Each one of these statements contained in the brief in sup-

[76] Bunting v. Oregon, 243 U.S. 426, 432 (1917).
[77] Frankfurter and Goldmark, Brief for defendant in error, Bunting v. Oregon, p. xi.
[78] Bunting v. Oregon, 243 U.S. 426, 437 (1917).
[79] Stettler v. O'Hara, 243 U.S. 629 (1917).

port of the contention that this is wise legislation, might upon further investigation be found to be erroneous, each conclusion of fact may be found afterwards to be unsound—and yet the constitutionality of the act would not be affected thereby. This court is not burdened with the duty of passing upon the disputed question whether the legislature of Oregon was wise or unwise, or probably wise or unwise, in enacting this law. The question is merely whether, as has been stated, you can see that the legislators had no ground on which they could, as reasonable men, deem this legislation appropriate to abolish or mitigate the evils believed to exist or apprehended. If you cannot find that, the law must stand.[80]

But the Court split evenly four to four, and the Oregon statute was allowed to stand.

The Brandeis brief had proved itself useful in providing support for several social welfare measures. But in the final analysis it was not, as one critic has observed, "an irresistible force."[81] In the case of Block v. Hirsh,[82] decided in 1921, the Court upheld an emergency housing statute enacted by Congress for the capital. Justice Holmes observed that a legislative declaration of fact "is entitled at least to great respect." But he also stated, "It is true that a legislative declaration of facts that are material only as the ground for enacting a rule of law . . . may not be held conclusive by the Courts. . . ."[83]

It is clear that when the Court wished to uphold social welfare measures, it generally accepted the validity of facts contained in Brandeis briefs. But whenever it chose to reject such legislation, the Court found extralegal data spurious and unconvincing.[84] Thus, despite the submission of a Brandeis brief in the case of Adkins v. Children's Hospital,[85] decided in 1923, the Court struck down a federal statute that fixed minimum-wage standards for

[80] Brief for Stettler v. O'Hara, reprinted in Brandeis, *The Curse of Bigness*, pp. 65–66.

[81] Marion E. Doro, "The Brandeis Brief," 11 *Vanderbilt Law Review* 783, 792 (1958).

[82] Block v. Hirsh, 256 U.S. 135 (1921).

[83] *Ibid.*, p. 154.

[84] Norman J. Small, ed., *The Constitution of the United States of America* (Washington, D.C.: U.S. Government Printing Office, 1964), p. 1097.

[85] Adkins v. Children's Hospital, 261 U.S. 525 (1923).

women in the District of Columbia. The purpose of the brief
was to call the Court's attention to the existence of a factual
relationship between the earnings of women and morality. But
according to Justice Sutherland, who spoke for the majority,
the recent gains in the political and civil status of women had all
but eliminated any significant differences between the two sexes
and therefore negated any need for special legislation affecting
women. Sutherland thus curtly dismissed the principal rationale
of this type of legislation, the psychology and the special societal
role of the female, which was first announced by the Court in
the Muller case, then fifteen years old. "The relation between
earnings and morals," Sutherland noted, "is not capable of
standardization. It cannot be shown that well paid women safe-
guard their morals more carefully than those who are poorly
paid."[86] Referring to the Brandeis brief, which contained much
extralegal data in support of this rejected hypothesis, Sutherland
remarked derisively, "We have also been furnished with a large
number of printed opinions approving the policy of the minimum
wage, and our own reading has disclosed a large number to the
contrary. These are all proper enough for the consideration of
the law making bodies, since their tendency is to establish the
desirability or undesirability of the legislation; but they reflect
no legitimate light upon the question of its validity, and that is
what we are called upon to decide. The elucidation of that
question cannot be aided by counting heads."[87]

This Brandeis brief, in addition, contained documentation of
the beneficial effects produced by the statute. But Justice Sutherland was decidedly unimpressed with the brief: "A mass of
reports, opinions of special observers and students of the subject,
and the like, had been brought before us in support of this
statement, all of which we have found interesting but only mildly
persuasive."[88] Sutherland's attitude toward the Brandeis brief
was evidently shared by Chief Justice Edward D. White, who is
reported to have picked up the brief during the proceedings and

[86] *Ibid.*, p. 556.
[87] *Ibid.*, p. 560.
[88] *Ibid.*

to have remarked, "Why, I could compile a brief twice as thick to prove that the legal profession ought to be abolished."[89]

While the Court in striking down the statute had waved aside a substantial body of extralegal data, it offered no factual refutation of the hypothesis concerning earnings and morality. Sutherland's legal logic was faulty. He conceded that after the passage of the act the wages of women and the conditions affecting them had improved. Yet he stated, "Convincing indications of the logical relation of these desirable changes to the law in question are significantly lacking."[90] However, Sutherland never denied specifically that such a relation did exist. In effect, his presumption that social welfare legislation was unconstitutional was facilely extended to extralegal data, which was presumed to be inconsequential. As a result, the Court held that the act violated the due-process clause of the Fifth Amendment.

It is clear that Sutherland's opinion was poorly reasoned. Justice Holmes in a dissenting opinion quipped, "It will need more than the Nineteenth Amendment to convince me that there are no differences between men and women, or that legislation cannot take those differences into account." Holmes observed that a "reasonable man" would have accepted the existence of the relation between the law and its claimed effects. The belief in such a cause-and-effect relation, Holmes noted, was after all "fortified by a very remarkable collection of documents. . . ."[91] Even the normally conservative Justice Taft wrote a dissenting opinion: "It is not the function of this Court to hold congressional acts invalid simply because they are passed to carry out economic views which the Court believes to be unwise or unsound."[92]

Yet in the case of Wolff Packing House Co. v. Court of Industrial Relations,[93] decided in the same term, Taft suggested that he was in general no more eager than Sutherland to presume

[89] White quoted in Alpheus Thomas Mason, *The Supreme Court from Taft to Warren* (New York: W. W. Norton, 1964), p. 31.
[90] Adkins v. Children's Hospital, 261 U.S. 525, 560 (1923).
[91] *Ibid.*, p. 570 (dissenting opinion).
[92] *Ibid.*, p. 562 (dissenting opinion).
[93] Wolff Packing House Co. v. Court of Industrial Relations, 262 U.S. 522 (1923).

the relevance and validity of legislative facts drawn in support of a measure designed to produce industrial reform. Under the Kansas Industrial Relations Act the legislature had established an industrial court; it was empowered, with respect to industries affected with the public interest, to make factual findings, to fix wages and terms of employment, and in general to adjust disputes. The act was based on the principle first announced in Munn v. Illinois:[94] property affected with a public interest is subject to public regulation.

Taft implied that his only presumption would be the old formula—"Freedom is the general rule, and restraint the exception. The legislative authority to abridge can be justified only by exceptional circumstances."[95] Therefore, he dismissed the Kansas contention that a business engaged in the preparation of food was "clothed" with the public interest. Although this factual premise had been accepted by the Kansas Supreme Court, Taft emphasized that "the mere declaration by a legislature that a business is affected with a public interest is not conclusive of the question whether its attempted regulation on that ground is justified."[96] He went on to observe, "It has never been supposed, since the adoption of the Constitution, that the business of the butcher, or the baker, the tailor, the wood chopper, the mining operator or the miner was clothed with such a public interest that the price of his product or his wages could be fixed by state regulation."[97] No working rule, he argued, can be easily established by which the Court could determine when a business has become "clothed with a public interest." The closest the Court could come in devising such a principle would be to make determinations "by the process of exclusion and inclusion. . . ."[98] The result of this nebulous process was the holding that the Kansas act violated the due-process clause of the Fourteenth Amendment.

It should be noted that although the Court had dismissed the

---

[94] Munn v. Illinois, 94 U.S. 113 (1877).
[95] Wolff Packing House Co. v. Court of Industrial Relations, 262 U.S. 522, 534 (1923).
[96] *Ibid.*, p. 536.
[97] *Ibid.*, p. 537.
[98] *Ibid.*, p. 539.

state's factual contention, it still made no explicit finding that the business in question was not affected with the public interest. Nor did the Court explain factually why the act was unreasonable. In the Munn case the Court had applied the public-interest formula by assuming that a necessary set of facts existed. The application of the traditional principle of presumptive constitutionality in the Munn case made an independent investigation of facts unnecessary. In the Wolff case the Court likewise did not bother to investigate the facts; it simply presumed that the facts did not exist. The Court had in effect repudiated the factual doctrine announced in the Munn case. This was done through the application of the new principle of presumptive unconstitutionality, which, as we have seen, had emerged concurrently with the Court's defensive attitude toward property in substantive due-process adjudication. The practice of this new principle excused the Court from the task of validating legislative facts. On the contrary, the informal application of the new principle implied that such facts were implicitly erroneous or at best spurious.

Despite Brandeis's constant factual remonstrations from the bench, the Court often abjured factual decision-making. For example, in the case of Jay Burns Baking Co. v. Bryan,[99] decided in 1924, the Court overturned a Nebraska statute that provided restrictions to guard against short-weight bread loaves. Speaking through Justice Pierce Butler, the Court held that the statute violated the Fourteenth Amendment since it imposed on bakers restrictions, in terms of the baking process, that were "unreasonable" and "arbitrary." Although Butler feebly attempted to sketch a technical description of the bread-making process, to show that bakers could not reasonably conform to the statute, his opinion was relatively free of factual analysis. Butler nevertheless suggested that there was evidence to prove that the statute presented "an intolerable burden upon bakers," but these facts were not included in his opinion.

Brandeis, on the other hand, used thirty-six comprehensive factual footnotes in a seventeen-page dissenting opinion to demonstrate that legislators had reasonable cause to believe that such

[99] Jay Burns Baking Co. v. Bryan, 264 U.S. 504, 520 (1924).

prohibitions were necessary to prevent unfair competition. His data were drawn from various state statutes, reports of several state and local weight and measurement departments, reports of congressional hearings, federal administrative reports, local ordinances, and the Federal Trade Committee on the Baking Business. Much of his evidence, Brandeis admitted, was not in the record, but it was the duty of the Court to acquire knowledge whenever it had to perform the delicate task of judging. There was, he argued, ample evidence in the record to sustain the statute. If the record contained conflicting evidence, this was not a problem for the Court, for its function was not to weigh evidence. Instead, he observed, "Put at its highest, our function is to determine, in the light of all facts which may enrich our knowledge and enlarge our understanding, whether the measure, enacted in the exercise of an unquestioned police power, and of a character inherently unobjectionable, transcends the bounds of reason. That is, whether the provision, as applied, is so clearly arbitrary or capricious that legislators, acting reasonably could not have believed it to be necessary or appropriate for the public welfare."[100]

The Brandeis brief, and for that matter the Brandeis dissent, were designed to impart a new realism to constitutional law. As a lawyer and a judge, Brandeis argued that facts were indispensable to informed decision-making. As he wrote with great eloquence in the Jay Burns case, "Unless we know the facts on which legislators may have acted, we cannot properly decide whether they were . . . unreasonable, arbitrary, or capricious. Knowledge is essential to understanding; and understanding should precede judging. Sometimes, if we would guide by the light of reason, we must let our minds be bold."[101] Indeed, Brandeis's factual approach to law was so bold that Harold J. Laski wrote to Holmes that he and Roscoe Pound had agreed that if Holmes "could hint to Brandeis that judicial opinions aren't to be written in the form of a brief it would be a great relief to the world."[102]

---

[100] *Ibid.*, p. 534 (dissenting opinion).
[101] *Ibid.*, p. 520.
[102] Mark De Wolfe Howe, ed., *Holmes-Laski Letters,* 2 vols. (Cambridge, Mass.: Harvard University Press, 1953), 1: 127.

The Brandeis brief was a double-edged weapon. Brandeis consistently advocated that the Court should have at its disposal extralegal data relevant to the issues at hand.[103] "Whether a law enacted in the exercise of the police power is justly subject to the charge of being unreasonable," he wrote in Truax v. Corrigan, "can ordinarily be determined only by a consideration of the contemporary conditions, social, industrial and political, of the community to be affected."[104] In general, Brandeis was requesting the Court to take an objective sociological reading of society and its needs. This would allow the Court to appreciate the evils to be remedied and the overall welfare objectives of the legislature. But he realized, as did the founding fathers, that "government is not an exact science." Thus he urged the Court to also take into consideration public opinion or the public's conception of the prevailing social evils and their appropriate remedies.[105] According to Brandeis, the Court should be able to find two types of extralegal facts. It should be capable of sociological insight or a scientific understanding of society, and it should also be receptive to the desires of the people or able to comprehend the popular will. In the final analysis the Brandeis brief rested on the theory that the high bench should not only be able to approximate a Platonic council of social scientists, but that it should also be a tribunal of pollsters.

The impact on concepts of constitutional law of the Brandeis brief was as its collaborators had intended. It ultimately brought a "new flexibility" to law in general, and in particular it helped refine the concept of due process into a modern legal doctrine suitable for application as a rule of law to problems stemming from new social and economic conditions.[106] Judicial notice had traditionally meant that the Court was left to its own resources in gathering whatever extralegal data it might need in order

[103] For example, in Hammond v. Schappi Bus Line, 275 U.S. 164 (1927), finding the essential facts of the record to be either vague or missing, Brandeis for the Court returned the case to the district court for an adequate determination of the facts.

[104] Truax v. Corrigan, 257 U.S. 312, 356 (1921) (dissenting opinion).

[105] *Ibid.,* p. 357.

[106] Edward S. Corwin, "Social Planning under the Constitution," in *American Constitutional History: Essays by Edward S. Corwin,* ed. Alpheus Thomas Mason and Gerald Garvey (New York: Harper Torchbooks, 1964), p. 120,

to render more informed decisions. The main contribution of the Brandeis brief was to make extralegal data readily available to the Court. Consequently the "reasonableness" of social welfare legislation was not to be determined solely on the basis of legal reasoning confined to an intellectual vacuum. Instead the Brandeis brief gave rise to the hope that legal policy would be formulated on the basis of the same empirical considerations that guided the making of legislative policy.[107] Indeed, the chief aim of Brandeis's crusade both on and off the bench was to insure that the Court was aware of social facts in interpreting the Constitution. The conception of reasonableness that flowed from legal requirements would then be tempered by the Court's understanding of the needs of the people.

It is, of course, difficult to assess the precise impact and degree of influence the Brandeis brief has had on the Court. The initial success of government lawyers who employed the brief was partially facilitated by the reluctance of opposing counsel to file briefs containing contradictory data.[108] And interestingly enough, the Brandeis brief did not gain wide popularity until after 1937.[109] Government lawyers, however, were quick to recognize the benefits to be gained from the use of Brandeis briefs. For example, the use of economic data by government lawyers was planned deliberately in the first five cases to reach the Court from the new National Labor Relations Board. The board created a special Division of Economic Research, which conducted elaborate industrial studies for the express purpose of providing board attorneys with extralegal data for presentation to the Court.[110] That the Brandeis brief did prove useful is suggested by the fact that out of nineteen select cases where economic data were employed by one party and not by the other,

---

[107] See Sheldon Glueck, "The Social Sciences and Scientific Method in the Administration of Justice," 167 *Annals of the American Academy of Political and Social Science* 106, 115 (1933).

[108] Jerome Frank, *Courts on Trial* (Princeton, N.J.: Princeton University Press, 1950), pp. 211–12.

[109] Clement E. Vose, *Caucasians Only: The Supreme Court, the NAACP, and the Restrictive Covenant Cases* (Berkeley and Los Angeles: University of California Press, 1959), p. 65.

[110] David Ziskind, "The Use of Economic Data in Labor Cases," 6 *University of Chicago Law Review* 607, 624 (1939).

the former was successful sixteen times and the latter only three times.[111]

The Exhaustion of Subtantive Due Process

The Brandeis brief from its outset was an important factor in the Court's interpretation, especially with respect to property rights, of the two due-process clauses. To be sure, the Brandeis brief was not always a decisive factor in such adjudication. As late as 1936, in the case of Morehead v. New York,[112] the Court persevered in its restrictive property conception of due process. It struck down an act that set minimum wages for women calculated in relation to the reasonable value of their services. The act was promulgated with a factual background that purported to demonstrate the need for the legislative action. But the Court interpreted these facts to mean that the act would "unreasonably restrain" women in their competition with men and would "arbitrarily" deprive them of opportunities to work.[113] In holding the act unconstitutional, Justice Butler reiterated the old saw "Freedom of contract is the general rule and restraint the exception."[114] In effect, the Court had cast aside vital legislative facts. This action suggested that while the Court was prepared to use extralegal facts, by no means did facts necessarily cut a neat channel in which the power of judicial review automati-

[111] *Ibid.* The cases in which economic data were used successfully were Lochner v. New York, 198 U.S. 45 (1905); Muller v. Oregon, 208 U.S. 412 (1908); Hawley v. Walker, 232 U.S. 718 (1914); Miller v. Wilson, 236 U.S. 373 (1915); Bosley v. McLaughlin, 236 U.S. 385 (1915); Bailey v. Drexel Furniture Co., 259 U.S. 20 (1922); Coronado Coal Co. v. United Mine Workers, 268 U.S. 295 (1925); Santa Cruz Fruit Packing Co. v. N.L.R.B., 303 U.S. 453 (1938); N.L.R.B. v. Jones and Laughlin, 301 U.S. 1 (1937); N.L.R.B. v. Fruehauf Trailer Co., 301 U.S. 49 (1937); N.L.R.B. v. Friedman–Harry Marks Clothing Co., 301 U.S. 58 (1937); Associated Press v. N.L.R.B., 301 U.S. 103 (1937); Washington Va. and Maryland Coach Co. v. N.L.R.B., 301 U.S. 142 (1937); Senn v. Tile Layers Protective Union, 301 U.S. 468 (1937); New Negro Alliance v. Sanitary Grocery Co., 303 U.S. 552 (1938); and Consolidated Edison Co. v. N.L.R.B., 304 U.S. 555 (1939). Unsuccessful uses were in Adkins v. Children's Hospital, 261 U.S. 525 (1923); Schechter Corp. v. United States, 295 U.S. 495 (1935); and Morehead v. New York ex rel. Tipaldo, 298 U.S. 587 (1936).

[112] Morehead v. New York ex rel. Tipaldo, 298 U.S. 587 (1936).

[113] *Ibid.*, p. 617.

[114] *Ibid.*, p. 611.

cally flowed. The Court's finding of facts, despite the influence of the Brandeis brief, remained as problematic as its interpretation of law. For as Morris Cohen once wrote, "It is simply not true that the facts themselves suggest the appropriate hypothesis to everyone who looks at them."[115] On the other hand, Chief Justice Hughes dissented in the Morehead case, stating that he could not understand how the facts could be ignored. "We are not at liberty to disregard these facts. We must assume that they exist and examine respondent's argument from that standpoint."[116]

In 1937 the Court reversed itself in the case of West Coast Hotel Co. v. Parrish,[117] which marked the practical end of its restrictive property conception of substantive due process. This time the Court upheld a Washington minimum-wage law for women and minors. A switch in time had saved nine, one news columnist remarked.[118] The Court had finally shed its old negative attitude toward social welfare legislation. In doing so, Chief Justice Hughes clearly affirmed that the "Constitution does not speak of freedom of contract."[119] Moreover, he stated, "We may take judicial notice of the unparalleled demands for relief which arose during the recent period of depression . . ."; it was unnecessary for the Court "to cite official statistics to establish what is of common knowledge through the length and breadth of the land." Even though "no factual brief has been presented," Hughes wrote, "there is no reason to doubt that the state of Washington has encountered the same social problem that is present elsewhere."[120] Thus, without the aid of a Brandeis brief, the Court had reinterpreted the due-process clause in the context of a critical finding of extralegal fact.

Substantive due process did not receive a formal theoretical burial until 1963, when a unanimous Court in the case of Ferguson v. Skrupa announced that it refused to return to the time

[115] Morris R. Cohen, *Reason and Nature: The Meaning of the Scientific Method* (New York: Free Press, 1964), p. 80.
[116] Morehead v. New York ex rel. Tipaldo, 298 U.S. 587, 627 (1936).
[117] West Coast Hotel Co. v. Parrish, 300 U.S. 379 (1937).
[118] See Drew Pearson and Robert S. Allen, *The Nine Old Men* (Garden City, N.Y.: Doubleday, Doran and Co., 1937).
[119] West Coast Hotel Co. v. Parrish, 300 U.S. 379, 391 (1937).
[120] *Ibid.*, p. 399.

when laws were voided because they were thought "unreasonable," "unwise," or "incompatible with some particular economic
or social philosophy."[121] Justice Black's opinion was, appropriately
enough, based on Holmes's Lochner dissent:

> We refuse to sit as a "superlegislature to weigh the wisdom of
> legislation," and we emphatically refuse to go back to the time
> when courts used the Due Process Clause "to strike down state
> laws, regulatory of business and industrial conditions, because
> they may be unwise, improvident, or out of harmony with a par-
> ticular school of thought." Nor are we able or willing to draw
> lines by calling a law "prohibitory" or "regulatory." Whether the
> legislature takes for its textbook Adam Smith, Herbert Spencer,
> Lord Keynes, or some other is no concern of ours.[122]

Undoubtedly the Brandeis brief helped inspire a veritable
revolution in judicial interpretation. Under the influence of the
brief, the Court became wary of deciding cases on the basis of
abstract formulas like "business affected with a public interest,"
"freedom of contract," and "direct" and "indirect" effects. The
Court's long-brewing reaction against the old mechanical jurisprudence was evident when Chief Justice Hughes protested in
1937, "We are asked to shut our eyes to the plainest facts of our
national life and to deal with the question of direct and indirect
effects in an intellectual vacuum."[123] To be sure, at least with
respect to the due-process clauses, "the mechanical application
of legal formulas [was] no longer feasible."[124]

Once the Court abandoned the principle of presumptive unconstitutionality, which had often been applied informally to
social welfare legislation, the original cause that inspired
the Brandeis brief disappeared. Prior to the Muller case, as Felix
Frankfurter had written, "social legislation was supported before the courts largely *in vacuo*—as an abstract dialectic between
'liberty' and 'police power,' unrelated to a world of trusts and
unions, of large scale industry and all its implications." The
Brandeis brief and its collection of extralegal data, Frankfurter

[121] Ferguson v. Skrupa, 372 U.S. 726, 729 (1963).
[122] *Ibid.*, pp. 731–32.
[123] Labor Board v. Jones Laughlin, 301 U.S. 1, 41 (1937).
[124] Wickard v. Filburn, 317 U.S. 111, 124 (1942).

suggested, "mark[ed] an epoch in the disposition of cases presenting the most important present day constitutional issues."[125] But while the Court had abandoned its mechanical interpretation of due process, at this point the future role of the Brandeis brief was far from clear.

[125] Felix Frankfurter, ed., *Mr. Justice Brandeis* (New Haven, Conn.: Yale University Press, 1932), p. 52.

CHAPTER FIVE

The Court and Social Science: The Development of a Cautious Relationship

The Insufficiency of the Court's Extralegal Expertise

Even before the Court began to be immersed more quickly in substantive due-process adjudication, there could be no doubt that narrowly drawn issues as well as broad constitutional questions were resolved more easily and rationally on the basis of valid extralegal data as opposed to factual assumptions derived from judicial introspection. For example, in the case of Gorham Co. v. White,[1] decided in 1872, the Court was faced with an extremely narrow question that still called for extralegal expertise. The question was whether a patent right for a silver design had been violated. In answering this question, Justice William Strong reasoned that "if, in the eye of an ordinary observer, giving such attention as a purchaser usually gives, two designs are substantially the same, if the resemblance is such as to deceive such an observer, inducing him to purchase one supposing it to be the other, the first one patented is infringed by the other."[2] But the Court's decision was based solely on its own notion of what the public might perceive, there being no way for it to determine whether the public was able to discriminate between the two designs. In similar fashion in the case of McLean

---

[1] Gorham Co. v. White, 14 Wallace 511 (1872).
[2] *Ibid.*, p. 528.

v. Flemming,[3] decided in 1878, the Court ruled that the question
of whether a trademark right had been infringed could be resolved on the probable ground of whether an ordinary purchaser
was likely to be misled.[4] In rendering both these decisions, the
Court assumed that it knew what "ordinary" observers or pur-
chasers saw. But in both instances the Court failed to substantiate its extralegal knowledge, which apparently amounted to
nothing more than intuition or introspection.

In any event, the insufficiency of judicial introspection soon
became evident. As the industrial revolution in the United
States gathered momentum, socio-economic problems became increasingly complex. Besides adjudicating problems that called
in the first instance for the application of political prudence,
the Court was now called upon to provide answers to such
technical economic problems as what constituted reasonable railroad rates. In the important case of Smyth v. Ames,[5] decided
in 1898, the Court revealed quite clearly the inadequacy of its
extralegal expertise. Although the Court did announce an extralegal formula for resolving the knotty problem of reasonable rate
structures, the solution was so simplistic that it plagued and
vexed the judicial system for many years. Justice Harlan had
ruled for the Court that the reasonableness of a rate could be
determined by the "fair value" of the property being used by
the public. Fair value was a nebulously defined quantity: "The
original cost of construction, the amount expended in permanent improvements, the amount and market value of its bonds
and stock, the present as compared with the original cost of
construction, the probable earning capacity of the property
under particular rates prescribed by statute, and the sum required to meet operating expenses, are all matters for consideration, and are to be given such weight as may be just and right in
each case."[6]

However, Harlan's economic formula was so vague and inadequate that it still left "to the courts, for separate determina-

[3] McLean v. Flemming, 6 Otto 245 (1878).
[4] *Ibid.*, p. 251.
[5] Smyth v. Ames, 169 U.S. 466 (1898).
[6] *Ibid.*, pp. 546–47.

tion in every instance, the fairness of rates contested."[7] As a result of the insufficiency of the Court's economic expertise, judicial rate-making remained a confused and troubled problem in constitutional law until the high bench finally agreed in 1944 to accept rates determined by administrative commissions. At this time Justice Frankfurter bluntly characterized the Smyth formula as a "hodgepodge."[8]

If the law was, as Roscoe Pound had suggested, "a science of social engineering," then the Court could hardly adjudicate technical issues in a competent fashion unless the justices were properly trained or were at least willing to accept on-the-job training.[9] No one was presumptuous or impudent enough to ask the justices to return to school. But, nevertheless, the Court's handling of the Smyth case did make it apparent that it required a better understanding of the objectives and effects of legislation on which it acted as a final arbiter. Although the Brandeis brief was an enlightening legal vehicle, the Adkins case[10] clearly showed that the educative influence of the brief was by no means compelling. Acutely aware of the insufficiency of the Court's extralegal expertise, Pound wrote in 1925, "We need to work out a better apparatus of informing the courts as to the social background of the statutes on which they pass, so that instead of viewing them consciously or unconsciously on the background of the pioneer society of the frontier era of our institutions, or on the abstract background of the formal, abstract economics of a generation ago, they may be judged with reference to the actual environment of the industrial society of to-day."[11]

Indeed, throughout the 1920s an influential body of jurists directed a steady fusillade of criticism at the Court, demanding

[7] Carl Brent Swisher, *American Constitutional Development*, 2nd rev. ed. (Boston: Houghton Mifflin, 1954), p. 404.

[8] Federal Power Commission v. Hope Natural Gas Co., 320 U.S. 591, 627 (1944).

[9] Roscoe Pound, *Justice according to Law* (New Haven, Conn.: Yale University Press, 1951), p. 30.

[10] Adkins v. Children's Hospital, 261 U.S. 525 (1923).

[11] Pound quoted in National Consumers' League, *The Supreme Court and Minimum Wage Legislation* (New York: New Republic, Inc., 1925), p. xxvii.

in effect a more realistic jurisprudence.[12] The general thrust of much of this criticism was that lawmakers—courts as well as legislatures—required a working familiarity with social science. Writing in 1930, one observer insisted, "The time has arrived when the grim hard facts of modern psychological inquiry must be recognized by our law makers despite the havoc they may create in the established institutions. . . . Legal definitions are essential but they too must rest on the facts of modern science and not medieval folklore."[13]

Slowly toward the Use of Social Science

Progressive jurists, as we have seen, tended to regard social science as a medicine that, once administered, would immediately cure the Court's negative attitude toward legislative social planning. However, it was clear that the term "social science" or disciplines purporting to be social science had no spellbinding effect whatever on the Court. The Court's complacent and somewhat misconceived impression of social science was demonstrated in the case of United States v. Sprague,[14] decided in 1931. Sprague had been acquitted in a district court of violating the national prohibition act. In dismissing the indictment, the district court had used political science data. According to Justice Owen J. Roberts, the district court had dismissed the indictment "by resorting to 'political science,' the 'political thought' of the times, and a 'scientific approach to the problem of government.' "[15]

The appellee, Sprague, had ingeniously though fruitlessly attempted to convince the Court through "contemporary political literature" that amendments to the Constitution affecting the liberty of the citizen, as opposed to amendments changing the federal machinery, must be ratified by conventions and not by state legislatures. He referred to such works as Elliot's and

[12] See Wilfrid E. Rumble, Jr., *American Legal Realism: Skepticism, Reform, and the Judicial Process* (Ithaca, N.Y.: Cornell University Press, 1968).

[13] Nathaniel Cantor, "Law and the Social Sciences," 16 *American Bar Association Journal* 385, 387 (1930).

[14] United States v. Sprague, 282 U.S. 716 (1931).

[15] *Ibid.*, p. 730.

Farrand's notes on the constitutional convention, *The Federalist Papers*, Jameson's *The Constitutional Convention*, Ford's *Essays on the Constitution*, the *Works of Hamilton*, the papers of Washington, and other documents. Since the Eighteenth Amendment was not ratified by state conventions, Sprague contended that it was invalid. But the Supreme Court, unlike the district court, was not susceptible to arguments drawn from "political science." In reversing the decision of the district court, Justice Roberts ruled that despite political science findings to the contrary, the Constitution was not problematic on the contested point. It should be noted, however, that what the Court took to be political science was actually nothing more than pure historical record.

The Sprague case indicates that the high bench was not overly impressed with extralegal data that it mistakenly believed was social science. Significantly, the case suggests that the Court did not have a clear idea of the nature of social science in the first place. Yet in 1935 in the case of Stewart Dry Goods Co. v. Lewis[16] the Court saw fit to substitute its knowledge of economics for that of the legislature. In striking down a Kentucky graduated sales tax calculated on annual gross retail sales, the Court had assumed that the economic hypothesis underlying the tax was invalid. As Justice Roberts pointed out, the act rested on the "general proposition [that] increased volume of sales results in increased profits and increased ability to pay the tax." The "duty" of the Court in evaluating the tax, Roberts emphasized, "is to ascertain its nature and effect."[17] He noted that expert witnesses during the trial proceedings, using various extralegal data, had attempted to prove that a general ratio existed between an increased volume of sales and increased profits. Nevertheless, Roberts rejected this proof, along with the legislature's economic hypothesis, and announced firmly that "the gross sales of a merchant do not bear a constant relation to his net profits. . . ."[18] As for the economic data offered in support of the tax, Roberts wrote, "The best that can be said for this evidence is that, aver-

[16] Stewart Dry Goods Co. v. Lewis, 294 U.S. 550 (1935).
[17] *Ibid.*, p. 555.
[18] *Ibid.*, p. 558.

aging the results of the concerns making the reports, it is true 'generally speaking' . . . that profits increase with sales." Yet he added, "So many exceptions and reservations must be made that averages are misleading."[19] On the basis of its finding of extra-legal fact, the Court held that the tax categories were arbitrary and therefore violated the equal-protection clause of the Fourteenth Amendment.

To be sure, the Court had proceeded far beyond Brandeis's theory of the legal utility of extralegal data. Brandeis had argued that the mere existence of extralegal data, offered in support of a contested statute, confirmed that the legislature had reasonable grounds for its judgment. Whether the data in question were valid or not, Brandeis contended, was of no concern to the Court. Nevertheless, it is clear enough that in this instance the Court had disputed the validity of extralegal data presented in support of a statute. The Court, of course, had dismissed extralegal data before. But in view of the singular and express economic hypothesis at issue, the Stewart case raised the problem of the validity of extralegal data in an unusually conspicuous way. This problem, it has already been suggested, was bound to arise sooner or later regardless of Brandeis's theory, because the distinction he drew between the "existence" and the "validity" of facts, while acceptable perhaps for the purposes of law, was certainly questionable as a matter of general logic. A more pressing question brought into focus by the Stewart decision was whether the Court was adequately equipped and informed to be able to pass competent judgment on technical, economic, and social problems.

Justice Cardozo thought otherwise. In a dissenting opinion he argued that it was not the function of the Court to choose between "competing economic theories professed by honest men on grounds not wholly frivolous."[20] He cited the Harvard Bureau of Business's research bulletins in support of the legislature's economic hypothesis and, in line with Brandeis's theory of the legal utility of extralegal data, contended that the existence and not the validity of such data was the primary concern of the

[19] *Ibid.*, p. 559.
[20] *Ibid.*, p. 569 (dissenting opinion).

Court. "How far the teachings of these tables are to be credited as accurate," he insisted, "is not for us to say."[21] Since reputable economists had supported the legislature's economic hypothesis, Cardozo stated that the tax should not have been invalidated even if the legislature had endorsed a hypothesis "in the face of . . . conflicting judgments pronounced by men of learning." The legislature was free to make its own judgment, and if "their conclusion is not arbitrary, it is not for us to set them right."[22]

Although one observer was certain that the relationship between law and social science was burgeoning,[23] the Supreme Court apparently was not eager to use social science findings, even though it continuously made judgments that were political, economic, sociological, or psychological in nature.[24] In the case of Steward Machine Co. v. Davis,[25] decided in 1937, in which the Court upheld the Social Security Act of 1935, probably one of the most important pieces of social welfare legislation to date, Justice Cardozo's use of economic data in his majority opinion was sparse and merely incidental. But Cardozo had little reason, in view of the legal objections that had been raised against the act, to explain his opinion in terms of social science findings.

The act had been attacked on several grounds. The appellee argued that the tax was not a uniform duty, import, or excise as required by Article I, Section 8, of the Constitution. In addition, it was charged that several arbitrary exceptions to the tax brought the statute into conflict with the Fifth Amendment. Finally, the statute was assailed as a violation of the Tenth Amendment because it purportedly invaded the powers reserved to the states. Justice Cardozo was able to rebut these charges by clarifying the legal theory of the permissible use of the federal tax power. He thus emphasized the nature of the tax power and drew attention to comparable taxes previously

[21] *Ibid.*, p. 574 (dissenting opinion).
[22] *Ibid.*, p. 575 (dissenting opinion).
[23] See Robert C. Angell, "The Value of Sociology to Law," 31 *Michigan Law Review* 512, 513 (1933).
[24] For example, in holding the Railroad Retirement Act of 1934 unconstitutional, the Court reasoned that the act could not fulfill its stated objective of providing contentment and security for the workers because such objectives did not "encourage loyalty and continuity of service." See Retirement Board v. Alton R. Co., 295 U.S. 330, 374 (1935).
[25] Steward Machine Co. v. Davis, 301 U.S. 548 (1937).

enacted. In general, the record of the contested statute provided Cardozo with more than enough facts to construct a reasoned opinion. Although Cardozo's opinion did not depend on extralegal facts, Justice McReynolds in a dissenting opinion displayed his deep distrust of any argument that departed from the traditional style of syllogistic legal discourse. He observed that the decision denied the relevance of the Tenth Amendment and "opens the way for practical annihilation of this theory; and no cloud of words or ostentatious parade of irrelevant statistics should be permitted to obscure that fact."[26]

Curiously enough, even the appointment of the comparatively liberal law professor Felix Frankfurter to the high bench in 1939 did not make the Court more receptive to the use of social science. Although Frankfurter had helped pioneer the Brandeis brief, his practical interest in social science apparently left him suspicious of its status as a science. In 1929 he had written, "We are still heady with the wine that we have begun to sip . . . from the new loving cup of the social sciences. We are still largely in the social stage of the social sciences."[27] He continued, "The ultimate concern of the social sciences . . . is the conquest of knowledge leading, one hopes, eventually to new and important insights into the good life of society. But we are still at the very beginning of this effort and the methods, the criteria, even the aims of the social sciences are still at large and still unshapen."[28]

Undoubtedly modern social science finally did come of age with the famous Hawthorne Works studies, a massive research project begun in the mid 1920s and carried on for almost a decade. These studies, regarded as the "*single* most important social science research project ever conducted in industry," demonstrated the mounting success of social science in explaining and ultimately manipulating human behavior.[29] Indeed, one con-

---

[26] *Ibid.*, p. 599 (dissenting opinion).
[27] Felix Frankfurter, *Law and Politics: Occasional Papers of Felix Frankfurter, 1913–1938*, ed. Archibald MacLeish and E. F. Prichard (New York: Capricorn Books, 1962), p. 290.
[28] *Ibid.*, p. 296.
[29] Loren Baritz, *The Servants of Power: A History of the Use of Social Science in American Industry* (Middletown, Conn.: Wesleyan University Press, 1960), p. 77.

clusion arrived at by the sociologist Elton Mayo, who partici-
pated in the studies, was that "the typical institutions of the indus-
trialized world were organized for conflict instead of cooperation."[30] Mayo and his associates believed that social science could
be used to eliminate industrial conflict. But, unfortunately, to
Mayo "industrial cooperation meant that labor should do as management said."[31] Be that as it may, the Hawthorne studies did suggest that social science was an applied as well as a theoretical
science. But the Court made no haste to use social science findings, possibly, among other reasons, because it considered such
findings to be tentative.

Yet despite any reluctance to recognize the scientific status of
social science, the Court's use of social science, either implicit or
explicit, seemed inevitable. After all, the subject of law was
social behavior. Therefore, cases were bound to arise that would
almost literally invite social science explanation. By Frankfurter's own admission, for example, the case of Haley v. Ohio,[32]
decided in 1948, suggested that social science explanation was
decidedly relevant to constitutional law. In the Haley case
the Supreme Court reversed the murder conviction of a fifteen-
year-old Negro boy on the ground that his "voluntary" confession
had been obtained through coercion. Speaking for the Court,
Justice William O. Douglas noted that even though a jury had
established the fact of the voluntary character of the confession,
such a finding did not "foreclose the independent examination
which it is our duty to make. . . ."[33]

The decision about whether the confession was voluntary or
coerced, Douglas suggested by implication, required psychological understanding. He pointed out that "age fifteen is a tender
and difficult age for a boy of any race," and circumstances that
"would leave a man cold and unimpressed can overawe and over-
whelm a lad in his early teens." Moreover, he noted, "This is the
period of great instability which the crisis of adolescence produces. A 15 year old lad, questioned through the dead

[30] *Ibid.*, p. 112.
[31] *Ibid.*, p. 113.
[32] Haley v. Ohio, 332 U.S. 596 (1948).
[33] *Ibid.*, p. 599.

of the night by relays of police, is a ready victim of the inquisition."[34] On the basis of psychological inference, Douglas concluded that the confession was coerced and therefore violated the due-process clause of the Fourteenth Amendment.

Despite his skeptical attitude toward social science, Justice Frankfurter concurred, making Douglas's implicit psychological point explicit. The character of the confession, Frankfurter emphasized, "is not a matter of mathematical determination." "Essentially, it invites psychological judgment—a psychological judgment that reflects deep, even if inarticulate, feelings of our society. Judges must divine that feeling as best they can from all relevant evidence and light which they can bring to bear for a confident judgment of such an issue. . . ."[35] Although Frankfurter suggested that the case depended "on an evaluation of psychological factors, or, more accurately stated, upon the pervasive feelings of society regarding such psychological factors," he noted that it was not possible for the Court to resort to social science data. "Unfortunately, we cannot draw upon any formulated expression of the existence of such feeling. Nor are there available experts on such matters to guide the judicial judgment."[36] Nevertheless, Frankfurter concluded, "Our Constitutional system makes it the Court's duty to interpret those feelings of society to which the Due Process Clause gives legal protection. Because of their inherent vagueness the tests by which we are to be guided are most unsatisfactory, but such as they are we must apply them."[37]

True enough, in the Haley case the Court was concerned not with psychology as a science but instead with psychological judgment. At the same time, however, if the duties of the Court required it to exercise such judgment—if, in other words, social science insight was germane to the decisional process, as Frankfurter had in effect admitted—then it certainly could be asked whether it was fitting for the Court to exercise psychological or sociological judgment without at least formally con-

[34] *Ibid.*
[35] *Ibid.*, p. 603 (concurring opinion).
[36] *Ibid.*, p. 605 (concurring opinion).
[37] *Ibid.*

sulting relevant social science literature. The necessity for sup-
plementing judicial insight with social science insight again
became apparent in the case of Beauharnais v. Illinois,[38] decided
in 1952. Here the Court sustained an Illinois statute prohibiting
the public exhibition of literature that "exposes the citizens, of
any race, color, creed or religion to contempt, derision, or
obloquy."[39] On behalf of the Court, Justice Frankfurter noted
that in view of the history of racial and religious propaganda,
the Court would be denying "experience" if it held that the legislature "was without reason in seeking ways to curb false or mali-
cious defamation of racial and religious groups, made in public
places and by means calculated to have a powerful emotional
impact on those to whom it was presented."[40] However, Frankfurter noted, while the objectives of the legislature were reasonable, there was no scientific proof that the statute was effective. "Only those lacking responsible humility," he observed,
"will have a confident solution for problems as intractable as the
frictions attributable to differences of race, color, or religion."
If the legislative remedy did not work or in turn created new
problems, "it is the price to be paid for the trial-and-error inherent in legislative efforts to deal with obstinate social issues."
The due-process clause, Frankfurter emphasized, "does not require the legislature to be in the vanguard of science—especially
sciences as young as human ecology and cultural anthropology."[41]

However, Frankfurter continued, "Long ago this Court recognized that the economic rights of an individual may depend for
the effectiveness of their enforcement on rights in the group,
even though not formally corporate, to which he belongs. . . .
Such group-protection on behalf of the individual may, for all we
know, be a need not confined to the part that a trade union plays
in effectuating rights abstractly recognized as belonging to its
members."[42] But despite overt sociological statements regarding
the relationship of the individual to the group, Frankfurter

[38] Beauharnais v. Illinois, 343 U.S. 250 (1952).
[39] *Ibid.*
[40] *Ibid.,* p. 261.
[41] *Ibid.,* p. 262.
[42] *Ibid.*

emphasized, "it is not within our competence to confirm or deny claims of social scientists as to the dependence of the individual on the position of his racial or religious group in the community. It would, however, be arrant dogmatism," he added, "quite outside the scope of our authority . . . for us to deny that the Illinois Legislature may warrantably believe that a man's job and his educational opportunities and the dignity accorded him may depend as much on the reputation of the racial and religious group to which he willy-nilly belongs, as on his own merits."[43] Therefore, on behalf of the Court, Frankfurter ruled that the rights of speech and press guaranteed by the First Amendment had not been infringed because libelous statements directed at groups were no more deserving of constitutional protection than libelous statements made against individuals.

It is interesting to note, especially in view of Frankfurter's long-standing skepticism regarding the scientific status of social science, that the legal equation drawn between individual and group libel was based on a factual assumption that was also a matter of critical concern to modern social scientific thought. The equation was grounded, of course, on the important social science hypothesis advanced by George Herbert Mead and Charles Horton Cooley. It stated in effect that the individual or social self reflected the estimation made of it by its reference group or depended for its definition and meaning to a large extent on "the generalized other." Curiously, however, Frankfurter did not formally allude to social science findings but, instead, pointedly denied the competence of the Court to assess any such findings. It is ironic that Frankfurter, while disavowing social science, still used implicitly a basic sociological tenet in his legal reasoning.

Indirectly the Court's treatment of social science was paradoxical. The Beauharnais case suggested that the high bench was not quite ready to make formal use of social science in order to define the fact situation of a major constitutional case. Yet the Beauharnais case does indicate that even for the judicial mind,

---

43 *Ibid.*, p. 263.

the perspective of modern social science had become a thing "taken for granted."[44] By 1952 the relationship of constitutional law and modern social science might have been formally aloof and distant, but a closer reading of the Beauharnais case reveals that it was implicitly intimate.

The Tension between Law and Social Science

It should not be very surprising that the path from the Court's formal recognition of the Brandeis brief in 1908[45] to its formal use of modern social science two years after the Beauharnais decision was both tortuous and graded. As Holmes had observed earlier, "Judges commonly are elderly, and are more likely to hate at sight any analysis to which they are not accustomed, and which disturbs repose of mind, than to fall in love with novelties."[46] To be sure, when the Court granted its approval of the Brandeis brief, at the same time recognizing the legal relevance of nascent social science, the occasion was marked by the underlying tension between law and social science. Perhaps only the great presence and persuasive pleading of Louis Brandeis saved his unique brief from stillbirth. As one observer of the oral argument in the Muller case has reported,

> When Brandeis began to speak, the Court showed all inertia and elemental hostility which courts cherish for a new thought, or a new right, or even a new remedy, for an old wrong, but he visibly lifted all this burden, and without orationizing or chewing the rag he reached them all and even held Pitney quiet. . . .
> . . . It was so clear that something had happened in the Court today that even Chas. Henry Butler saw it and he stopped me afterwards on the coldest corner in town to say that no man this winter had received such close attention from the Court as B. got today.[47]

[44] Cf. Alfred Schutz, "The Social World and the Theory of Social Action," 27 *Social Research* 203 (1960).

[45] Muller v. Oregon, 208 U.S. 412 (1908).

[46] Oliver Wendell Holmes, *Collected Legal Papers* (New York: Peter Smith, 1952), p. 230.

[47] William Hitz to Felix Frankfurter, Dec., 1914, quoted in Clement E. Vose, "The National Consumers' League and the Brandeis Brief," 1 *Midwest Journal of Political Science* 267, 280 (1957).

The Brandeis brief encountered resistance from conservative justices because they chose to deny the lawmaking power of the Court; for that reason they "usually looked with disdain on any tendency to stray beyond law books into the mundane realm of facts."[48] By virtue of temperament and as a result of their professional training, judges were not likely to feel comfortable with, or be able to master easily, the new disciplines of the social sciences. Legal education, with its heavy emphasis on the casebook method, was a parochial endeavor that stifled rather than encouraged the exploration of collateral sciences. As William O. Douglas, later a justice, wrote in 1936 with respect to legal education, "The content and nature of our law curricula were pretty well set over a generation ago. . . . The objective at the time these curricula were crystallized was pretty largely the education of country practitioners. . . . What were conceived to be the requirements of general practice of that era fashioned the contents of the courses."[49] The chief concern of legal education, Douglas noted, was the common-law system. Thus he stated, "The emphasis was on the meaning and the application of the legal words of art, the nature of various legal proceedings, the basic factors in legal strategy, the philosophies of the system of common law and equity." As a result the training of lawyers is "in large part inappropriate. They have in effect been trained for one profession while they practice in another."[50]

Not only did legal education dissuade the lawyer from the broader study of social science, but legal practice was divorced from the working perspective of social science. Lawyers, it would seem, are oriented to the needs of their clients, while judges are immersed in the exigencies of particular cases. It follows that the working logic of law begins with deduction, insofar as jurists try to interpret and apply rules to fit particular

[48] Alpheus Thomas Mason, *The Supreme Court from Taft to Warren* (New York: W. W. Norton, 1964), p. 196.

[49] William O. Douglas, *Democracy and Finance: The Addresses and Public Statements of William O. Douglas as Member and Chairman of the Securities and Exchange Commission,* ed. James Allen (New Haven, Conn.: Yale University Press, 1940), pp. 285–86.

[50] *Ibid.,* p. 286.

fact situations. On the other hand, given the logic of scientific method, induction precedes deduction, with social scientists hypothesizing in order to discover generalizations or laws consistent with empirical data. But the legal and social science perspectives diverge still further. Social science is the explanation of group behavior, while the operation of law focuses on individual behavior. In other words, social science is primarily the explanation of social and political processes; the criminologist, for example, is concerned with the social category of criminals. Judges and lawyers, on the other hand, are more likely to perceive criminology in terms of a particular criminal act.[51]

Moreover, the jurist is likely to be confused after his initial contact with social science. Law represents codified and authoritative pronouncements concerning individual acts. Social science, however, by no means displays unanimity and agreement in the analysis of critical social problems. The lack of hierarchical construction in the social sciences did not facilitate the jurist's easy access to social science material, and it undoubtedly compounded the task of the jurist who may have wanted to utilize the findings of social science.

Finally, and most decisively, the Court's cautious approach to the temple of social science, and the underlying tension between law and social science, are understandable in terms of the distinct fundamental philosophical styles or drifts of the two disciplines. In the final analysis law is a practical art, while social science is ultimately a theoretical pursuit. This means that by and large the practitioners of law—lawyers—are essentially advocates. Social scientists, on the other hand, strive for impartial or value-free explanation. Law, quite clearly, no matter how equitable, is a form of political rule. As such, law seeks to fulfill the partial objectives of a political order. Rousseau emphasized that the relationship between science and politics is fraught with tension. A political society, Rousseau explained, is a closed society animated by parochial teachings. Society requires stability and conformity, and it extracts obedience from the citizenry through the apotheosization of law, which is ultimately based

[51] Samuel M. Fahr, "Why Lawyers Are Dissatisfied with the Social Sciences," 1 *Washburn Law Journal* 161, 163 (1961).

on myth and dogma. The Constitution—after all, the ultimate norm—is based on political values that are sustained by faith alone.[52] Science, on the other hand, is a universal calling that definitionally weakens the particular bonds of patriotism. Since science begins with skepticism, it inevitably comes into conflict with political truths. Scientists, then, as a result of their training, are in a loose sense political subversives. Thus social scientists are more likely to revere and follow their own truths than the political values that sustain the law.[53]

It can be surmised that this underlying tension between law and social science colored the development of the Court's cautious relationship with social science. Supreme Court justices in general, as guardians of the law, were not likely to be magnetically drawn to the perspective of social science. As sociologist Peter Berger has explained, "There is a debunking motif inherent in sociological consciousness. The sociologist will be driven time and again, by the very logic of his discipline, to debunk the social systems he is studying. . . . The roots of the debunking motif in sociology are not psychological but methodological."[54] In view of all this, the bar as well as the bench understandably did not welcome, immediately and enthusiastically, the intrusion of social science expertise into its conservative realm. As one observer has stated, perhaps hyperbolically, the major source of legal resistance to social science has been the lawyer's "fear of the loss of his age-old function as intellectual broker, and of his ultimate replacement—in terms of power and prestige—by the specialist and expert."[55]

[52] No one regarded the Constitution with greater reverence than Justice Black. As he put it, "That Constitution is my legal bible; its plan of our government is my plan and its destiny my destiny. I cherish every word of it, from the first to the last, and I personally deplore even the slightest deviation from its least important commands." See Hugo L. Black, *A Constitutional Faith* (New York: Alfred A. Knopf, 1968), p. 66.

[53] Jean Jacques Rousseau, "First Discourse," in *The Social Contract and Discourses*, tr. G. D. H. Cole (London: Everyman's Library, 1963). Cf. Leo Strauss, "On the Intention of Rousseau," 14 *Social Research* 445 (1947).

[54] Peter Berger, *Invitation to Sociology: A Humanistic Perspective* (Garden City, N.Y.: Doubleday Anchor Books, 1963), p. 38.

[55] Julius Cohen, "Factors of Resistance to the Resources of the Behavioral Sciences," 12 *Journal of Legal Education* 67, 68 (1959).

CHAPTER SIX

Racial Discrimination and the Equal-Protection Clause

The Separate-but-Equal Formula

Before World War II the Supreme Court had used extralegal facts primarily in the review of legislation designed to effect social and economic reform. And as we have seen, the Court's increasingly critical approach to the problem of fact-finding in due-process adjudication led eventually to the development of a more realistic jurisprudence. But not until the late forties did the high bench begin to take a hard, consistent look at the facts of racial segregation. Indeed, the legal struggle of the black American for the equality solemnly described by the Declaration of Independence as the natural right of all men had languished prior to the war, despite the broad guarantee of the equal-protection clause of the Fourteenth Amendment, which specified that no state shall "deny to any person within its jurisdiction the equal protection of the law." Although some progress in the area of civil rights was made after the war, not until 1954 did the Court discover in the equal-protection clause a warrant with which to attack the entrenched system of racial segregation, which had long victimized Negroes and other minority groups.

Though the Fourteenth Amendment had been ratified in 1868, racial relations following the Reconstruction era had deteriorated to the point, as Christopher Lasch has written, "that the great question was no longer whether Negroes should be allowed to vote but whether they should be allowed to live; not whether they should be educated in the same schools as white children but whether they should go to school at all."[1] In view of the abysmal plight of the Negro, the Court's overall reluctance to invalidate racial segregation contrasted sharply with its original view of the purpose and scope of the Fourteenth Amendment. As mentioned previously, the Court first interpreted the amendment in 1873, in the Slaughterhouse Cases, as applying basically to Negroes; its express purpose, according to Justice Samuel F. Miller, was the protection of the rights and freedom of the recently emancipated Negro.[2]

The Court's clearly enunciated conviction about the primary purpose of the Fourteenth Amendment was reaffirmed seven years later in the case of Strauder v. West Virginia.[3] Justice William Strong announced that the amendment "was designed to assure to the colored race the enjoyment of all the civil rights that under the law are enjoyed by white persons, and to give to that race the protection of the general government, in that enjoyment, whenever it should be denied by the States."[4] Moreover, in terms of the history of the amendment, the Court stated explicitly that "its design was to protect an emancipated race, and to strike down all possible legal discriminations. . . ." This protection was not to be restricted by the limitations of legal terminology. The Fourteenth Amendment, Justice Strong affirmed, "makes no attempt to enumerate the rights it [was] designed to protect. It speaks in general terms, and those are as comprehensive as possible."[5]

In the same year the Court reiterated again that the main purpose of the Civil War amendments was "to take away all possibility of oppressions by law because of race or color."[6] But in the Civil Rights Cases,[7] decided in 1883, the Court advanced a more cautious interpretation of the Fourteenth Amendment. In this instance the Court invalidated the Civil Rights Act of

[1] Christopher Lasch, The Agony of the American Left (New York: Vintage Books, 1969), p. 19.
[2] Slaughterhouse Cases, 16 Wallace 36 (1873).
[3] Strauder v. West Virginia, 100 U.S. 303 (1880).
[4] Ibid., p. 306.
[5] Ibid., p. 310.
[6] Ex Parte Virginia, 100 U.S. 339, 345 (1880).
[7] Civil Rights Cases, 109 U.S. 3 (1883).

1875, which was intended to guarantee Negroes equal accommodations in public conveyances, inns, and places of amusement, on the ground that the Fourteenth Amendment applied to state action alone. Although the Court had restricted the practical application of the amendment, Justice Joseph P. Bradley did state, "It nullifies and makes void all State legislation, and State action of every kind, which impairs the privileges and immunities of citizens of the United States, or which injures them in life, liberty or property without due process of law, or which denies to any of them the equal protection of the laws."[8]

Nevertheless, the Court had retreated from its previously broad interpretation of the Fourteenth Amendment. This retreat was accelerated with the appearance in 1890 of the "separate-but-equal" formula, which effectively emasculated the equal-protection clause. The separate-but-equal formula was later used principally to condone racial segregation in the field of public education, under the guise of simulated equality. The formula itself was first heard by the Court in a case in which a Mississippi statute requiring all passenger trains to provide "equal-but-separate facilities for the white and colored races" was upheld.[9] But this decision was rendered solely under the commerce clause on the ground that the statute did not apply to interstate commerce. No mention was made of the Fourteenth Amendment. After this decision the separate-but-equal formula was not used to decide any case until 1896. The classic use of the formula in this year came, as we have already seen, in the case of Plessy v. Ferguson,[10] which also involved railroad transportation.

Not until three years later, in the case of Cumming v. Board of Education,[11] did the Court apply the separate-but-equal formula to school facilities, but it did so only by implication. In the Cumming case the Court did not find any discrimination and, therefore, declined to enjoin a local school board from providing funds for a white high school, despite the fact that for eco-

---

[8] *Ibid.*, p. 11.
[9] Louisville, N.O. & T. Ry. v. Mississippi, 133 U.S. 587 (1890).
[10] Plessy v. Ferguson, 163 U.S. 537 (1896). For an extensive discussion of the separate-but-equal formula, see Note, " 'Separate-but-Equal': A Study of the Career of a Constitutional Concept," 1 *Race Relations Law Reporter*, 283 (1956).
[11] Cumming v. Board of Education, 175 U.S. 528 (1899).

nomic reasons the operation of a black high school had been suspended. A significant note in Justice Harlan's opinion was his statement that the control of education was a matter primarily reserved to the states. Harlan added, however, that this control did not entirely rule out the possibility of federal intervention. Clearly "the education of the people in schools maintained by state taxation is a matter belonging to the respective States, and any interference on the part of Federal authority with the management of such schools cannot be justified except in the case of a clear and unmistakeable disregard of rights secured by the supreme law of the land."[12]

Nine years later, in the case of Berea College v. Kentucky,[13] the Court moved closer to an explicit application of the separate-but-equal formula. It upheld a Kentucky statute that prohibited persons and corporations from maintaining an integrated school. But Justice Brewer in this instance did not view the Fourteenth Amendment as controlling. Instead he ruled on the narrow ground that the state, under its power to control corporations, could forbid private schools from integrating their students. In a dissenting opinion Justice Harlan called for the federal intervention he had alluded to briefly in his Cumming opinion. In his view the statute violated the Fourteenth Amendment. "Have we become so inoculated with prejudice of race," Harlan asked, "that an American government, professedly based on the principles of freedom, and charged with the protection of all citizens alike, can make distinctions between such citizens in the matter of their voluntary meeting for innocent purposes, simply because of their respective races?"[14] The Court's positive response to Harlan's query did not come until almost fifty years later.

There were no further decisions regarding education until 1927, when the separate-but-equal principle was used in the case of Gong Lum v. Rice,[15] although Chief Justice Taft for the Court did not explicitly refer to the phrase. Court action was brought after a young Chinese girl, Martha Lum, was denied admission

---

[12] *Ibid.*, p. 545.
[13] Berea College v. Kentucky, 211 U.S. 45 (1908).
[14] *Ibid.*, p. 69 (dissenting opinion).
[15] Gong Lum v. Rice, 275 U.S. 78 (1927).

to a white school simply because she was not a member of the Caucasian race. Gong Lum, on behalf of his daughter, did not challenge the validity of segregated schools or ask for the establishment of a separate Chinese school, but he did claim that in the absence of a Chinese school, Martha Lum should be permitted to attend the white school. The Court ruled that since Martha Lum had the option of attending either a "school which receives only colored children of the brown, yellow or black races" or a private school, and in view of the state's right to provide the method of public school education, there had been no denial of the equal protection of the laws as provided for by the Fourteenth Amendment.[16] With the Court's stamp of approval on separate school systems, and its express recognition of the primacy of state control over education, racial segregation in public education became constitutionally entrenched.

More Critical Fact-Finding

The legal relegation of Negroes to inferior secondary schools and the complete lack of any first-class Negro institutions of higher learning imposed permanent social and political disabilities on an already much abused people. Almost from its inception in 1910 the NAACP had been concerned with segregation and discrimination in the field of education. Not only did the association believe that these practices harmed the Negro, but it also felt that an uneducated Negro populace compromised the general welfare of the nation.[17] The association's legal effort to win equality in education focused in particular on professional graduate schools. Since fewer people were involved in graduate education, it was thought that less resistance to integration would be encountered at this level of education. The NAACP's legal efforts in this area seemed promising. At first the association attempted to win separate equality—the actual implementation of the separate-but-equal formula. This, it was believed, might make school segregation all but impossible in the South through

[16] *Ibid.*, p. 85.
[17] Charles Flint Kellogg, *NAACP: A History of the National Association for the Advancement of Colored People* (Baltimore: Johns Hopkins Press, 1967), p. 187.

the imposition of an unsustainable economic burden on already faltering school systems. In an extreme instance the NAACP could have brought, according to its legal advisors, "an attack on segregation at a graduate school of nuclear physics—requiring a separate-but-equal cyclotron."[18]

There was a good reason for the association's optimism that the Court might be persuaded to recognize the separate-but-equal formula as a flagrant legal fiction. By the late thirties the Court was disowning other legal fictions that it had once used to invalidate social welfare legislation. To be sure, due-process adjudication was reflecting a greater fidelity to economic and social realities.

In 1935 in the case of Norris v. Alabama[19] the Court indicated that it would also discharge its fact-finding function more vigorously in instances where it was alleged that federal rights had been violated in contravention of the equal-protection clause of the Fourteenth Amendment. Eight Negro boys were found guilty of rape in Alabama in the Norris case; the Supreme Court overturned the conviction on the ground that Negroes had been systematically excluded from jury service in violation of the equal-protection clause. The Court documented this exclusion with statistics and, in doing so, manifested a scrupulous attitude toward fact-finding that became indispensable to the continuing legal struggle of the Negro for civil rights. Chief Justice Hughes left no doubt that in the future, when a federal right was claimed in a state court, the Supreme Court would be prepared to examine for itself the relevant fact situations. Accordingly, Hughes wrote:

> That the question is one of fact does not relieve us of the duty to determine whether in truth a federal right has been denied. When a federal right has been specially set up and claimed in a state court, it is our province to inquire not merely whether it was denied in express terms but also whether it was denied in substance and effect. If this requires an examination of evidence, that examination must be made. Otherwise, review by this Court

[18] Jack Greenberg and Herbert Hill, *Citizen's Guide to Desegregation* (Boston: Beacon Press, 1955), p. 58.
[19] Norris v. Alabama, 294 U.S. 587 (1935).

would fail of its purpose in safeguarding constitutional rights. Thus, whenever a conclusion of law of a state court as to a federal right and findings of fact are so intermingled that the latter control the former, it is incumbent upon us to analyze the facts in order that the appropriate enforcement of the federal right may be assured.[20]

In view of the Supreme Court's later use of social science to establish facts relevant to the invalidation of public school segregation, Hughes's statement of the Court's firm resolve to find facts for itself was significant. Clearly the Court could serve as an effective guardian of civil rights only if it was prepared to define fact situations for itself. Hughes had announced the Court's preparedness in cases likely to come under the equal-protection clause. The Norris case revealed minimally that in enforcing the equal-protection clause, the high bench would review the finding of facts in a state court as critically as the prior finding of law.

Shortly afterward, in the case of Missouri ex rel. Gaines v. Canada,[21] decided in 1938, the Court began to look sternly at the issue of racial segregation, insofar as it tested for the first time the adequacy of the separate-but-equal formula in the realm of public education. Petitioner Gaines brought suit after he had been denied admission to the Law School of the University of Missouri, charging that the university's arbitrary action violated the equal-protection clause of the Fourteenth Amendment. Since Missouri did not maintain a separate law school for Negroes, it had offered to pay Gaines's expenses at a law school in an adjacent state in order to provide him with advantages comparable to those available to white Missourians. Chief Justice Hughes, however, was not misled by this segregation ploy and went to the heart of the issue when he sought to determine the concrete meaning of the equal-protection clause in terms of the actual facilities available to Negroes. Hughes wrote, "The fact remains that instruction in law for negroes is not now afforded by the State, either at Lincoln University or elsewhere within the State, and that the State excludes negroes from the advantages of the

[20] *Ibid.*, pp. 589–90.
[21] Missouri ex rel. Gaines v. Canada, 305 U.S. 337 (1938).

law school it has established at the University of Missouri."[22] Whether the facilities of out-of-state law schools were comparable to those available to whites in Missouri, Hughes reasoned, was not a material question.

In appraising directly the separate-but-equal formula, Hughes avoided all esoteric discussion of the definition of equality. He emphasized that on the face of the record Missouri had not in the first instance provided two schools that could be compared. Therefore, Hughes concluded, if the Negro has to leave the state in order to receive a legal education, this by itself "is a denial of the equality of legal right to the enjoyment of the privilege which the State has set up, and the provision for the payment of tuition fees in another State does not remove the discrimination."[23]

The primary significance of Hughes's opinion was the Court's forthright examination of the condition of equality. Moreover, for the first time the Court seriously appraised the effect of the separate-but-equal formula in the field of public education. As soon as the Court posed the question of the meaning of "equal facilities in separate schools," the promise of simulative equality provided by the separate-but-equal formula was bound to be revealed as a transparent legal fiction. As Robert Harris has written, "What makes the Gaines case unusual is that the Court looked beyond the formula to question the fiction, and in law to question a fiction is to kill it."[24] The Gaines case by no means rendered school segregation indefensible, but it did make it more vulnerable to future legal assault. Gaines himself, shortly after his admission to the University of Missouri Law School, mysteriously dropped out of sight and was not heard from again.

Tocqueville emphasized that equality is the primary condition of democracy.[25] But while the principle of equality before the law has generally been accepted as the basic prerequisite of a democratic society, an understanding of its theoretical nature,

---

[22] *Ibid.*, p. 345.

[23] *Ibid.*, pp. 349–50.

[24] Robert J. Harris, "The Constitution, Education, and Segregation," 29 *Temple Law Quarterly* 409, 416 (1956).

[25] Alexis de Tocqueville, *Democracy in America*, ed. Phillips Bradley, 2 vols. (New York: Vintage Books, 1961).

and of the means for its practical application, has long been a subject of dispute.[26] Since there was no Negro law school in Missouri, in the Gaines case the question of equality was easily resolved. However, once the Court was called upon to decide whether two separate school systems—or, indeed, separateness itself—were compatible with the requirement of the equal-protection clause, then judicial interpretation would necessarily entail a sociological and psychological understanding of racial segregation.

The Criterion of Race and a New Presumptive Principle

With the outbreak of World War II, the legal battle for civil rights waned. Indeed, the war led to gross violations of civil rights and saw the Court dutifully acquiesce to the dictates of military security. For example, in the case of Korematsu v. United States,[27] decided in 1944, the Court sustained a civilian exclusion order that required the wholesale removal of Americans of Japanese ancestry from the West Coast. Justice Black, for the Court, justified the decision on the ground that the action in question was based solely on military need. He denied that Korematsu was excluded from the specified area "because of hostility to him or his race" and insisted instead that "he *was* excluded because we are at war with the Japanese Empire," and that the military actually had no choice but to adopt proper security measures.[28] The crucial factual issue on which the case turned was whether the political loyalty of Japanese-Americans could legitimately be questioned. Without adequate explanation the Court assumed that their loyalty was in doubt, and although Justice Black maintained that there was "evidence of the dis-

[26] Aristotle noted that democracy arose because of the opinion that those who are equal in one respect should be absolutely equal in all respects; similarly, oligarchy arose from the opinion that those who were unequal in one respect should be unequal in all respects. See *Politics*, 1301a. The problem of equality and inequality is clearly at the root of Aristotle's discussion of justice. However, he did not spell out in a concrete fashion how equality could be achieved in a democracy that maintained respect for differences of merit and wealth.

[27] Korematsu v. United States, 323 U.S. 214 (1944).

[28] *Ibid.*, p. 223.

loyalty on the part of some,"[29] he noticeably failed to substantiate or clarify this charge.

Justice Frank Murphy, on the other hand, dissented, arguing that "justification for exclusion [was] sought . . . mainly upon questionable racial and sociological grounds . . ." beyond the expertise of military judgment.[30] Murphy took issue with the commanding general's report, which depicted Japanese-Americans as " 'a large, unassimilated, tightly knit racial group, bound to an enemy nation by strong ties of race, culture, custom and religion' . . . given to 'emperor worshipping ceremonies' and to 'dual citizenship.' "[31] In countering what he considered to be "misinformation, half-truths and insinuations,"[32] Murphy referred to other sociological studies that pointed to the lack of correlation between certain customs and religious practices and loyalty to the United States.[33] Murphy therefore reasoned that the general's report, based upon its tenuous "racial and sociological considerations," should not be given any special consideration, as a normal military judgment might receive.[34] The Court's decision, Murphy concluded, represented the "legalization of racism."[35]

The Korematsu decision suggested that the Court was willing to act on an unproven "sociological" judgment, even though the supporting evidence was far from unimpeachable.[36] Yet by implication the case indicated that modern social science could be a critical factor in constitutional adjudication. However, the Korematsu case threw no definitive light upon the possibility of effectively presenting the Court with social science evidence in civil rights cases. Whether social science could be used to persuade the Court to take drastic action to insure equal conditions for the Negro was a question that remained to be answered. If social science findings were to be used to challenge

[29] *Ibid.*
[30] *Ibid.*, pp. 236–37 (dissenting opinion).
[31] *Ibid.*, p. 237 (dissenting opinion).
[32] *Ibid.*, p. 239 (dissenting opinion).
[33] *Ibid.*, p. 237, n. 4 (dissenting opinion).
[34] *Ibid.*, p. 240 (dissenting opinion).
[35] *Ibid.*, p. 242 (dissenting opinion).
[36] See Jacobus Ten Broek *et al., Prejudice, War and the Constitution* (Berkeley and Los Angeles: University of California Press, 1968), pp. 261–321.

legislation that the Court presumed on its face to be constitutional, then any flaws or weaknesses in such studies might cause the Court to discard them. If, however, the Court did not apply the traditional principle of presumption to segregation legislation, then it might readily use social science findings, even if they were of a tentative nature.

Curiously enough, Justice Black's Korematsu opinion indicated that the traditional principle of presumption, at least in the future, would not apply to legislation based on racial prejudice. Black wrote accordingly, "It should be noted, to begin with, that all legal restrictions which curtail the civil rights of a single racial group are immediately suspect." But he added, "That is not to say that all such restrictions are unconstitutional. It is to say that courts must subject them to the most rigid scrutiny. Pressing public necessity may sometimes justify the existence of such restrictions; racial antagonism never can."[37]

Despite the Court's failure in the Korematsu case to condemn racial discrimination, it had at least suggested that it was prepared to abandon the traditional principle of presumptive constitutionality in cases where classifications were unreasonably based on the criterion of race. The emergence of the Court's new principle of presumption was suggested again in the case of Oyama v. California,[38] decided in 1948. In the Oyama case the Court invalidated a California statute that forbade aliens ineligible for citizenship to acquire, own, occupy, lease, or transfer agricultural lands. Although the statute was struck down on the narrow ground that it violated the right of citizens "to own land anywhere in the United States," Chief Justice Fred M. Vinson saw fit to endorse the new presumptive principle first announced by Black. With respect to "the question whether discrimination between citizens on the basis of their racial descent" could be justified, Vinson clearly stated, "Here we start with the proposition that only the most exceptional circumstances can excuse discrimination on that basis in the face of the equal protection clause. . . ."[39] In retrospect, the Oyama

[37] Korematsu v. United States, 323 U.S. 214, 216 (1944).
[38] Oyama v. California, 332 U.S. 633 (1948).
[39] *Ibid.*, p. 646.

decision indicates that the Court was moving toward the total invalidation, on constitutional grounds, of racial segregation in the public sector.

Segregation under Attack

In the same term the Court cautiously resumed its critical appraisal of racial segregation in the field of public education. In the case of Sipuel v. Oklahoma[40] the high bench reversed a judgment of the Oklahoma Supreme Court refusing a writ of mandamus to a Negro who had been denied admission to the Law School of the University of Oklahoma, the only such institution in the state. In a *per curiam* judgment the Court held that the petitioner's right to a legal education had been violated and that "the State must provide it for her in conformity with the equal protection clause of the Fourteenth Amendment and provide it as soon as it does for applicants of any other group."[41] The Sipuel ruling did not affect the status of the separate-but-equal formula, which still remained legally viable, as a second *per curiam* decision later in the year demonstrated. In Fisher v. Hurst[42] the Court upheld an Oklahoma district court's order that either a Negro be admitted to the Law School of the University of Oklahoma until a separate school for Negroes was ready, or no applicants at all be accepted at the law school until a separate one was established. This decision added new vitality to the separate-but-equal formula and prompted Justice Wiley B. Rutledge to write a dissenting opinion. Rutledge argued that the Sipuel decision had not been followed, and despite its apparent ambiguity, he protested that in his "comprehension the equality required was equality in fact, not in legal fiction."[43] Justice Rutledge's call for a factual equality, as opposed to a fictional one, constituted an open invitation for an examination of the factual reality of racial segregation, long masked by an untenable legal formula.

[40] Sipuel v. Oklahoma, 332 U.S. 631 (1948).
[41] *Ibid.*, p. 633.
[42] Fisher v. Hurst, 333 U.S. 147 (1948).
[43] *Ibid.*, p. 152 (dissenting opinion).

The viability of the separate-but-equal formula as a legal endorsement for racial segregation from 1896 to 1948 undoubtedly reflected the Court's retreat from its original broad interpretation of the Fourteenth Amendment. However, on the heels of the Fisher decision the Court in the case of Shelley v. Kraemer,[44] also decided in 1948, ruled that the judicial enforcement of restrictive covenants among private individuals was a violation of the equal-protection clause. Of particular significance was the wide latitude Chief Justice Vinson ascribed to the intentions of the framers of the Fourteenth Amendment: "Whatever else the framers sought to achieve, it is clear that the matter of primary concern was the establishment of equality in the enjoyment of basic civil and political rights and the preservation of these rights from discriminatory action on the part of the States based on consideration of race or color."[45] The Shelley decision demonstrated that the Court was moving toward a broader interpretation of the Fourteenth Amendment and a more vigorous enforcement of the civil rights of Negroes.

The NAACP's attack on racial segregation was beginning to show good results, but the separate-but-equal formula had still not been discredited. In the late forties the association reevaluated its legal strategy. Officials of the association decided that nothing but a frontal assault upon the separate-but-equal formula could effectively serve the cause of civil rights. Yet according to Thurgood Marshall, this "doctrine had become so ingrained that overwhelming proof was sorely needed to demonstrate that equal educational opportunities for Negroes could not be provided in a segregated system."[46] In view of the now established prestige and respectability of social science, especially in regard to its successful application in industry, it appeared that social science findings might be accepted by the Court as the convincing evidence the association sought. One observer at the time confirmed this possibility; he wrote that the day was coming when it would be necessary to consult

[44] Shelley v. Kraemer, 334 U.S. 1 (1948).
[45] *Ibid.*, p. 23.
[46] Thurgood Marshall, "An Evaluation of Recent Efforts to Achieve Racial Integration in Education through Resort to the Courts," 21 *Journal of Negro Education* 316 (1952).

the social psychologist before any legislation was designed to regulate human behavior in conflict situations.[47] However, the convergence of law and social science was still far from complete. According to David Riesman, for example, law and psychology do mingle at their peripheries, "but these meeting grounds are rather like the parlor in the Victorian home in which the girl and her suitor can get together—but not get together too much."[48]

Nevertheless, the NAACP hoped to consummate the relationship between law and social science. Social science testimony was first presented in the case of Sweatt v. Painter,[49] decided in 1950. The association attempted to prove in the light of social science evidence that racial segregation in education constituted an unreasonable statutory classification because Negroes in a learning situation tended to respond the same as white students. The NAACP presented social science testimony to this effect in order to demonstrate that there was no reasonable or understandable factual basis to statutes requiring racial segregation.[50]

The Sweatt case was almost identical to the Gaines case, although in the former the state of Texas had hurriedly established a separate law school for Negroes, expecting that the new, separate-but-equal law school would satisfy the requirements of the equal-protection clause. However, it was clear to the members of the Supreme Court, from their position at the pinnacle of the legal profession, that the Negro law school opened in 1947 was not equal to the University of Texas Law School. While a comparison of the two schools would involve intangibles, no one could state with more authority than the Court itself that the white law school "possesses to a far greater degree those qualities which are incapable of objective measurement but which make for greatness in a law school."[51] But the

[47] Thomas A. Cowan, "The Relation of Law to Experimental Social Science," 96 *University of Pennsylvania Law Review* 484, 491 (1948).

[48] David Riesman, "Some Observations on Law and Psychology," 19 *University of Chicago Law Review* 30, 32 (1951).

[49] Sweatt v. Painter, 339 U.S. 629 (1950).

[50] Marshall, "An Evaluation," pp. 319–20.

[51] Sweatt v. Painter, 339 U.S. 629, 634 (1950).

Court, in line with tradition, declined to raise issues broader than necessary in deciding the immediate controversy. Therefore, in ordering Sweatt's admission to the University of Texas Law School as a requirement of the equal-protection clause, the Court passed over the social science evidence. As Chief Justice Vinson explained, "Because of this traditional reluctance to extend constitutional interpretations to situations or facts which are not before the Court, much of the excellent research and detailed argument presented in these cases is unnecessary to their disposition."[52] The NAACP had won its victory, but the campaign continued.

On the same day, in the case of McLaurin v. Oklahoma State Regents,[53] the high bench reversed a district court judgment that had sustained a grotesque number of patently discriminatory practices designed to segregate internally a Negro attending the University of Oklahoma. As Chief Justice Vinson pointed out, the student McLaurin was required "to sit apart at a designated desk in an anteroom adjoining the classroom; to sit at a designated desk on the mezzanine floor of the library, but not to use the desks in the regular reading room; and to sit at a designated table and to eat at a different time from the other students in the school cafeteria."[54] Such restrictions, Vinson said, made it difficult for McLaurin to pursue graduate training, since they set him apart from other students. While Vinson's opinion did not contain any social science findings, it was apparent that the Court had based its decision on psychological considerations.

The chief justice reasoned that "such restrictions impair and inhibit" McLaurin's "ability to study, to engage in discussions and exchange views with other students, and, in general, to learn his profession."[55] Receiving an education under such conditions, Vinson concluded, deprived McLaurin of his right to the equal protection of the laws. Although Vinson admitted

[52] *Ibid.*, p. 631.
[53] McLaurin v. Oklahoma State Regents, 339 U.S. 637 (1950).
[54] *Ibid.*, p. 640.
[55] *Ibid.*, p. 641.

that the Court's decision might not ameliorate personal discrimination, it would at least remove state-imposed restrictions
that deprived the appellant of the opportunity to gain the
acceptance of his peers on the basis of his own merits.[56] The
Supreme Court had thus for the second time in the same year
disavowed racial segregation in the field of public education
without constitutionally invalidating it.

The Vinson Court, although not generally considered
libertarian-minded, had manifested a circumspect regard for
Negro civil rights. Under Vinson's tenure the Court moved
toward a direct factual appraisal of the separate-but-equal formula. In 1953 President Eisenhower nominated Earl Warren as
chief justice of the Supreme Court. By no means a flaming
liberal, Warren's first opinion was striking in two respects. The
Warren Court met the problem of racial segregation head on,
and did so through a conspicuous use of modern social science.

[56] *Ibid.,* p. 642.

CHAPTER SEVEN

Modern Social Science
and the Brown Case

Prelude to Decision

The case of Brown v. Board of Education of Topeka[1] first reached the Court on appeal in October, 1952, when the justices decided to hear simultaneously three cases involving public school segregation in the states of Kansas,[2] South Carolina,[3] and Virginia.[4] In November the Court granted *certiorari* for a case in which Delaware's highest court had ordered the admission of Negro children to previously all-white schools, much to the dismay of school officials.[5] In the same month the Court granted *certiorari* in the case of Bolling v. Sharpe,[6] which involved public school segregation in the District of Columbia. The four state cases, all coming under the equal-protection clause of the Fourteenth Amendment, were later disposed of in a single opinion. Because the suit in the District of Columbia came under the Fifth Amendment, a separate opinion was later required. But because the Supreme Court felt that the issues

[1] Brown v. Board of Education of Topeka, 347 U.S. 483 (1954).
[2] Brown v. Board of Education of Topeka, 98 F. Supp. 797 (1951).
[3] Briggs v. Elliot, 98 F. Supp. 529 (1951).
[4] Davis v. County School Board of Prince Edward County, 103 F. Supp. 337 (1952). The three state cases were placed on the docket in an intermediate order. See Brown v. Board of Education of Topeka, 344 U.S. 1 (1952).
[5] Gebhart v. Belton, 91 A. 2d 137 (1952). The writ was granted concurrently with the other three state cases.
[6] Bolling v. Sharpe, 344 U.S. 873 (1952).

in all five cases were comparable, it decided to hear all oral arguments together.

Over the years the various legal challenges to public school segregation had not prompted the Court to confront directly the central issue of the constitutionality of racial segregation. As we have seen, the Court had previously ruled in several instances that the separate-but-equal formula had not been adequately implemented. Yet this formula itself had never been formally rejected.[7] Consequently it was generally recognized in the legal community that a convincing factual showing of inequality inherent even in an ideal application of the formula would be required before the Supreme Court would invalidate public school segregation on broad constitutional grounds.[8]

The NAACP Legal Defense and Educational Fund, the legal arm of the parent organization, filed suits against Kansas, South Carolina, Virginia, Delaware, and the District of Columbia, calculating that it could produce the necessary factual evidence. The NAACP had worked for some time with social scientists. Just as Brandeis had relied on nascent social science to convince the Court of the reasonability of social welfare legislation, the NAACP hoped to use modern social science to convince the Court that racial segregation was an unreasonable exercise of the legislative power. Accordingly, in the words of one observer, "in each case, an unusual type of evidence was presented on behalf of the Negro children: testimony from social scientists to the effect that segregation often inflicted serious psychological harm on children subjected to it."[9] But legal opinion in some quarters remained skeptical that available social science findings could be relied on to undermine the separate-but-equal formula.[10] Indeed, NAACP lawyers themselves were not entirely certain that modern social science findings would be admissible

[7] See Ralph F. Bischoff, "One Hundred Years of Court Decisions: Dred Scott after a Century," 6 *Journal of Public Law* 411, 418 (1957).

[8] Note, "Grade School Segregation: The Latest Attack on Racial Discrimination," 61 *Yale Law Journal* 730, 734 (1952).

[9] Daniel M. Berman, *It Is So Ordered: The Supreme Court Rules on School Segregation* (New York: W. W. Norton, 1966), p. 14.

[10] "Grade School Segregation," p. 737.

in the courts.[11] The subsequent action of the trial courts was inconclusive in this respect.

In the Kansas case the district court endorsed the testimony offered by social scientists that public school segregation had a detrimental effect on Negro children. The court acknowledged that segregation caused a sense of inferiority that affected the motivation of children to learn. However, despite this finding of fact, the district court upheld the constitutionality of segregated schools. In the South Carolina case the district court upheld school segregation as a matter of legislative policy. The court emphasized that it was not at liberty to interfere with the preserve of the legislature simply on the basis of theories put forward by a few educators and sociologists. The Virginia court heard conflicting expert testimony and, as a result, ignored social science evidence. In contrast, the chancery court in the Delaware case accepted social science testimony to the effect that school segregation created a mental health problem for Negro children. Consequently the chancery court granted an injunction ordering the admission of Negro children to previously all-white schools.

At this point it was not at all clear from the respective actions of the four courts whether the Supreme Court might use such distinctive and unique extralegal data as modern social science. Although the Court had used extralegal facts on many other occasions, modern social science could not be regarded as simply another form of extralegal data. Even though the Brandeis brief was over forty years old at the time, few legal observers were led to such a simplistic equation. There existed wide differences between the methodology of the nascent social science in the Brandeis brief and that of modern social science.[12] Thus it was open to question whether the Supreme Court would accept social science findings as a binding definition of the pertinent fact situation. As we have already seen, the Supreme

[11] Kenneth B. Clark, "Desegregation: An Appraisal of the Evidence," 9 *Journal of Social Issues* 1 (1953).

[12] More to the point, the Brandeis brief was not properly the work of professional social scientists and in this sense did not suggest the possible clash of rival professional disciplines.

Court was not likely to be favorably predisposed to new things. Moreover, the tension implicit between law and social science was an additional factor, although a covert one, that mitigated against the Court's ready acceptance of social science findings. Yet as one observer has pointed out, "Every successful use of technical information by the law has had to travel the path from strangeness to indispensability."[13]

While lawyers questioned the legal utility of social science, some social scientists believed that the relationship between law and social science would develop best if left alone, especially if no deliberate legal uses of social science were made.[14] Behind this reluctance to encourage social science to serve the normative purposes of law was the view, far from uncommon in various social science disciplines, that the utility of social science, like natural science, was restricted by an unbridgeable dichotomy between facts and values. For some social scientists, law simply reflected policy or value judgments. Social science, unlike law, was simply concerned with facts. Many social scientists could not understand how facts and values were related. Without doubt, Max Weber had good reason for referring to values as "that unfortunate child of misery of our science."[15]

On the other hand, Dr. Kenneth B. Clark, who served as a liaison between NAACP lawyers and social scientists, rejected the orthodoxy that there was no linkage between facts and values. Clark, a noted social psychologist, believed that moral implications were inevitable in all social behavior and that one

---

[13] Michael O. Finkelstein, "The Application of Statistical Decision Theory to the Jury Discrimination Cases," 80 *Harvard Law Review* 338, 376 (1966).

[14] Philip Selznick, "The Sociology of Law," 12 *Journal of Legal Education* 521, 522 (1960).

[15] Max Weber, "'Objectivity' in Social Science and Social Policy," in Maurice Natanson, ed., *Philosophy of the Social Sciences: A Reader* (New York: Random House, 1963), p. 414. The proponents of a value-free social science seemed to overlook Weber's definition of the "cultural sciences" as "those disciplines which analyze the phenomena of life in terms of their cultural significance." Weber goes on to say, "The *significance* of a configuration of cultural phenomena and the basis of this significance cannot however be derived and rendered intelligible by a system of analytical laws (*Gesetzesbegriffen*), however perfect it may be, since the significance of cultural events presupposes a *value-orientation* towards these events. The concept of culture is a *value-concept*. Empirical reality becomes 'culture' to us because and insofar as we relate it to value ideas" (p. 382).

of the major goals of social science was to seek a description and verification of moral laws.[16] Much of the leading social science testimony at the trial level was delivered by Clark. The role of social science, according to Clark, was to provide NAACP lawyers "with the kind of information which, within the framework of the law, would differentiate fact from opinion, knowledge from prejudice, and predictions based upon past biases from those based upon careful and detailed analyses of past events."[17]

The factual evidence demonstrating that racial segregation per se constituted inequality was contained in the NAACP brief as a social science appendix entitled "The Effects of Segregation and the Consequences of Desegregation: A Social Science Statement."[18] This relatively short statement, extensively documented, summarized social science findings on the general effects of segregation and specifically on the effects of school segregation. The statement emphasized that "segregated schools impair the ability of the child to profit from the educational opportunities provided him."[19] It pointed out that segregation caused "guilt feelings," a "distorted sense of social reality," and "mutual suspicion, distrust and hostility."[20] These feelings of "inferiority and doubts about personal worth" were attributed "to living in an underprivileged environment only insofar as the latter is itself perceived as an indicator of low social status and as a symbol of inferiority."[21] The child, it was reported, "may be able to cope with ordinary expressions of prejudice by regarding the prejudiced person as evil or misguided; but he cannot readily cope with symbols of authority, the full force of the authority of the State—the school or the school board, in this instance—in the same manner." In short, the statement concluded, "enforced segregation is psychologically detrimental to the members of the segregated group."[22]

[16] Kenneth B. Clark, *Prejudice and Your Child*, 2nd ed. (Boston: Beacon Press, 1966), p. 38.
[17] *Ibid.*, p. 214.
[18] "Appendix to Appellants' Briefs: Statements by Social Scientists . . . ," reprinted in 2 *Social Problems* 227 (1955).
[19] *Ibid.*, p. 228.
[20] *Ibid.*, p. 229.
[21] *Ibid.*
[22] *Ibid.*, p. 230.

The social science statement on the effects of segregation was signed by thirty-five distinguished social scientists. Among them were Gordon W. Allport, Hadley Cantril, Otto Klineberg, R. M. MacIver, Paul Lazarsfeld, Robert Merton, and Robert Redfield. The Court was thus informed of the most recent findings of modern social science, agreed upon and endorsed by leading representatives of its various fields. It was made clear to the Court that social science literature in the field of race had changed dramatically since the time of the Plessy case. Actually the transition away from the fixed notion of Negro inferiority had begun as early as 1925. And by 1930 the amount of social science literature that purported to prove the inferiority of the Negro had declined markedly.[23] The social science statement informed the Court of the critical fact that "much, perhaps all, of the observable differences among various racial and national groups may be adequately explained in terms of environmental differences."[24] Modern social science, as the Court could plainly see, had decisively rejected the psychological and sociological assumptions that underlay the Plessy decision. The Court, in effect, was asked to reject them also.

Oral Argument

On Tuesday afternoon, December 9, the Supreme Court began to hear oral argument in the five school segregation cases. Robert L. Carter, assistant counsel of the NAACP Legal Defense and Educational Fund, appeared first for the appellants and relied heavily on social science findings in his argument. Carter told the Supreme Court:

> It was testified that racial segregation, as practiced in the City of Topeka, tended to relegate appellants and their group to an inferior caste; that it lowered their level of aspiration; that it instilled feelings of insecurity and inferiority with them, and that it retarded their mental and educational development, and for these reasons, the testimony said, it was impossible for the Negro children who were set off in these four schools to secure, in fact

[23] I. A. Newby, *Jim Crow's Defense: Anti-Negro Thought in America, 1900–1930* (Baton Rouge: Louisiana State University Press, 1965), pp. 50–51.
[24] "Appendix," p. 231.

or in law, an education which was equal to that available to white children in the eighteen elementary schools maintained for them.[25]

Carter's emphasis on social science findings, which he described as the "heart of our case,"[26] did not elicit an unusually critical reaction from the Court. The immediate concern of the justices was to question whether the Constitution permitted statutory classifications based solely on the criterion of race.

Of all the participating justices, Frankfurter demonstrated the keenest interest in the fact situation of racial segregation and was most cognizant of the novelty of social science testimony presented in the trial courts. Frankfurter's questions suggested that a psycho-sociological understanding of racial segregation was relevant to the disposition of the cases. He asked Carter, "What is the root of this legislation? What is it based on?"[27] Not satisfied with Carter's simple answer—race—Frankfurter replied, "Yes, I understand that. I understand all this legislation. But I want to know why this legislation, the sole basis of which is race—is there just some wilfulness of man in the states or some, as I say, of man's inhumanity to man, some ruthless disregard of the facts of life?"[28] But despite Frankfurter's leading questions, there was no way of knowing whether the Court would accept the "heart" of the NAACP case or use the facts of social life as verified by the findings of modern social science.

An affirmative answer to this question was vital to the success of the NAACP's case. The association was gambling plainly enough on the persuasiveness and authority of social science evidence. Thurgood Marshall, appearing for the appellants later in the afternoon, raised directly the problem of the legal relevance of social science testimony. He asserted that social science witnesses "stand in the record as unchallenged as experts in

[25] "Oral Argument in the Supreme Court, Brown v. Board of Education, Case No. 8," in Leon Friedman, ed., *Argument: The Oral Argument before the Supreme Court in Brown v. Board of Education of Topeka, 1952–55* (New York: Chelsea House, 1969), p. 13.
[26] *Ibid.*, p. 18.
[27] *Ibid.*, p. 24.
[28] *Ibid.*, p. 25.

their field, and I think we have arrived at the stage where the courts do give credence to the testimony of people who are experts in their fields."[29] Marshall's assertion was not questioned by the Court.

Shortly afterward Justice Frankfurter intimated that the Court would be receptive to social science findings, and not merely in the form of testimony. Frankfurter queried Marshall, "Can we not take judicial notice of writings by people who competently deal with these problems? Can I not take judicial notice of Myrdal's book without having him called as a witness?"[30] Marshall replied that the Court could notice Myrdal's book but that portions should not be read out of context. Frankfurter then proceeded to answer his own question: "That is a different point. I am merely going to the point that in these matters this Court takes judicial notice of accredited writings, and it does not have to call the writers as witnesses." Frankfurter then observed, "How to inform the judicial mind, as you know, is one of the most complicated problems. It is better to have witnesses, but I did not know that we could not read the works of competent writers."[31]

Frankfurter had ostensibly indicated that modern social science was germane to the process of judicial interpretation. However, he was careful to point out that the role of social science was strictly related to the finding of fact. As for the finding of law, Frankfurter emphasized that social science would have no bearing on the matter of whether the Constitution permitted statutory classifications based on race. If race was a constitutionally justifiable criterion, Frankfurter noted, ". . . then I do not care what any associate or full professor in sociology tells me. If it is in the Constitution, I do not care about what they say. But the question is, is it in the Constitution?"[32]

During the oral argument Frankfurter alone demonstrated a special interest in the possibility that the Supreme Court might use modern social science. Although he asserted that the Court

[29] *Ibid.*, p. 37.
[30] *Ibid.*, p. 63.
[31] *Ibid.*
[32] *Ibid.*, p. 65.

could cite social science testimony or take judicial notice of social science findings, he remained skeptical, as in the past, of the scientific nature of such findings. During the oral argument in the Delaware case Frankfurter had remarked that he did not consider psychological testimony to be the equivalent of mathematical pronouncements. "If a man says three yards, and I have measured it, and it is three yards, there it is," Frankfurter stated. "But if a man tells you the inside of your brain and mine, and how we function, that is not a measurement, and there you are."[33] The judicial use of psychology would, according to Frankfurter, bring the Court to "a domain which I do not yet regard as science in the sense of mathematical certainty."[34] This did not mean that Frankfurter lacked respect for psychology: "I simply know its character. It can be a very different thing from . . . things that are weighed and measured and are fungible." Frankfurter appeared to be as wary of social science as he was in 1928. "We are dealing here," he said, "with very subtle things, very subtle testimony."[35]

The Supreme Court's first round of oral argument in the segregation cases threw doubt on primary questions of law and fact. It was not clear that the Fourteenth Amendment was intended to prohibit public school segregation. Thus the Court, especially in view of the general reluctance of Congress to face the issue of segregation, had to determine first whether it could appropriately use the judicial power to invalidate public school segregation. If the scope of the ambiguously worded Fourteenth Amendment could not be ascertained by the study of history, then a determination of the effects of segregation might be doubly important. A clear delineation of the fact situation, or the effects of segregation, could help the Court determine whether statutes prescribing school segregation conflicted with the general objectives of the amendment.

If the definition of the fact situation was to become the crucial element in the process of judicial interpretation, as it had often been in the past, then social science findings would be decidedly

[33] *Ibid.*, p. 172.
[34] *Ibid.*
[35] *Ibid.*, p. 173.

relevant to the issue at hand, and the Court's use of these findings would logically follow. Frankfurter had granted the relevance of social science testimony. But he had also questioned the status of social science. The conclusion of the oral argument left open the possibility that the Court might use modern social science, but it went no further.

The Framers' Intentions

After hearing oral argument, the Supreme Court reserved decision. In June, 1953, the Court asked for further argument on five questions, which it posed in an intermediate order.[36] The order gave some indication that the Court was sympathetic to a ruling that would abolish racial segregation in all public schools, but the justices appeared to be searching for the appropriate grounds for such a landmark ruling. Questions one and two of the order sought to uncover evidence that would clarify whether Congress or the ratifying state legislatures understood that the Fourteenth Amendment abolished segregation in public schools. In addition, the Court asked for evidence showing that the framers of the amendment understood that Congress, under Section 5, might abolish such segregation. The Court also asked whether the framers "in the light of future conditions" contemplated judicial interpretation of the amendment that would result in the invalidation of school segregation. In effect, the Court was asking opposing counsel whether extralegal data could furnish the basis for a decision. However, it was clear from question three that the Court was also preparing for the possibility that historical data might be inconclusive. If the recourse to history did not provide an adequate basis for interpreting the amendment, the Court obviously would have to look elsewhere. Accordingly the Court asked in question three, "On the assumption that the answers to question 2(a) and (b) do not dispose of the issue, is it within the judicial power, in construing the Amendment, to abolish segregation in public schools?"[37] On the basis of the additional assumption

---

[36] Miscellaneous Orders, 345 U.S. 972 (1953).
[37] *Ibid.*

that public school segregation was unconstitutional, the Court asked in questions four and five how a decree ordering integration might be formulated.

The overall tenor of the order left no doubt that the high bench was moving toward a momentous decision. Insofar as the Court had never addressed itself to the issue of the constitutionality of public school segregation per se, it would be making precedent, and its decision would amount to judicial legislation. Obviously intertwined with the legal problems of judicial interpretation was the informal but no less important problem of judicial policy-making.

The Court had posed clearly the basic historical question. The justices were asking for clarification of the intentions of the framers of the Fourteenth Amendment. But the Court had carefully formulated the basic historical question in two parts. In question one the Court had asked whether the framers intended or "understood" that the amendment would have the immediate effect of prohibiting public school segregation. In question two the Court asked whether it was the "understanding" of the framers that future Congresses acting under the amendment could ban public school segregation or whether the Court "in light of future conditions" could construe the amendment to the same end.

NAACP lawyers were at first elated with the Court's questions and looked forward to the opportunity of amassing historical data that would convince the Court that the Fourteenth Amendment was intended, among other things, to invalidate public school segregation. According to Alfred Kelly, one of the many scholars called on by the NAACP to conduct historical research, there was a consensus among lawyers and men of learning that the justices had already made up their minds and that the order was simply a favorable omen. In Kelly's words the justices appeared to be saying that

> we would like to dispose of the Plessy rule, for once and for all, as constitutionally outmoded and incompatible with the realities of the Negro's role in contemporary American society. But we are fearfully embarrassed by the apparent historical absurdity of such

an interpretation of the 14th amendment, and equally embar-
rassed by the obvious charge that the Court will be legislating if
it simply imposes a new meaning on the amendment without regard to historical intent. Therefore, learned counsel, produce for
us in this Court a plausible historical argument that will justify
us in pronouncing, in solemn and awful sovereignty, that the 14th
amendment properly was intended by its authors to sanction its
abolition by judicial fiat.[38]

Needless to say, there was no readily available statement of
the framers' intentions. Counsel for the states, under the direction of John W. Davis, would also be combing the historical
record with the assistance of scholars. And, obviously, the
NAACP's initial optimistic assessment of the Court's order could
be wrong. Indeed, history might conceivably show that the
amendment was not intended to prohibit public school segregation at the time or in the future. As Thurgood Marshall is
reported to have remarked later, "What looked like a 'golden
gate' might 'turn out to be a booby trap with a bomb in
it.' "[39]

Both sides enlisted the services of professional scholars in the
preparation of their historical briefs. The NAACP, in particular,
received the help of distinguished historians and constitutional
experts. John Frank, Walter Gellhorn, Milton Konvitz, Howard
K. Beale, C. Vann Woodward, and John Hope Franklin were
but a few of the noted authorities that assisted in the preparation of the NAACP brief.

The Civil Rights Act of 1866 posed a key problem for association historians. The Thirty-ninth Congress had passed the act
only three months before approving the final draft of the Fourteenth Amendment. The act and the amendment were generally
believed to be related. The Senate had first reported a draft
of the Civil Rights Act that contained a general prohibition of
discriminatory practices worded broadly enough to cover school

---

[38] Alfred H. Kelly, "An Inside View of Brown v. Board," 108 *Congressional
Record—Senate* 17931, 17932 (1962).

[39] Alfred H. Kelly, "The School Desegregation Case," in John A. Garraty, ed.,
Quarrels That Have Shaped the Constitution (New York: Harper and Row, 1964),
p. 260.

segregation. However, in the House, John A. Bingham spearheaded an attack on the Senate draft that resulted in the elimination of a section giving the act wide latitude. Bingham also happened to be the principal draftsman of the Fourteenth Amendment. If, as Kelly has suggested, the Civil Rights Act was rewritten to avoid legislating against segregation, and if the amendment was passed simply to "constitutionalize" the act, then it would be difficult to argue that the framers intended to prohibit school segregation.[40] But the reasons for Bingham's opposition to the Senate's broad draft of the act are no clearer than his specific intentions with respect to the amendment. It is possible that Bingham opposed the first draft of the act because he believed that the proper means for eliminating racial segregation was a constitutional amendment. In other words, Bingham may have opposed the first draft of the Civil Rights Act because in his judgment Congress lacked the power to legislate in a sweeping fashion against segregation. On the other hand, it is possible that Bingham may not have been an extreme civil libertarian and may have had serious reservations about both an act and an amendment that forbade all forms of racial segregation. In short, legal counsel focusing on this single historical problem had several alternative courses of conjecture.

Opposing counsel, with the United States acting as *amicus curiae*, filed lengthy briefs detailing the intentions of specific framers as well as of the Thirty-ninth Congress in general. In addition, the reactions of state legislatures and conventions that ratified the amendment were exhaustively examined. Association and state counsel argued respectively that the framers did or did not intend the amendment to provide for the immediate or eventual abolition of school segregation.[41] Lee J. Rankin, U.S. Assistant Attorney General, took the middle course. The United States argued that the intentions of the framers could not be determined conclusively on the basis of historical data.[42] The briefs submitted by all the parties in response to

[40] Kelly, "An Inside View," p. 17933.
[41] See John L. Fletcher, Jr., *The Segregation Case and the Supreme Court*, Boston University Studies in Political Science, no. 4 (1958).
[42] Friedman, ed., *Argument*, p. 241.

the question of historical intent, as Alexander Bickel has stated, "must surely have amounted to the most extensive presentation of historical materials ever made to the Court."[43]

To be sure, the historical arguments submitted to the Court were not prepared by disinterested or neutral bystanders; they were prepared within the framework of the American system of legal advocacy. The key assumption of this system is that the truth emerges through the clash of ideas and evidence, even though opposing counsel might in their zeal bend or distort both relevant and irrelevant facts.[44] The NAACP brief was obviously designed to produce the most favorable gloss on history possible within the boundaries of credibility. According to Kelly, the NAACP selectively interpreted history: "It presented, indeed, a great deal of perfectly valid constitutional history. But it also manipulated history . . . carefully marshalling every possible scrap of evidence in favor of the desired interpretation and just as carefully doctoring all the evidence to the contrary, either by suppressing it when that seemed plausible, or by distorting it when suppression was not possible."[45] This did not mean, Kelly has stated, "that we were engaged in formulating lies. . . . But we were using facts, emphasizing facts, bearing down on facts, sliding off facts, quietly ignoring facts, and above all interpreting facts in a way to do what Marshall said we had to do—'get by those boys down there.' "[46]

At the same time, counsel for the states were hardly innocent of the craft of advocacy. Their historical brief also "doctored, distorted, twisted, and suppressed" historical data as vigorously as the NAACP's.[47] Even the U.S. brief, it may safely be presumed, was carefully formulated within the guidelines of the Eisenhower administration's southern policies. No doubt the administration was somewhat uneasy about siding too forcefully with

[43] Alexander M. Bickel, "The Original Understanding and the Segregation Decision," 69 *Harvard Law Review* 1 (1955).

[44] Edmund Morris Morgan, *Some Problems of Proof under the Anglo-American System of Litigation* (New York: Columbia University Press, 1956), p. 3.

[45] Alfred H. Kelly, "Clio and the Court: An Illicit Love Affair," in Philip B. Kurland, ed., *The Supreme Court Review* (Chicago: University of Chicago Press, 1965), p. 144.

[46] Kelly, "An Inside View," p. 17934.

[47] Kelly, "Clio and the Court," p. 144.

the NAACP position. Certainly the justices could hardly have been unaware of all these difficulties and for the time being would sit as a Supreme Court of history.

Historical Reargument

On December 7, 1953, the Court began to hear argument on the school segregation cases within the framework of the questions contained in the intermediate order. The high bench first heard Spottswood Robinson for the NAACP, who pointed out that during the congressional debates on the Fourteenth Amendment there occurred only one specific reference to school segregation. Robinson told the Court that Representative Andrew Jackson Rogers had characterized Bingham's first draft of the amendment as a dangerous proposal that would undermine the foundation of government and threaten the liberties of the people. The amendment, Rogers had charged, would probably eliminate school segregation, among other things. Robinson then explained to the Court that since Bingham had not disputed Rogers's appraisal of the amendment, the principal framer surely must have agreed with Rogers's estimation of the scope of the amendment.

The NAACP's dubious test for ascertaining Bingham's intentions provided a good example of the kind of historiography employed by opposing counsel. However, Justice Frankfurter indicated quickly that the Court was not likely to be persuaded by simple-minded interpretations of historical data. Indeed, Frankfurter practically demolished Robinson's argument when he inquired, "You think if an opponent gives an extreme interpretation of a proposed statute or constitutional amendment in order to frighten people on the other side, and the proponents do not get up and say 'Yes, that is the thing we want to accomplish,' that means they believe it, do you?"[48] In short, the opening exchange left no doubt that the high bench was acutely aware of the liabilities of sundry theories of historical intent.

Counsel for the states argued in general that congressional

[48] Friedman, ed., *Argument*, p. 188.

silence with respect to school segregation demonstrated that the amendment was not intended to apply to public schools. However, John W. Davis conceded that the debates did not provide enough clear and specific evidence to allow the Court to ascertain the intention of the framers. "I do not think that is possible," Davis stated, yet the action of Congress was a "far more reliable source" for answering the question of intent.[49] The failure of Congress to integrate schools in the District of Columbia, Davis argued, demonstrated that the amendment was not intended to apply to school segregation. Obviously the amendment did not restrict Congress, but would Congress destroy school segregation in the states and then institute such segregation in the District?[50] But Davis's theory of intent was also weak. As the Assistant Attorney General noted later, the immediate action of Congress was also inconclusive, since it did not exercise detailed supervision of the District until 1871.

The Court had listened to conflicting historical versions of the intentions of the framers. Counsel for the United States in the face of this discord had argued that historical evidence did not support the contentions of either side. The advocative stretching of historical data by both sides was enlightening in one sense. The Court undoubtedly saw that the historical search for the meaning of the Fourteenth Amendment was futile. During the course of historical reargument Justice Stanley F. Reed looked beyond history and touched on what proved to be the basic problem of judicial interpretation raised by the Brown case. That is, the Court by accepting the segregation cases for review, and in the light of argument and reargument, had demonstrably chosen to interpret the meaning of the Fourteenth Amendment. But as Justice Reed observed, "What is striking to me, if you lay aside the history, lay aside what has happened, and the intentions as expressed in Congress, then we have nothing left except the bare words."[51] But Reed had overlooked one thing. The Court might be left without conclusive historical data, but it did have at its disposal a coherent and authoritative

[49] *Ibid.*, p. 208.
[50] *Ibid.*, p. 212.
[51] *Ibid.*, p. 251.

definition of the crucial fact situation. And as we have suggested —as the Brown case itself later demonstrated—"constitutional adjudication depends as much on 'what are the facts?' as on 'what is the law?' "[52]

The Opinion

On May 17, 1954, the Court handed down its long-awaited decision on the constitutionality of public school segregation in the historic case of Brown v. Board of Education of Topeka.[53] Eighteen months had elapsed since the first three segregation cases had been placed on the court docket. The long period of time the Court took in reaching its final decision underscored the delicacy and complexity of the school segregation issue. The process of judicial interpretation had been almost open-ended, owing to the relative ambiguity of the wording of the Four-teenth Amendment. But this did not necessarily make judicial interpretation easy. For one thing the political factor of enforce-ment, if the Court chose to invalidate school segregation, almost certainly complicated the task of judicial interpretation. As Frankfurter had observed during the first round of oral argu-ment, "Nothing could be worse, from my point of view, than for this Court to make an abstract declaration that segregation is bad and then have it evaded by tricks."[54] Undoubtedly the delay in the decision-making process had afforded the Court an opportunity to assess how the Eisenhower administration would act on the civil rights plank the Republicans had ad-vanced during the 1952 presidential election. This is not to imply that the Court was guided only by political considerations, but it is to acknowledge that justices do have an ear for politics. Therefore, as Edward McWhinney has pointed out, "it is difficult to see how the court could rationally avoid giving some atten-tion to the question of what the federal executive, as the chief

[52] Arthur S. Miller and Ronald F. Howell, "The Myth of Neutrality in Con-stitutional Adjudication," in Leonard W. Levy, ed., *Judicial Review and the Supreme Court: Selected Essays* (New York: Harper Torchbooks, 1967), p. 224.
[53] Brown v. Board of Education of Topeka, 347 U.S. 483 (1954).
[54] Friedman, ed., *Argument*, p. 48.

law-enforcement agency in the United States federal system, would be likely to do."[55] Indeed, in view of the extreme political sensitivity of the segregation issue, the Court's opinion would have to express a high degree of both legal and political rationality.

Chief Justice Earl Warren, who had replaced Fred Vinson in time for the second round of oral argument, delivered the Court's unanimous opinion, without doubt "simple, lucid, non-legal and most understandable." These qualities, along with its comparative brevity, gave Warren's opinion "the flavour and tone of a great historical document."[56] The chief justice emphasized three factual themes throughout the course of his opinion: the inconclusiveness of history, the role of education in contemporary society, and the psycho-sociological effects of racial segregation.

Warren first turned to the problematic question of the framers' intentions. He noted that oral reargument had "covered exhaustively consideration of the Amendment in Congress, ratification by the states, then existing practices in racial segregation, and the views of proponents and opponents of the Amendment."[57] However, quickly disposing of the nettlesome question of historical intent, the chief justice stated, "This discussion and our own investigation convinced us that, although these sources cast some light, it is not enough to resolve the problem with which we are faced. At best, they are inconclusive."[58]

Having summarily dismissed the basic historical question in no uncertain terms, Warren explained that the "most avid proponents of the post-War Amendments undoubtedly intended them to remove all legal distinctions among 'all persons born or naturalized in the United States.'" Yet, he pointed out, the opponents of the amendments "just as certainly, were antagonistic to both the letter and spirit of the Amendments and wished

[55] Edward McWhinney, "An End to Racial Discrimination in the United States? The School-Segregation Decisions," 32 *Canadian Bar Review* 545, 547 (1954).

[56] Robert A. Liston, *Tides of Justice: The Supreme Court and the Constitution in Our Time* (New York: Delacorte Press, 1969), p. 37.

[57] Brown v. Board of Education of Topeka, 347 U.S. 483, 489 (1954).

[58] *Ibid.*

them to have the most limited effect." With respect to others in Congress and state legislatures, what was in their minds "cannot be determined with any degree of certainty."[59]

An additional reason for the inconclusiveness of the history of the amendment as it related to schools, Warren suggested, was the "status of public education at that time."[60] Citing historical sources, Warren pointed out that the development of public education at the time of the Thirty-ninth Congress was immature and uncertain. "As a consequence, it is not surprising that there should be so little in the history of the Fourteenth Amendment relating to its intended effect on public education."[61]

The Court had briskly answered the first two questions of its intermediate order. The basic historical question had been swept aside. In removing the process of judicial interpretation from a historical matrix, the chief justice had freed the Court from the binding power of past conditions. Not only had the Court cast history aside, but at the same time the high bench declared itself free from the restraints of both dictum and precedent.

The chief justice then proceeded to expound on the critical role of public education in American life. He mentioned briefly the appearance of the separate-but-equal formula in the Plessy case and its subsequent application to the field of education. Warren also noted that the formula had not been re-examined in any of the education cases. But in this instance, he affirmed, the "question is directly presented." The present Negro and white schools, in terms of tangible factors, were now either equal or were being equalized. But equality could not be measured only on the basis of tangible factors. "We must look instead," he emphasized, "to the effect of segregation itself on public education."[62]

Having announced that the present fact situation, and not the past, was controlling, Warren bore down on this crucial point. "In approaching this problem, we cannot turn the clock

---

[59] *Ibid.*
[60] *Ibid.*
[61] *Ibid.*, p. 490.
[62] *Ibid.*, p. 492.

back to 1868 when the Amendment was adopted, or even to
1896 when *Plessy v. Ferguson* was written." It was necessary,
he continued, to "consider public education in the light of its
full development and its present place in American life throughout the Nation." Only in this way could it be determined that
segregation violated the equal-protection clause.[63]

There followed an assessment of the role of education in a
democratic society. Education, Warren observed, "is perhaps the
most important function of state and local governments."[64] It
is required "in the performance of our most basic public responsibilities, even service in the armed forces." Indeed, education "is the very foundation of good citizenship."[65] The chief
justice then described the psycho-sociological significance of
education: "Today it is a principal instrument in awakening
the child to cultural values, in preparing him for later professional training, and in helping him to adjust normally to his
environment." Therefore, no child could reasonably expect to
succeed in contemporary society if he was denied the equal
"right" to educational opportunities.[66]

Warren then posed the fundamental question of law and
fact. "Does segregation . . . in public schools solely on the
basis of race, even though physical facilities and other 'tangible'
factors be equal, deprive the children of the minority group of
equal educational opportunities?" For a unanimous Court, Warren answered, "We believe that it does."[67]

The Supreme Court had infused new meaning into the Fourteenth Amendment. Judicial interpretation was based neither on
history nor on precedent. Instead the newly revealed meaning
of the equal-protection clause flowed from a social science definition of the crucial fact situation. Chief Justice Warren had so
far avoided the use of technical legal terminology. Similarly,
the Court's finding of fact was stated in a direct fashion, free
from the obscurities of social science terminology. Warren accordingly wrote that to separate children "from others of similar

[63] *Ibid.*, p. 493.
[64] *Ibid.*
[65] *Ibid.*
[66] *Ibid.*
[67] *Ibid.*

age and qualifications solely because of their race generates a feeling of inferiority as to their status in the community that may affect their hearts and minds in a way unlikely ever to be undone."[68] Reiterating this crucial finding of fact, first stated by the Kansas court, the chief justice continued:

> Segregation of white and colored children in public schools has a detrimental effect upon the colored children. The impact is greater when it has the sanction of the law; for the policy of separating the races is usually interpreted as denoting the inferiority of the negro group. A sense of inferiority affects the motivation of a child to learn. Segregation with the sanction of law, therefore, has a tendency to [retard] the educational and mental development of Negro children and to deprive them of some of the benefits they would receive in a racial[ly] integrated school system.[69]

The Court then clearly acknowledged its implicit use of nineteenth-century social science in the Plessy case. Warren repudiated this use in an appropriate manner by formally and expressly citing the findings of modern social science. "Whatever may have been the extent of psychological knowledge at the time of *Plessy v. Ferguson,* this finding is amply supported by modern authority." There followed in footnote eleven a reference to seven social science studies:

> K. B. Clark, Effect of Prejudice and Discrimination on Personality Development (Midcentury White House Conference on Children and Youth, 1950); Witmer and Kotinsky, Personality in the Making (1952), c. VI; Deutscher and Chein, The Psychological Effects of Enforced Segregation: A Survey of Social Science Opinion, 26 J. Psychol. 259 (1948); Chein, What are the Psychological Effects of Segregation under Conditions of Equal Facilities?, 3 Int. J. Opinion and Attitude Res. 229 (1949); Brameld, Educational Costs, in Discrimination and National Welfare (MacIver, ed., 1949), 44–48; Frazier, The Negro in the United States (1949), 674–681. And see generally Myrdal, An American Dilemma (1944).[70]

[68] *Ibid.,* p. 494.
[69] *Ibid.*
[70] *Ibid.*

The factual finding of psychological harm caused by school segregation, documented by modern social science, constituted an empirical rejection of the separate-but-equal formula. The Court's finding of fact and its subsequent finding of law were inextricably combined. As the chief justice wrote, "We conclude that in the field of public education, the doctrine of 'separate but equal' has no place. Separate educational facilities are inherently unequal."[71] The Court therefore held that school segregation violated the equal-protection clause of the Fourteenth Amendment. The Court had advanced a social science definition, in this instance, of the democratic condition of equality. More important, the Court's definition was at the same time one of law.

On the same day, in the case of Bolling v. Sharpe,[72] the Court also struck down school segregation in the District of Columbia. In this separate decision, necessitated by the fact that the equal-protection clause applies only to the states, Chief Justice Warren announced for a unanimous Court that "the concepts of equal protection and due process, both stemming from our American ideal of fairness, are not mutually exclusive."[73] The chief justice emphasized that "classifications based solely upon race must be scrutinized with particular care, since they are contrary to our traditions and hence constitutionally suspect."[74] The Court therefore held that public school segregation constituted an arbitrary deprivation of liberty in violation of the due-process clause of the Fifth Amendment. As in the Brown case, the issue of relief was returned to the docket for reargument.

Well aware of the profound impact its decisions would have on the structure of American society, the Court refrained from issuing an immediate decree ordering the termination of public school segregation. Instead it restored both cases to the docket and asked for reargument on the problem of relief in terms of questions four and five of the intermediate order.

[71] *Ibid.,* p. 495.
[72] Bolling v. Sharpe, 347 U.S. 497 (1954).
[73] *Ibid.,* p. 499.
[74] *Ibid.*

Significance of the Court's Use of Modern Social Science

The Brown and Bolling decisions—especially Brown, for this case represented class action and was therefore binding on all public school districts—were stunning legal victories for the NAACP.[75] The high bench had dealt a cataclysmic legal blow to a southern society based on racism. The Brown decision had the effect of severing the nerve center of a social structure dependent on the belief that the Negro was not a human counterpart of the white man. In ruling that the Negro was legally entitled to attend the same school as his white peer, the Court directly undermined the racial mythology of the South.[76] The Brown decision was actually more than a legal attack on legislation predicated on racism. In broader cultural terms Chief Justice Warren's opinion symbolized the confrontation between mythology and empiricism. In the context of judicial discourse legal rationality in the Brown case was formally and deliberately expressed as empiricism, rejecting the ideology and mythology implicitly contained in the Plessy case.[77] Herein lies the significance of the Supreme Court's use of modern social science. Broadly speaking, the explanation of the Court's use of social science is twofold. It relates to the general development of American jurisprudence as part of the larger and overarching evolution of the American scientific cultural order.

The call for a sociological jurisprudence by such leading jurists as Holmes, Brandeis, Pound, and Cardozo was, as we have seen, tantamount to a plea for a more realistic constitutional law. Realism in law, as Brandeis repeatedly argued, could only be achieved if the Court paid closer attention to the "facts of life." The Brandeis brief and Brandeis's factual judicial opin-

---

[75] The Brown decision also paved the way for a series of *per curiam* decisions that held segregation unconstitutional in a number of municipal facilities. For example, segregation was invalidated in public parks—Holcombe v. Beal, 347 U.S. 974 (1954); public housing—Housing Authority v. Banks, 347 U.S. 974 (1954); and public beaches—Mayor and City Council of Baltimore v. Dawson, 350 U.S. 877 (1955).

[76] Anthony Lewis, *Portrait of a Decade: The Second American Revolution* (New York: Random House, 1964), p. 5.

[77] Plessy v. Ferguson, 163 U.S. 537 (1896).

ions reflected the basic tenet of sociological jurisprudence—
that abstract principles of law could be neither interpreted nor
applied in a responsible manner without an understanding of
the needs of the people and the effects of law. Constitutional
adjudication in the twentieth century, of both property rights
and civil rights, revealed a general tendency on the part of the
Court to emphasize its fact-finding prerogative. With respect
to due-process adjudication, the general trend between 1908
and 1937 toward an emphasis on facts, as opposed to abstract
policy preferences, was not unalterably stated once and for all
in a single definitive decision. On the contrary, general trends
in constitutional law develop more slowly and usually in a less
dramatic fashion. However, in developing the due-process
clause, to use the words of Sanford Kadish, "the Court has not
been content to rest upon a frankly avowed subjective choice,
but rather has attempted to rest choice upon criteria outside its
personal idiosyncratic judgement."[78] The same can be said for
the Court's interpretation and application of the equal-protection clause from 1948 to 1954. The basic point is that the
Court's pronounced interest in fact-finding represented a long
trend in judicial interpretation; empirically defined facts
gradually became more important or superseded facts drawn
from judicial introspection. In other words, the Court's use of
social science in the Brown case confirmed the success of efforts
first made in the Muller case[79] to have constitutional law pro-
pounded in the light of reliable extralegal data rather than of
arbitrary judicial biases. In all certainty, the gradual rise of an
empirically oriented jurisprudence was not an isolated cultural
movement but inevitably revealed the legal facet of a cultural
order thoroughly permeated with—and wholly distinguished
by—empiricism.[80]

The pervasive and profound influence of science in American
culture has been widely discussed. For example, as early as
1941 sociologist Pitirim Sorokin pointed out that the primary

[78] Sanford H. Kadish, "Methodology and Criteria in Due Process Adjudication:
A Survey and Criticism," 66 *Yale Law Journal* 319, 321 (1957).
[79] Muller v. Oregon, 208 U.S. 412 (1908).
[80] See, for example, Bernard Barber, *Science and the Social Order* (London:
Allen and Unwin, 1953).

concept of knowledge in the United States was rapidly becoming identical with empiricism.[81] More recently, the celebrated social critic Herbert Marcuse has stated that the process or transformation which Sorokin had described, whereby science emerged as the only form of knowledge popularly thought to be legitimate or sound, had virtually been completed. Indeed, Marcuse has gone so far as to suggest that American culture is now wholly dominated by scientific method;[82] in other words, scientific thinking is the standing order of the day.[83]

Insofar as science has come to be accepted as the primary "source of truth,"[84] it should not be surprising that the Supreme Court used modern social science to find the factual effects of racial segregation. On the contrary, what is surprising is the length of time that elapsed before the Court did eventually make use of social science findings. Social science had long been used with great success in both industry and government as well as in the military.[85] But as we have seen, cultural lag between social science and law is understandable in terms of

[81] Pitirim A. Sorokin, *The Crisis of Our Age: The Social and Cultural Outlook* (New York: E. P. Dutton, 1941). Sorokin suggested that in a "sensate" or empirically oriented culture, science replaces all other kinds of knowledge, such as theology and speculative philosophy. It is clear, he wrote, that "our principal body of truth is scientific." In view of the pre-eminence of science, "a nexus of empirical, sensory knowledge derived from observation of, and experimentation with, sensory facts," the only true, generally accepted definition of social reality derived from the application of scientific method. "The essential character of this logico-sensory fabric of thought is revealed," Sorokin concluded, "by the fact that terms 'scientific' and 'true,' 'unscientific' and 'false' are used as synonymous" (pp. 102–3).

[82] Herbert Marcuse, *One-Dimensional Man: Studies in the Ideology of Advanced Industrial Society* (Boston: Beacon Press, 1969).

[83] Marcuse writes that there has emerged "a pattern of *one-dimensional thought and behavior* in which ideas, aspirations, and objectives that, by their content, transcend the established universe of discourse and action are either repelled or reduced to terms of this universe." More important, "they are redefined by the rationality of the given system and of its qualitative extension." Therefore, social reality and the given standard of rationality are intimately related to the development of scientific method. The common feature of the American cultural order, or what Marcuse calls one-dimensional thought, "is a total empiricism in the treatment of concepts . . ." (*ibid.*, p. 12).

[84] Cf. Don K. Price, *The Scientific Estate* (New York: Oxford University Press, 1965), p. 125.

[85] See, for example, Samuel A. Stouffer *et al.*, *The American Soldier: Adjustment during Army Life*, 2 vols. (Princeton, N.J.: Princeton University Press, 1949).

the underlying tension that exists between the two professions. In addition, the rigidity of legal procedures and the Court's dependence on the legal brief as its primary source of extra-legal data left the high bench somewhat insulated from research developments in the social sciences. Chief Justice Warren himself has pointed out that "the law is slow to move. In the past, seldom has it anticipated conditions and evolved methods to remedy them."[86]

The making of rules—the art of judicial interpretation—is surely a complex process. Because several alternative courses of action are always open in the decisional process, and since the Court will invariably take into account political factors when rendering a decision, especially in an epoch-making case, a total understanding of how and why a landmark opinion such as Brown is written can never be reached. However, an understanding of a judicial opinion (aside from the psychological motivations of the justices) is possible within the framework of three points of reference. They are (1) the alternative courses of legal decision-making, (2) the nature of judicial authority, and (3) the dominant cultural standard of rationality. Most important, the intersection of these three points of reference makes fully apparent the significance of the Supreme Court's use of modern social science.

It is conceivable, although not probable, that the Court might have decided the Brown case by avoiding altogether the constitutional issue of segregation. The Court has often noted that it would avoid passing on constitutional issues if some other ground was available. Judicial ingenuity in this respect is not to be underestimated. The Court could have retained the separate-but-equal formula by ordering its implementation in any number of ways. For example, the Court could have returned the four state cases to the district courts for separate fact-finding in each instance. When and if inequality in each instance was established, the states could have been granted time to equalize their facilities, or the facilities could have been

[86] Earl Warren, "Science and the Law: Change and the Constitution," 12 *Journal of Public Law* 3, 5 (1963).

integrated pending their equalization.[87] However, the series of education cases from Gaines to McLaurin[88] would seem to have forestalled such alternatives. In addition, the endless litigation that would have resulted was not a prospect the Court would have been pleased to entertain.

A different alternative the Court could have opted for was the rejection of the separate-but-equal formula and the constitutional invalidation of public school segregation on the basis of earlier precedents. The chief justice did refer in passing to several nineteenth-century cases in which the Court had defined the scope of the Fourteenth Amendment, insofar as it pertained to Negroes, in very broad terms.[89] However, this would have meant backtracking past several later precedents in which school segregation had been condoned, and for this reason there was little to recommend such a course of action.

A more likely alternative, one which the Court openly and formally pondered, was to hold that school segregation was incompatible with the meaning of the Fourteenth Amendment as revealed in the historical light of the intentions of its framers. A historical exegesis of the intentions of the framers would have been considered synonymous with the original meaning of the amendment. Once ascertained, the Court could have sidestepped its previous checkered interpretations of the equal-protection clause and would have been able to proclaim, with a minimum of embarrassment, that the freshly unearthed original truth of the amendment required an end to school segregation. If reliable and convincing historical data had been available, the Court could have used history to proclaim the revealed truth of the amendment. Ostensibly, then, any subsequent quarrel with the Court's decision would have to be picked with the framers and not with the judiciary. But the Court soon realized that while history may have provided the simplest

---

[87] See Robert A. Leflar and Wylie H. Davis, "Segregation in the Public Schools —1953," 67 *Harvard Law Review* 377, 387–92 (1954).

[88] Missouri ex rel. Gaines v. Canada, 305 U.S. 337 (1938); McLaurin v. Oklahoma State Regents, 339 U.S. 637 (1950).

[89] Strauder v. West Virginia, 100 U.S. 303 (1880); Ex Parte Virginia, 100 U.S. 339 (1880).

solution to the problem of judicial interpretation, it was obviously too simple.

The paucity of historical data bearing on the intentions of
the framers with respect to school segregation turned out to be
the clearest and most convincing historical fact the Court could
cite, despite the diligent and inventive historical research prof-
fered by opposing counsel. Indeed, there has been no ensuing
controversy over the Court's reluctant conclusion that history
was at best inconclusive. In his distinguished and most comprehensive study of the framers' intentions, Alexander Bickel
found no flaw in the Court's reading of history. Bickel has
confirmed that the Fourteenth Amendment, like the Civil Rights
Act of 1866, "carried out the relatively narrow objectives of the
Moderates, and hence, as originally understood, was meant to
apply neither to jury service, nor to suffrage, nor to antimis-
cegenation statutes, nor to segregation."[90] If the amendment
had been a statute, Bickel went on to suggest, the Court might
not have possessed sufficient discretion for a broad interpretation applying to public school segregation. But the amendment
was, after all, a part of the Constitution.[91] And as the intermediate order revealed, the Court was interested in the immediate
and long-range purposes of the amendment. The important point
is, according to Bickel, that "the Radical leadership succeeded
in obtaining a provision whose future effect was left to future
determination." The fact that the framers expected Congress to
act under the amendment is not significant. "It indicates no
judgment about the powers and functions properly to be exercised by the other branches."[92]

In view of the lack of historical data, and the difficulty under
the best of circumstances of ascertaining the intentions of legislators, the appeal to history had to be abandoned.[93] If the
meaning of the Fourteenth Amendment was not to be found
in the past, then there was nowhere else to look but at the

[90] Bickel, "The Original Understanding," p. 58.
[91] *Ibid.*, p. 59.
[92] *Ibid.*, p. 64.
[93] See William Anderson, "The Intentions of the Framers: A Note on Constitutional Interpretation," 49 *American Political Science Review* 340 (1955).

present. The Court thus turned to the present role of education in contemporary society. It took judicial notice of the vital importance of education and then posed the critical question of fact: did racially segregated schools provide equal educational opportunities for Negro children? The separate-but-equal formula had been found in the Plessy case not to have resulted in a factual denial of equality with respect to transportation.[94] Since there was no inequality in fact, the Court had ruled that the legal requirements of the equal-protection clause had not been violated. In the Brown case, given the inadequacy of history, the Court posed a comparable factual question: what were the effects of school segregation? Did segregation harm Negro children, thereby creating conditions of factual inequality?

In the Plessy case the Court was unaware of any extralegal data suggesting that segregation harmed the Negro or placed him in a condition of factual inequality. Indeed, insofar as the Court was familiar with the prevailing conception of social science, and Justice Brown's language suggests that the Court was profoundly influenced by current "social science" theories, it had no reason to believe that segregation was harmful or did place the Negro in a position of factual inequality. The holdings in both the Plessy and Brown cases followed from the Court's critical finding of fact. Since equality in both cases was viewed in terms of the effects of segregation on the Negro, judicial interpretation in both instances necessarily involved sociological judgments. In this sense the sociological question was inherent in the terms of the Fourteenth Amendment.[95] In short, the fact situation in both cases proved to be a crucial determinant of the process of judicial interpretation.

Under what influence did the Court establish its finding of fact, or, more precisely, what was the source of the Court's finding of extralegal fact? In the Plessy case Justice Brown did not formally or explicitly quote current social science findings; in the Brown case Chief Justice Warren assuredly did.

[94] Plessy v. Ferguson, 163 U.S. 537 (1896).
[95] Arthur E. Sutherland, Jr., "The American Judiciary and Racial Segregation," 20 *Modern Law Review* 201, 208 (1957).

The two cases clearly differ in this sense. Yet a more important point of comparison is the validity of the Court's factual finding of the effects of racial segregation. In the Plessy case Justice Brown's discussion of racial segregation, although relating to transportation, did reveal the factual assumption that segregation in both transportation and education was not harmful. Racial segregation, Brown wrote, does "not necessarily imply the inferiority of either race to the other. . . ." Then he continued, "The most common instance of this is connected with the establishment of separate schools for white and colored children. . . ."[96] Racial segregation did not impose upon the Negro "a badge of inferiority." If the Negro interpreted segregation to signify inferiority, he reasoned, that is because the Negro chooses to believe that he is inferior. In other words, the "Court clearly conceived it to be its task to show that segregation did not really disadvantage the Negro. . . ."[97]

Brown did not bluntly state that the Negro was inferior. But the idea of biological inferiority was the underlying factual assumption of his opinion—an assumption, it may be added, that is characteristic of racist thought in general. This assumption is pointedly revealed by Brown's reference to "racial instincts" and was undoubtedly drawn from the prevailing theories of social science. Since the Court used extralegal facts drawn from the current ideas of social science or, properly speaking, social Darwinism, it was most appropriate that in the Brown case the Court used modern social science to overturn the Plessy decision and its pseudoscientific factual assumptions. In this sense the decision that invalidated racial segregation was no more dependent on social science than the decision that had previously sanctioned it.[98]

Further comparison of the Plessy and Brown cases reveals a most interesting point. Nowhere in his opinion did Chief

[96] Plessy v. Ferguson, 163 U.S. 537, 544 (1896).

[97] Charles L. Black, "The Lawfulness of the Segregation Decisions," 69 *Yale Law Journal* 421, 422 (1959–60).

[98] Cf. Arnold M. Rose, "Sociological Factors in the Effectiveness of Projected Legislative Remedies," 11 *Journal of Legal Education* 470, 477 (1959), and Kenneth B. Clark, "The Social Scientist as an Expert Witness in Civil Rights Litigation," 1 *Social Problems* 5 (1953).

Justice Warren suggest that the Plessy case was wrongly decided as a matter of law. What Warren unequivocally challenged and rejected was Justice Brown's finding of fact. Warren's
reference to "psychological knowledge" in 1896 suggests that
in the context of nineteenth-century social science, the Plessy
decision was a rational interpretation of the Fourteenth Amendment. In other words, Warren reasoned that the Plessy decision
became "bad because of the growth of public education . . .
into the all-encompassing and grandiose thing it had become by
1954, and because of advances in psychological knowledge."[99] Warren's legal reasoning then leads to an inescapable
conclusion. The factual finding of psychological harm was the
crucial determinant in the Court's interpretation of the Fourteenth Amendment.

The significance of the Court's use of modern social science becomes clearer as alternative courses of action open to the Court
are eliminated. Insofar as the fact situation emerges as the crucial
determinant of Warren's opinion, the question remains open
whether the Court's use of social science to establish the factual
finding of harm was merely a *pro forma* use of extralegal data,
or whether the Court earnestly relied on modern social science to
discover the pertinent facts. Briefly stated, how meaningful was
the Court's use of social science?

It is possible that the Supreme Court could arrive at a decision for one set of reasons but in its written opinion present
for public consumption a second set of reasons. It is also not
beyond the realm of possibility that the proverbial Negro porter
told the chief justice that school segregation was harmful, and the
chief justice then attributed this most hypothetical extralegal fact
to the social scientists named in footnote eleven. In a less speculative vein, it is also possible for the Court to have found that
segregation meant inequality on the basis of its own authority,
without formally alluding to modern social science at all. While
this is all possible, speculation along these lines is fruitless; the
private motivations, encounters, and professional calculations of
the justices are no more open to public inspection than are the

[99] Robert J. Harris, "The Constitution, Education, and Segregation," 29 *Temple
Law Quarterly* 409, 430 (1956).

motivations, encounters, and calculations of politicians, generals, and other decision makers. More important, such speculation ignores the nature of the Court's authority and the primary function of a judicial opinion.

Needless to say, the Supreme Court has no command of troops to order compliance with its decisions. Indeed, the authority of the high bench may be defined ultimately as moral in nature. The Court's moral authority is not only based on the functions assigned to it by the Constitution, but it also derives from the manner in which those functions are performed. Judicial opinion-writing, like the power of judicial review itself, is not formally prescribed by the Constitution. However, both have become customary, and the legitimacy of judicial review is rarely questioned. The moral authority of the Court flows from the judicial opinion, whose function is to provide a rational explanation for a given legal decision. This is the primary purpose of a judicial opinion, and it should not be confused with the act of rationalizing an arbitrary judicial decision.

Surely there is a difference between a rational legal opinion and a rationalized but nonetheless arbitrary judicial decision. Admittedly, the distinction between a rational explanation in law and an arbitrary decision that has been rationalized cannot be understood in the precise terms of a geometric theorem. But the distinction does reflect the fundamental character of law, which is generally considered to be reason. Curiously enough, Governor Charles Evans Hughes's classic observation, "The Constitution is what the judges say it is," helps clarify this point. There is, of course, a measure of truth in Hughes's remark, but only a measure, and surely not the full truth. The Court does interpret the Constitution, but the justices are not free to declare arbitrarily that the Constitution means anything they please. Hughes's words have suggested to some that judges are free to be arbitrary; this fallacy occurs because judicial interpretation and the authority of the Court to perform it are not commonly distinguished. To be sure, the two are intimately related, but they are not one and the same thing. As H. L. A. Hart has pointed out, " 'The score is what the scorer says it is' is not the scoring rule: it is a rule providing for the authority and finality of his application of the scoring rule in particular cases."[100] In other words, the general requirement that the process of judicial interpretation should result in rational explanations of law is the real rule of scoring. For analytical purposes it is worth distinguishing this rule from the closely related question of the Court's problematic authority to interpret the Constitution.

At the same time the requirement that judicial opinions should represent rational explanations of law is difficult to distinguish in practice from the problem of judicial authority, because the nature of that authority compels the Court to exercise reason and to provide rational explanations of law rather than rationalizations of arbitrary decisions. This is not to imply that the Court has never rationalized an arbitrary decision. The important point is that if rationalizations of arbitrary decisions were the predominant historical mode of the judicial opinion, the moral authority and consequently the power of the Court would soon be eroded.

Needless to say, the Court is in a sense a nondemocratic institution. As Archibald Cox has written, "Court decrees draw no authority from the participation of the people. Their power to command consent depends upon more than habit or even the deserved prestige of the Justices." Therefore, the authority of the Court flows, as Cox has put it, "from the continuing force of the rule of law—from the belief that the major influence in judicial decisions is not fiat but principles which binds the judges as well as the litigants. . . ."[101] Moreover, even if a judicial opinion were simply a convenient vehicle for rationalizing arbitrary or biased decisions, it could not effectively serve this function for long. Once promulgated, a judicial opinion becomes binding upon the Court in no small way as *stare decisis*. Ironically, then, even if judicial opinions were arbitrary rationalizations of law, they would still constrain the Court to write opinions compatible with previous rationalizations of law; the Court would become bound in a web of contradictions. In other words, the notion that a judicial opinion is simply a rationalization of an arbitrary de-

[100] H. L. A. Hart, *The Concept of Law* (Oxford: Clarendon Press, 1963), p. 140.
[101] Archibald Cox, *The Warren Court: Constitutional Decision as an Instrument of Reform* (Cambridge, Mass.: Harvard University Press, 1968), p. 21.

cision leads to the *reductio ad absurdum* that the Court would be driven to be consistently arbitrary. This is not to say that the primary function of opinion-writing cannot on occasion be abused. But it is to suggest that in the absence of contrary evidence, the analysis of a judicial opinion can be based on the reasonable assumption that the Court means what it says.

The authority of the Court, it has already been suggested, depends on the rationality of its opinions and decisions. As Alexander Bickel has stated, "The process of the coherent, analytically warranted, principled declaration of general norms alone justifies the Court's function. . . ."[102] But even though the rationality of the Court's decisions may appear patently obvious to the justices, the rationality of law must be made intelligible to the public. The Court does this by explaining in a judicial opinion how legal principles are applied to fact situations. In other words, the Court is obliged to present a rational explanation of the process of judicial interpretation. This obligation has been very ably described by Paul Weiler:

> In order that adjudicative decisions be characterized by the quality of rationality which is a prerequisite for their moral force and acceptability, the arbiter must have some principles which he can utilize in explaining to himself and to the parties his reasons for deciding one way or the other. The arbiter is under a duty to articulate a reasoned basis for his decision (whether or not he writes an opinion), because he is not conceded the power of *enactment*. He is not considered to have a *legitimate* power to exercise a discretion to settle a matter just because it needs settling, and without giving reasons for deciding on the particular disposition he selects. Hence, he cannot merely confront an undifferentiated factual situation and decide by an intuitive "leap in the dark."[103]

It is therefore clear that the requirements of rationality serve as a limitation on the Court's discretion to find both law and fact. While the Court is not free to declare that the Constitution

[102] Alexander M. Bickel, *The Supreme Court and the Idea of Progress* (New York: Harper and Row, 1970), p. 96.
[103] Paul Weiler, "Two Models of Judicial Decision-Making," 46 *Canadian Bar Review* 406, 419 (1968).

means anything that it pleases, by the same token the Court cannot simply invent or manufacture facts. Definitions of fact situations that are patently arbitrary and false would undoubtedly embarrass the Court and seriously compromise its authority.

Circumstances in the Brown case apparently placed the Court in the difficult position of having to define a complex and subtle fact situation. The Court was ultimately faced with the factual question of the effects of school segregation on Negro children. But by no means were the psychological effects of segregation clear and apparent for all to see. Left to its own resources, the Court had no reliable way of knowing what these effects were.[104] That is, common knowledge was as reliable a guide to the psychological effects of racial segregation in 1954 as it is today with respect to the effects of pornography, capital punishment, and marijuana. Since judicial intuition was of no palpable help, and in the absence of convincing common knowledge, it is a reasonable assumption that the Court was informed and influenced by the research findings summarized in the social science appendix to the NAACP brief. The basic proof of this influence is, after all, the fact that the chief justice formally cited the findings of modern social science. Moreover, had the Court been able, perhaps by intuition, to state that segregation caused psychological harm, such a statement of fact might have appeared as a subjective and arbitrary finding, especially if the Court were unwilling or unable to disclose the source of its knowledge. Thus the requirements of legal rationality, somewhat flexible but requirements no less, in all likelihood obliged the Court to state the sources of its finding of extralegal fact. The Court did just this when it documented its factual finding of psychological harm in the celebrated footnote eleven.

Whether the Court earnestly used social science remains to some extent an open question because there is no sure way to divine judicial motivations. However, a number of relevant points have been made that do suggest an answer. The nature of law

---

[104] Only three of the presiding justices had southern backgrounds (Black, Clark, and Reed) and could conceivably have claimed some personal insight into the probable socio-psychological effects of racial segregation.

and the moral basis of judicial authority inhibit the Court from arbitrarily deciding cases. That is, the Court is customarily obliged to decide cases on the basis of reason and, in addition, to formulate rational explanations of the process of judicial interpretation. The Court, one may assume, means what it says, for even if it is duplicitous, the Court remains relatively bound by *stare decisis*. Since the Court used social science as part of its rational explanation of law, that use in itself is meaningful because it stands as a formal confirmation of social science as a significant element in the process of judicial interpretation. Whether the justices privately believed that social science findings were significant is not as important as the question of whether a judicial opinion is rational or arbitrary. If a judicial opinion is rational, the private reservations of the justices do not change this. Therefore, while the intensity of the Court's enthusiasm for the seven social science studies cannot be charted, in light of all that has been said, there is no apparent basis for doubting that the Court earnestly relied upon social science in order to find the factual effects of racial segregation.

It still remains to be seen whether the Court's use of social science can be logically characterized as a perfunctory or *pro forma* recourse to extralegal data. There are several important points concerning the nature of social science and its role in the Brown case that make such a perspective extremely doubtful. First, it has already been observed that modern social science is qualitatively different from the other kinds of extralegal data the Court has used in the past. Therefore, in at least a qualitative sense the Court's use of modern social science constituted an extension and not simply a continuation of the Court's traditional recourse to extralegal data.

Moreover, although the Court had previously used nascent social science, this use was restricted to the support of contested legislation. On the other hand, in the Brown case the Court used modern social science to invalidate segregation statutes. Brandeis had explained that the existence, not the validity, of extralegal data was the only criterion the Court needed to consider in using such data to support the reasonableness of legislation. In the Brown case the Court did not merely note the existence of seven social science studies but, instead, cited those studies as evidence of incontrovertible fact. Therefore, in a strict legal sense the Brown case represented an innovation in the Court's use of extralegal facts.[105] There is no reason to believe that the Court was unaware of the novel aspects of its use of modern social science. In short, then, the Court's use of social science in the Brown case cannot logically be considered a perfunctory or *pro forma* recourse to extralegal data.

One final but no less critical observation concerning a rational explanation of law, and the dominant standard of rationality in the cultural order, should reveal the full significance of the Court's use of modern social science. A question is open to speculation: would the Brown decision have been different in the absence of relevant modern social science findings? It is clear that the Plessy decision was different, and it must be read in the context of the theories of nineteenth-century social science. As we have seen, Chief Justice Warren refrained from criticizing the overall rationality of that decision. Instead he focused on the comparable fact situations in 1896 and 1954. The chief justice firmly emphasized that psychological knowledge had changed markedly since 1896. Warren's emphasis on psychological knowledge is important because it suggests that legal rationality is related to—indeed, is dependent on—the dominant standard of rationality in a given cultural order.

The notion of the Negro's biological inferiority, implicit in the Plessy case, can be properly regarded as a part of the mythology of American life. In 1896 this myth was compatible with what is now considered pseudosocial science. The Supreme Court in 1896 was not likely to find the facts that segregation was harmful and that separate facilities were inherently unequal, not merely because such facts were unknown but because such a finding of fact was not rational in the context of the prevailing mythology, reinforced, as it was, by current theories of social science.

In 1954 mythological assumptions concerning the Negro still circulated, if not uniformly throughout the nation, certainly throughout the South. Mythology, it may be noted, is not easily

[105] See Albert P. Blaustein and Clarence E. Ferguson, *Desegregation and the Law* (New Brunswick, N.J.: Rutgers University Press, 1957), p. 134.

countered. In his classic statement on myth Georges Sorel pointed out that "a myth cannot be refuted, since it is, at bottom, identical with the convictions of a group, being the expression of these convictions in the language of movement; and it is, in consequence, unanalysable into parts which could be placed on the plane of historical descriptions."[106] However, in 1954 mythology was no longer compatible with the dominant standard of rationality. Instead, as we have already seen, scientific method prescribed the dominant cultural standard of rationality, which was generally equated with or defined as empiricism. And as we have also suggested, Chief Justice Warren was obliged to set forth a rational definition of the fact situation. Indeed, the lingering presence of mythology made a rational finding of fact in the Brown case all the more necessary. Therefore, in view of the dominant cultural standard of rationality, and of the Court's obligation to provide rational explanations of law, Chief Justice Warren was not free to define the psychological effects of racial segregation in a way that contradicted the available findings of modern social science. If the Court had concluded that segregated schools were equal, it would have placed itself in the anomalous position of upholding, as one observer put it, "law based on self-induced blindness, on flagrant contradiction of known fact."[107] As Philip Kurland has stated, the Court would have made "a monkey of itself" if it ignored the fact, proved by social science, that the separate-but-equal formula was an excuse for a system that subordinated the Negro to an inferior position and deprived him of the equal educational opportunities guaranteed by the Fourteenth Amendment.[108]

The Court was free, of course, to select alternative legal grounds for deciding the issue of public school segregation. However, this is really not the point. What matters is that the Court's opinion had to be consistent with social reality. In other words, Chief Justice Warren's rational explanation of law had to reflect "a social reality which looks for verification to empiricism

---

[106] Georges Sorel, *Reflections on Violence,* tr. T. E. Hulme (New York: Collier Books, 1961), p. 50.

[107] Black, "Lawfulness of the Segregation Decisions," p. 427.

[108] Philip B. Kurland, "The Legal Background of the School Segregation Cases," in Clark, *Prejudice and Your Child,* pp. 151–52.

rather than to the norms of precedent and history."[109] The full significance of the Court's use of modern social science should now be apparent. As Kenneth Clark has stated, "The role of social science in the Brown decision was crucial, in the Court's opinion, in supplying persuasive evidence that segregation itself means inequality."[110] Actually the social science studies cited by the Court were not only crucial, but they may very well have been compelling.

[109] G. Theodore Mitau, *Decade of Decision: The Supreme Court and the Constitutional Revolution, 1954–1964* (New York: Charles Scribner's Sons, 1967), p. 58.

[110] Kenneth B. Clark, "The Social Scientists, the Brown Decision and Contemporary Confusion," in Friedman, ed., *Argument,* p. xxxvi.

CHAPTER EIGHT

Responses to the Court's Use of Social Science

Political Repercussions

The Supreme Court had severed the legal roots of racial segregation.[1] The Brown decision was "a pronouncement second in importance only to President Lincoln's Emancipation Proclamation," Benjamin Muse wrote, and "it inaugurated a period of painful awakening, of impulsive resistance, and of tension and hysteria to the point in many instances of violent convulsion."[2] If southern folkways and mores were to change in accord with the Court's decision, an efficacy William Graham Sumner denied to law, then the consequences would be "staggering."[3] The decision was a particularly bitter pill for the South to swallow because school integration was viewed widely as a harbinger of or, more bleakly, an impetus toward miscegenation. Governor James F. Byrnes of South Carolina openly voiced this fear: "One cannot discuss this problem without admitting that, in the South, there is a fundamental objection to integration. White Southerners fear that the purpose of many of those advocating integration is to break down social barriers in the period of adolescence and ultimately bring about intermarriage of the races. Because they

[1] Brown v. Board of Education of Topeka, 347 U.S. 483 (1954).
[2] Benjamin Muse, *Ten Years of Prelude: The Story of Integration since the Supreme Court's 1954 Decision* (New York: Viking Press, 1964), p. 1.
[3] Robert L. Carter, "Legal Background and Significance of the May 17th Decision," 2 *Social Problems* 215 (1955).

are opposed to this, they are opposed to abolishing segregation. This is not petty prejudice. It is a serious problem of race relations."[4]

Even if Chief Justice Warren's opinion had been routine in nature, it would still have generated enormous controversy. However, the Court's formal use of modern social science further exacerbated hostile reactions to the decision. Indeed, footnote eleven, containing the sources of the Court's social science finding of fact, became the most dispute-laden footnote in American constitutional law. The controversy over the Court's use of social science stemmed in part from the impression that its finding of fact had somehow diminished the legality of its decision. Because the distinction between law and fact, although theoretically clear, is usually difficult to make in practice and was particularly so in the Brown case, criticism to the effect that the decision was wholly based on social science rather than law had a ring of plausibility.[5]

Even responsible commentators obscured the basic point that the Court had used social science to define a fact situation, that is, to ascertain whether racially segregated schools were in fact equal. James Reston, for example, wrote in the *New York Times* that the Court relied more on "the social scientists than on legal precedents . . . the Court's opinion read more like an expert paper on sociology than a Supreme Court opinion."[6] The distinguished constitutional scholar Carl Brent Swisher stated that the "decision was based neither on the history of the amendment nor on precise textual analysis but on psychological knowledge. . . ."[7] And Alpheus Thomas Mason, the sympathetic biographer of Brandeis, declared, "Rather than rely on available

[4] James F. Byrnes, "Guns and Bayonets Cannot Promote Education," 41 *U.S. News and World Report* 100, 104 (1956). See also W. J. Weatherby, *Breaking the Silence: The Negro Struggle in the U.S.A.* (Harmondsworth: Penguin Books, 1965), pp. 17–18.

[5] See Eugene Cook and William I. Potter, "The School Segregation Cases: Opposing the Opinion of the Supreme Court," and H. Gifford Irion, "The Constitutional Clock: A Horological Inquiry," in Hubert H. Humphrey, ed., *School Desegregation: Documents and Commentaries* (New York: Thomas Y. Crowell, 1964).

[6] *New York Times*, May 18, 1954, p. 14.

[7] Carl Brent Swisher, *The Supreme Court in Modern Role* (New York: New York University Press, 1954), p. 158.

judicial precedents, the Court invoked two of the flimsiest of all our disciplines—sociology and psychology—as the basis of its decision."[8]

Facts, of course, may be crucial determinants in the process of judicial interpretation. But strictly speaking, decisions are based on legal principles and not facts. Because facts and law are so intimately related, it was easy for politicians to confuse and distort the Court's use of social science. Southern politicians conveniently forgot that the principle of equality was prescribed by the Constitution, not by modern social science. Thus many of them grossly claimed that the Brown decision was based solely on the work of disloyal social scientists.

With judicial interpretation being an esoteric process, especially for the general public, and social science sounding suspiciously like socialism, the Court's novel use of social science provided a ready subject for political polemics.[9] The political fire ranged from dark McCarthyite imputations of disloyalty on the part of social scientists cited by the Court to methodological criticism of social science. Governor Herman E. Talmadge of Georgia, in a book-length attack upon the decision, wrote, "Who are these authorities? What is their background? What has been the nature of their work in this field? What is their public record? What is their political background? What do they really believe?"[10] In a similar vein former Associate Justice James F. Byrnes stated, "Loyal Americans of the North, East, South and West should be outraged that the Supreme Court would reverse the law of the land upon no authority other than some books written by a group of psychologists about whose qualifications we know little and about whose loyalty to the United

[8] Mason quoted in the *New York Times*, May 18, 1956, p. 87.

[9] J. W. Peltason, *Fifty-eight Lonely Men: Southern Federal Judges and School Desegregation* (New York: Harcourt, Brace and World, 1961), p. 41. See also Clifford M. Lytle, *The Warren Court and Its Critics* (Tucson: University of Arizona Press, 1968), pp. 10–23.

[10] Herman E. Talmadge, *You and Segregation* (Birmingham, Ala.: Vulcan Press, 1955), p. 67. An indication of the lasting merit of this work was provided by Talmadge himself. When asked by this writer whether he could help locate a copy of the book, Talmadge replied, "I wished I could be of help to you in obtaining a copy. However, the company which published the book went out of business several years ago and there are no further copies available."

States there is great doubt."[11] Senator James Eastland charged in Congress that the Court had absorbed alien social doctrines that were opposed to the principles of the Constitution. These doctrines, he claimed, "can be traced to Karl Marx, and their propagation is part and parcel of the conspiracy to divide and destroy this Government through internal controversy. The Court adopts this propaganda as 'modern scientific authority.' "[12] Eastland saw the use of social science as part of a system of jurisprudence to be found only in Nazi Germany and the Soviet Union. More important, the loyalty of the social scientists cited by the Court was suspect, except for Kenneth B. Clark, who Eastland found to be merely disreputable because he was a "paid employee" of the NAACP.[13]

Political critics of the Brown decision also charged that social science had become the law of the land.[14] According to Byrnes, "The Court could not cite a single legal precedent in support of its decision. It cited only the writings of a group of psychologists."[15] Others contended that the Court had set itself up as "the final authority" on social science and had based its decision upon its own notion of psychology.[16] Numerous southern legislative resolutions were passed condemning the decision, particularly footnote eleven. "The South Carolina Act," for example, stated that the Court had relied upon "its own views of sociology and psychology."[17] Florida legislators declared:

> In reaching its conclusions the supreme court has disregarded its former pronouncements and attempted to justify such action by

[11] James F. Byrnes, "The Supreme Court Must Be Curbed," 40 *U.S. News and World Report* 50, 54 (1956).

[12] James O. Eastland, "Remarks on School Integration Cases in the United States Supreme Court," 101 *Congressional Record—Senate* 7119, 7120 (1955).

[13] *Ibid.*

[14] See Charles J. Block, *States' Rights: The Law of the Land* (Atlanta: Harrison Co., 1958), pp. 213, 250–51, and William D. Workman, *The Case for the South* (New York: Devin-Adair Co., 1960), pp. 26, 30, 197.

[15] Byrnes, "Guns and Bayonets," p. 101.

[16] See James Jackson Kilpatrick, *The Southern Case for School Segregation* (New York: Crowell-Collier Press, 1962), p. 105, and Alfred M. Scott, *The Supreme Court versus the Constitution* (New York: Exposition Press, 1963), p. 31.

[17] "The South Carolina Act of Feb. 14, 1956," 1 *Race Relations Law Reporter* 443, 444 (1956).

the expedient of imputing ignorance of psychology to men whose knowledge of the law and understanding of the constitution could not be impugned, and has expressly predicated its determination of the rights of the people . . . upon the psychological conclusions of Kotinsky, Brameld and Myrdal, and their ilk, rather than the legal conclusions of Taft, Holmes, Van Devanter, Brandeis and their contemporaries upon the bench.[18]

Social science itself, aside from its judicial use, was attacked as nonscientific and irrelevant. Peter A. Carmichael, professor of philosophy at Louisiana State University, intoned, "Sociology, as a distinct department of knowledge, has only a petty place. . . . It has no very strict technical requirements: no mastery of logic, mathematics, philosophy, law, or of other scientific grounds, except, perhaps elementary statistics."[19]

Curiously enough, Senator Strom Thurmond stated that the Court's use of social science was nothing new but was, instead, part of a long, insidious trend. According to the senator, Plessy v. Ferguson was probably the last case in this area based simply on law and that "did not take into account the sociological implications which since that time have been foisted upon the courts."[20] Thurmond concluded, "It certainly is not in the interest of the American people as a whole or the legal profession to argue extralegal considerations upon the Supreme Court as the basis for a decision of such constitutional importance."[21]

Modern Social Science and the Theory of the Brandeis Brief

The political criticism of the Court's use of social science can obviously be dismissed as polemics. On the other hand, Paul Freund thoughtfully suggested that the Court's use of "sociological writings is open to question" because it was not com-

---

[18] "Senate Concurrent Resolution No. 17—XX of the 1956 Special Session of the Florida Legislature, Approved August 1, 1956," 1 *Race Relations Law Reporter* 950 (1956).
[19] Peter A. Carmichael, *The South and Segregation* (Washington, D.C.: Public Affairs Press, 1965), p. 168.
[20] Strom Thurmond, "Remarks," 108 *Congressional Record—Senate* 17930 (1962).
[21] *Ibid.*, p. 17936.

patible with the original theory of the Brandeis brief.[22] Freund properly pointed out that the use of the Brandeis brief was traditionally limited to the purpose of supporting legislation. Thus the brief was used in conjunction with the traditional principle of presumptive constitutionality. Freund found no problem with a Brandeis brief used in this fashion, for "even a court that relies on the presumption in sustaining a statute does so more confidently and more comfortably if some factual foundation has been established for the validity of the law."[23] But when a Brandeis brief is used to attack legislation, then extralegal data take on a new significance; the primary issue is no longer the existence of such data but, rather, their validity.

Freund is, of course, correct in pointing out that Brandeis had emphasized that the mere existence of extralegal data was sufficient to establish that a legislature had reasonable grounds for enacting legislative remedies for given problems. However, Brandeis's presentation of nascent social science in the Muller case[24] cannot be related only to the traditional principle of presumptive constitutionality. As we have already seen, the principle of presumption has varied in both meaning and application, thereby obscuring the respective burdens of proof associated with the two categories of "attacking" and "supporting" legislation.

Yet we saw the traditional principle of presumptive constitutionality actually giving way to a new, informal presumptive principle that stated, in effect, that social welfare legislation interfering with the individual's freedom to contract was invalid. Therefore, although the early Brandeis briefs were used in support of social welfare legislation, in practice they were employed against this new presumptive principle. The Brandeis brief was first used in a period of constitutional crisis, when the Court stood behind the Constitution to block urgent social and economic reforms. Brandeis thus resorted to nascent social science for the ultimate purpose of facilitating social change. In a comparable way the civil rights movement, which gained legal momentum

[22] Paul A. Freund, *The Supreme Court of the United States: Its Business, Purposes, and Performance* (Cleveland: World Publishing Co., 1963), p. 152.
[23] *Ibid.*, p. 151.
[24] Muller v. Oregon, 208 U.S. 412 (1908).

in the late 1940s and early 1950s, reflected a second constitutional crisis. The question this time was whether the Court would be passive and continue to condone school segregation, or whether the high bench might be as vigorous in attacking segregation legislation as it had once been in attacking social welfare legislation.

It appears certain that the traditional principle of presumptive constitutionality operated in neither the Muller case nor the Brown case. Before the Brown decision the Court had suggested on several occasions that statutory discrimination based on the criterion of race was immediately suspect.[25] Indeed, on the same day that the Brown decision was handed down, the Court affirmed that "classifications based solely on race must be scrutinized with particular care. . . ."[26] Therefore, it is not at all clear that the traditional principle of presumptive constitutionality applied to segregation statutes. Instead the Court in 1954 may have taken the view that "when race is the criterion, the presumption of constitutionality is reversed."[27] As Freund has pointed out, the Court's use of social science "would be compatible with the theory of the Brandeis brief only if the usual presumption in favor of legislation is reversed in cases of racial classification. . . ."[28] Since there is good reason to believe that this was the Court's actual presumption in the Brown case, and bearing in mind that in the past there has been more than one presumptive principle, it appears that in both the Muller and the Brown cases Brandeis briefs were used by Courts operating under the presumption that the legislation in question was unconstitutional. In short, the Court's use of modern social science was not inconsistent with the theory of the Brandeis brief, at least not in terms of the two presumptive principles.

Be that as it may, it is certain that the Court did not say simply that social science findings "existed" but used social science findings to define as a "valid" fact the effects of racial segregation.

[25] Korematsu v. United States, 323 U.S. 214 (1944); Oyama v. California, 332 U.S. 633 (1948).
[26] Bolling v. Sharpe, 347 U.S. 497, 499 (1954).
[27] Janet G. Kohn, "Social Psychological Data, Legislative Fact, and Constitutional Law," 29 *George Washington Law Review* 136, 143 (1960).
[28] Freund, *Supreme Court of the United States*, p. 152.

While this is a different matter from simply concluding that extralegal data existed, such a difference does not really mean that the Brown case was incompatible with the theory of the Brandeis brief. As we have seen, Brandeis first introduced the brief as a result of his conviction that law should follow the facts rather than the arid proofs of abstract legal syllogisms. Needless to say, Brandeis held this conviction throughout his judicial career. As Freund has written about Brandeis, "No one attached more weight than he to the presumption of constitutionality attaching to the acts of the legislature; and yet he was rarely content to rest his judgment there without the confirmation that he found in a study of the context of legislation. In his opinions the technique of the Brandeis brief was generally employed to sustain the legislative judgment." However, there were occasions when "the same technique, reflecting the same insatiable passion to know, was employed to suggest that what had once been constitutional might be questionable in the light of facts that had markedly changed."[29]

Brandeis did more than suggest; he clearly stated that decisions affecting constitutional rights should be made in the context of apposite facts. In a concurring opinion in the case of St. Joseph Stock Yards Co. v. United States, decided in 1936, in which the Court affirmed that factual findings by legislative agencies were not necessarily conclusive, Brandeis pointed out that "a citizen who claims that his liberty is being infringed is entitled . . . to the opportunity of a judicial determination of the facts."[30] Moreover, Brandeis observed, "Whenever a legislative body regulates a subject within the scope of its power, *a presumption of constitutionality prevails, in the absence of some factual foundation of record for overthrowing the regulation. . . .*"[31] In other words, Brandeis indicated that the presumption of constitutionality gives way in the light of facts. Obviously, then, facts do provide the Court with grounds for invalidating legislation. Brandeis was hardly drawing a dis-

[29] *Ibid.*, p. 120.
[30] St. Joseph Stock Yards Co. v. United States, 298 U.S. 38, 77 (1936) (concurring opinion).
[31] *Ibid.*, p. 83. Emphasis supplied.

tinction between the "existence" and the "validity" of facts, since the criterion of existence applied only when the principle of presumptive constitutionality was intact. The presumption obviously could give way only in the presence of "valid" facts.

Brandeis's curious argument that the Court only needed to note the existence and not the validity of facts was legally sound because it rested on the traditional principle of presumptive constitutionality. But he never stated that the Court only needed to note the "existence" of facts when this principle did not operate. Thus we can draw the theoretical implications of the Brandeis brief to their logical conclusion. It appears almost certain that in view of Brandeis's insistence on the relevance of extralegal data to the decisional process, if such data were presented respectively by both sides to demonstrate that an act was or was not reasonable, the Court would of necessity have to consider not only the existence but also the validity of the data. For if the Court were to assume simply that the existence of any data in support of an act demonstrated the reasonableness of legislative action, despite the presentation of more reliable data to the contrary, the Court would not only be forfeiting its power of review but would also be flying in the face of reason.[32]

Brandeis was, after all, "the social scientist with a conscience."[33] No social scientist would distinguish logically between the existence and the validity of a fact. Brandeis made such a distinction because he believed that social welfare legislation *should* benefit from the presumption that it was constitutional. The original theory of the Brandeis brief was expressed in the context of supporting legislation simply because the initial legal objective of the Brandeis brief was limited. Obviously the original theory of the Brandeis brief was formulated in the context of supporting social welfare legislation because advocative strategy does not necessarily embrace legal battles that might be fought in the future. Nevertheless, it is clear that Brandeis's overall view of the role of facts in the process of judicial interpretation does suggest

[32] See Herbert Garfinkel, "Social Science Evidence and the School Segregation Cases," 21 *Journal of Politics* 37, 41 (1959).

[33] Samuel J. Konefsky, *The Legacy of Holmes and Brandeis* (New York: Collier Books, 1961), p. 152.

a rationale for a factual judicial inquiry into the possibility that legislation may be unconstitutional. Theoretically, then, the use of the Brandeis brief is not logically restricted to providing facts only to support the constitutionality of legislation. On the contrary, the theory of the Brandeis brief also calls for the presentation of extralegal data in order to demonstrate "a lack of 'reasonable' factual support" for contested legislative enactments.[34]

Brandeis was, in the final analysis, an advocate of social reform. He believed that the process of judicial interpretation would result in a rational application of legal principles to fact situations only as long as the Court was in command of the facts. In brief, then, it is not at all likely that Brandeis would have objected to the Court's use of modern social science for the purpose of ascertaining the relevant facts of racial segregation.

The Adequacy of Social Science Findings

The Supreme Court had relied on the mainstream of modern social science thought in finding that school segregation adversely affected the "hearts and minds" of Negro children. This psychological and sociological finding led to the Court's factual conclusion that racially segregated schools were inherently unequal. Unlike the historical arguments the Court had considered and then dismissed, the seven social science studies in footnote eleven were not deliberately prepared for the Brown litigation. One study (Deutscher and Chein) had been prepared in the hope that courts might eventually take notice of the findings of social science. Be that as it may, the studies cited by the Supreme Court, in stark comparison to the historical briefs, made no attempt to distort or conceal the adequacy of social science research in the field of race relations or, for that matter, to gloss over gaps in the relevant literature. Indeed, the candor and frankness of the studies made it relatively easy for the Court as a lay body to evaluate the adequacy of the available social science material relating to the problem of school segregation. To be sure, by

[34] Chester A. Newland, "Innovation in Judicial Techniques: The Brandeis Opinion," 42 *Southwestern Social Science Quarterly* 22, 29 (1961).

turning to social science, the Court was venturing beyond the restricted sphere of its legal expertise. It is therefore worth noting what the Court found.

The first of the seven studies cited by the Court primarily concerned the well-known "doll test," first conducted in 1940 by Kenneth B. Clark and his wife, Mamie.[35] The Clarks used two groups of Negro children, one from segregated schools in the South and the other from integrated schools in the North, to study the development of racial awareness in Negro children. The two groups, drawn from a sample of 253 children, were presented with identical brown and white dolls and given such instructions as "Give me the doll that is a nice doll" and "Give me the doll that looks bad." By correlating the number of positive and negative personal associations made with each doll, the Clarks attempted to demonstrate the attitude of the children toward their own race. In general, the Clarks found that Negro children more frequently preferred the white doll to the black doll or thought of the white doll as "nice" and the black doll as "bad." The study also indicated that "there are no significant quantitative differences between the Northern and Southern Negro children tested (children in mixed schools and children in segregated schools) in their knowledge of racial differences."[36] Southern children, in contrast to northern children, manifested fewer preferences to play with the white doll. In addition, the study revealed that southern children were less likely than northern children to reject or evaluate the brown doll in a negative fashion.[37]

The doll study did suggest that Negro children considered themselves less worthy than white children. But it did not identify school segregation as the independent variable that caused psychological harm. Indeed, as Clark noted later, the findings could superficially suggest that southern children suffered less from prejudice and discrimination than northern children. But such an interpretation, Clark explained, "would seem to be not only

[35] Kenneth B. and Mamie Clark, "Racial Identification and Preference in Negro Children," in Theodore M. Newcomb *et al.*, eds., *Readings in Social Psychology* (New York: Henry Holt, 1947), pp. 169–78.

[36] *Ibid.*, p. 174.

[37] *Ibid.*, pp. 177–78.

superficial but incorrect. The apparent emotional stability of the southern Negro child may be indicative only of the fact that through rigid racial segregation and isolation he has accepted as normal the fact of his inferior social status. Such acceptance is not symptomatic of a healthy personality."[38]

The study edited by Witmer and Kotinsky provided a cautious analysis of the various environmental factors that mold the development of human personality.[39] Although hesitant to claim full understanding of these factors, the editors did emphasize the primacy of various environmental factors as the fundamental determinants of mental health. Despite initial qualifications that much remained to be learned about personality development, the study pointed out that "the child who is not treated with respect as a child learns from not being treated with respect— learns that he is not worthy of respect (or learns so to feel in his inner heart, perhaps even without acknowledging it to himself), and that therefore others like him are not worthy of respect."[40] In addition, the school was singled out as having "a role which is not only strategic but indispensable in the development of the healthy personality."[41] But although a "wealth of material" was available on the origins and existence of and means for reducing prejudice and discrimination, the editors felt that the literature was not comprehensive enough to permit a statement on the precise effects of various forms of discrimination.[42]

The Deutscher and Chein study was actually a poll of social scientists deliberately conducted to enable courts to determine "whether prevailing social science opinion is that enforced segregation does or does not have detrimental effects. . . ."[43] To this

[38] Kenneth B. Clark, *Prejudice and Your Child,* 2nd ed. (Boston: Beacon Press, 1966), p. 45.

[39] Helen Leland Witmer and Ruth Kotinsky, eds., *Personality in the Making: The Fact-Finding Report of the Midcentury White House Conference on Children and Youth* (Palo Alto, Calif.: Science and Behavior Books, 1952).

[40] *Ibid.,* p. 237.

[41] *Ibid.,* p. 257.

[42] *Ibid.,* p. 136.

[43] Max Deutscher and Isidor Chein, "The Psychological Effects of Enforced Segregation: A Survey of Social Science Opinion," 26 *Journal of Psychology* 259, 265 (1948).

end, 849 social scientists were asked to answer a questionnaire on the psychological effects of racial segregation. A total of 517 social scientists responded, providing a striking picture of professional consensus on this issue in the various social science disciplines. Ninety percent of the total sample agreed that segregation had harmful psychological effects on the segregated group. Only 2 percent disagreed, 4 percent had no opinion, and the remaining 4 percent failed to answer the question. In brief, the poll presented a definitive overview of the mainstream of social science thought concerning the effects of school segregation.

The study by Isidor Chein stated that the principal effects of segregation, regardless of the physical facilities, were "feelings of inferiority and insecurity, self-doubt, self-ambivalence; feelings of isolation and of not belonging anywhere; cynicism; loss of initiative and efficiency, diminished sense of responsibility; ideas of persecution; displaced aggression; anti-social behavior; and disturbances in the sense of reality. . . ."[44] Similarly, Brameld found that segregation resulted in a "tremendous cultural loss" and general "social neurosis."[45] However, both Chein and Brameld noted that while a great deal of information had been gathered, sufficient data were not yet available on the precise effects of racial segregation.

E. Franklin Frazier's work was a general study of the American Negro.[46] He emphasized that the theory of separate-but-equal facilities had never worked out in practice. As a result, public school segregation always meant inferior schools and teachers for Negro children. He concluded that as a general result of discrimination, "the Negro has not been permitted to play a serious role in the economic and social life of the nation," and that "whites and Negroes do not know each other as human beings . . . for the simple reason that race prejudice and dis-

[44] Isidor Chein, "What Are the Psychological Effects of Segregation under Conditions of Equal Facilities?" 3 *International Journal of Opinion and Attitude Resolution* 229, 234 (1949).

[45] Theodore Brameld, "Educational Costs," in R. M. MacIver, ed., *Discrimination and National Welfare* (New York: Harper and Bros., 1949), p. 46.

[46] E. Franklin Frazier, *The Negro in the United States,* rev. ed. (New York: Macmillan, 1957), p. 677.

crimination has prevented normal human intercourse between the two races."[47]

Finally, the most comprehensive and elaborate study cited by the Court was Gunnar Myrdal's *An American Dilemma.*[48] This study, funded by the Carnegie Corporation, was published in 1944 after six years of research by a large team of scholars. Many distinguished social scientists—Ruth Benedict, Franz Boas, John Dollard, Ralph Linton, George Lundberg, Ashley Montagu, Robert E. Park, Edward Shils, W. J. Thomas, and Louis Wirth—assisted in the preparation of the 15,000-page manuscript. Myrdal's great study was reminiscent of Tocqueville's classic analysis of American society, *Democracy in America.* Myrdal, like Tocqueville, came to the United States as a neutral observer for the specific purpose of studying a critical and fundamental social problem. Tocqueville had posited that the primary prerequisite of a democratic society was the general condition of equality. Myrdal's study revealed a vast gulf between the American democratic credo, with its affirmation of equality, and the glaringly unequal status of the Negro. Myrdal stated unequivocally, "The whole system of discrimination in education in the South is not only tremendously harmful to the Negroes," but, he added prophetically, "it is flagrantly illegal, and can easily be so proven in the courts."[49]

In general, the social science studies cited by the Court were weak in three respects. First, although each of the studies affirmed that school segregation was psychologically harmful, school segregation was not identified as the sole environmental factor that caused such injury. Second, the studies did not define the precise psychological effects of school segregation. Finally, the studies indicated that the available empirical data on school segregation were limited and that many of the scientific hypotheses concerning the development of personality were still tentative.

On the other hand, the studies demonstrated that the main

[47] *Ibid.*

[48] Gunnar Myrdal, *An American Dilemma: The Negro Problem and Modern Democracy* (New York: Harper and Bros., 1944).

[49] *Ibid.*, p. 342.

body of social science literature confirmed that all significant achievement disparities between Negroes and whites could be explained in environmental rather than biological terms. Moreover, the studies revealed a veritable consensus among social scientists, and in the relevant literature, that the segregated school was a critical environmental factor that inflicted psychological harm on Negro children. In addition, it is important to note that the studies could hardly have misled the Court. They contained no exaggerated or unqualified claims. Instead the studies presented a balanced and modest description of the state of social science knowledge bearing upon the problem of school segregation. It may be true that social scientists had much to be modest about, but modesty and skepticism in science precede certainty. More important, the point should not be lost that despite the inherent limitations of social science research, and in this instance the apparent gaps in the relevant literature, the Supreme Court nevertheless deferred to the authority of modern social science. This suggests the acceptability or legitimacy of modern social science, even though its hypotheses are not as easily verified as those of natural science.

To be sure, the Court's finding of fact was completely in accord with the seven social science studies. These studies were neither misconstrued nor misused, and the Court did not claim more knowledge than the studies warranted. Indeed, all of Chief Justice Warren's factual dicta were compatible with the studies. The Court had found, as we have seen, that the school was a vital agency of socialization and, more broadly, that psychology had changed appreciably. Yet in view of the three weak points of the studies, it is important to reiterate the Court's precise finding of fact. Chief Justice Warren had found that public school segregation was harmful to Negro children and that segregated schools were therefore inherently unequal. The chief justice did not say or infer that segregated schools were the sole cause of psychological harm, nor did he attempt to present a detailed clinical description of that harm. Instead Warren stated that school segregation caused a sense of inferiority and ultimately inhibited the educational and mental development of Negro children. The factual finding of psychological harm was expressed in general terms. Segregation, Warren simply wrote, affected the "hearts and minds" of children "in a way unlikely ever to be undone." Finally, the chief justice did not state or infer that the social science findings were based on unlimited and direct empirical data that proved in mathematically precise terms that school segregation caused psychological harm. But he did say, quite plainly, that the Court's psycho-sociological finding of fact was "amply supported by modern authority." There was no exaggeration or deception in this statement. The studies, after all, were freely available, and the Court's use of them could be checked by anyone. From an ideal point of view, the social science literature on racial segregation was incomplete. Certainly many of the general conclusions of social science were (and remain) tentative. But the mainstream of social science thought did attest to the harm inflicted by school segregation. The Court had evaluated the effects of racial segregation in the light of all the available facts. It could hardly do more.

More than 500 social scientists had agreed that school segregation was harmful. Nevertheless, as I. A. Newby has written, a "small cadre of academic social scientists" not only took exception to the mainstream of social science thought but subsequently attempted to counter the Court's use of modern social science by establishing a "scientific" defense of segregation.[50] A handful of psychologists, including Henry E. Garrett, Frank C. J. McGurk, and Audrey Shuey, contributed to a literature of scientific racism.[51] The burden of this literature has been to prove that Negroes are biologically inferior to whites and therefore should be segregated. McGurk, for example, has contended that there is ample evidence to prove that there are important psychological differences between Negroes and whites. "These differences are, today, of about the same magnitude as they were two generations ago. These differences are not the result of differences in social and economic opportunities, and they will not disappear as the social and economic opportunities of Negroes and whites are

[50] I. A. Newby, *Challenge to the Court: Social Scientists and the Defense of Segregation, 1954–1966* (Baton Rouge: Louisiana State University Press, 1967), p. 63.
[51] *Ibid.*, p. 65.

equalized."[52] Needless to say, modern social science has long abandoned biological models for explaining social behavior. In short, McGurk's work, and scientific racism in general, have attracted little attention and hardly any support from the social science community.[53]

A few social scientists directly criticized the adequacy of the social science findings used by the Court. For example, A. James Gregor and Ernest van den Haag disputed the relevance and validity of the findings. Ironically, however, both agreed that the social science studies demonstrated that integrated schools were psychologically harmful to Negroes. Moreover, both Gregor and van den Haag have contended that school desegregation was objectionable because white children would be affected adversely.

Gregor argued that modern social science should not have been used by the Court because it was irrelevant, insubstantial, and not amenable to precise interpretation.[54] Gregor singled out the Clark study for criticism because it did not delineate the precise effects of school segregation on personality development. If modern social science does anything, Gregor wrote, it tends "to support racial separation in the schools at least throughout childhood and adolescence."[55] More important, the "special problem" for Gregor was not segregation but integration. "A white parent faces the issue of permitting his children, hitherto attending a racially homogeneous institution, to attend an institution where his children will be exposed to members of a group possessed, whatever the ultimate cause, of a higher index of delinquency, immorality, and communicable disease as well as a lower index of academic performance."[56] That is, white children will be brought into "regular and intimate contact with a group suffering significant social and psychological disabilities."[57]

[52] Frank C. J. McGurk, " 'Psychological Tests': A Scientist's Report on Race Differences," 49 *U.S. News and World Report* 92 (1956).

[53] One recent exception has been the suggestion by Arthur Jensen that genetic factors do help explain differences in IQ performances between Negroes and Caucasians. See Arthur R. Jensen, "How Much Can We Boost IQ and Scholastic Achievement?" 39 *Harvard Educational Review* 1 (1969).

[54] A. James Gregor, "The Law, Social Science, and School Segregation: An Assessment," 14 *Case Western Reserve Law Review* 621, 622 (1963).

[55] *Ibid.*, p. 626.

[56] *Ibid.*, p. 635.

[57] *Ibid.*

Although Gregor denied that school segregation was harmful, and that there was any conclusive evidence that the psychological disabilities of the Negro were caused by environmental factors, he nevertheless waved the red flag of integration by implying that it was detrimental to white children. But if there is no conclusive evidence that environmental factors contribute to mental health, it is hard to understand how Gregor could logically conclude that integration "can hardly lead to anything more than a real sense of inferiority on the part of the minority children and hostility on the part of their majority counterparts and their parents."[58]

Similarly, Ernest van den Haag attacked the Court's use of social science, in particular, the doll study, which he termed "pseudo scientific proof."[59] In subsequent testimony before the International Court of Justice in support of South Africa's policy of apartheid, van den Haag stated his unconditional disagreement with the principal social science findings reported by the Midcentury White House Conference on Children and Youth. These findings had figured prominently in the social science statement endorsed by thirty-five leading social scientists, and the White House report itself had been used by the Supreme Court. Not only did van den Haag claim on this occasion that there was no evidence to support the conclusions of the White House report or the Supreme Court's finding of fact, but he also charged imprudently that "whatever evidence appears in the body of the report . . . has been largely faked."[60] When the president of the International Court, Sir Percy Spender, rigorously questioned van den Haag on his allegation, he dropped his charge and tendered his apology.

Curiously enough, although van den Haag claimed that the Supreme Court's finding of fact could not be supported by modern social science, he did argue that racial segregation had harmful effects. "The Court's view that 'segregation with the

[58] *Ibid.*, p. 636.
[59] Ernest van den Haag, "Social Science Testimony in the Desegregation Cases: A Reply to Professor Kenneth Clark," 6 *Villanova Law Review* 69 (1960), reprinted, it may be noted, by the International Association for the Advancement of Ethnology and Eugenics, New York, p. 1.
[60] *I. C. J. Pleadings, South West Africa*, 10 (1966): 462.

sanction of the law' is humiliating," he wrote, "is doubtlessly true under historical circumstances."[61] Although segregation "inflicts an unhealthy mass humiliation," it is not known whether humiliation produces personality disorders.[62] However, van den Haag did not explain how it could be known that segregation produces an "unhealthy" effect and, at the same time, not be known that such an effect produces a disorder.

The Brown decision, van den Haag explained speciously, not only prohibited compulsory segregation but replaced it with compulsory congregation. The Fourteenth Amendment "was interpreted to mean that no group has the right to be separated from another on public property when the other's pride is hurt thereby." Consequently segregation becomes "a privilege of the rich."[63] Van den Haag concluded that the Court failed to realize that compulsory congregation was more harmful than compulsory segregation and quite possibly would increase the humiliation of the Negro.

In general, the small group of social scientists who criticized the adequacy of the studies used by the Court not only were critical of the methodology of those studies; they were also fundamentally opposed to integration.[64] Such critics as Gregor and van den Haag repeatedly emphasized that the studies did not prove that school segregation alone caused psychological harm, and that much of the available social science data applied only indirectly to school segregation. In this limited sense their criticism was correct. However, the overall argument that modern social science should have been disregarded by the Court does not logically follow unless the implicit premise of this argument is accepted—that social science findings can be tested in precisely the same manner as the findings of natural science, and that the only social science findings worthy of consideration are those exhibiting the same degree of validity as the findings of natural science. In other words, the criticism of Gregor and van den

[61] Van den Haag, "Social Science Testimony," p. 3.

[62] Ralph Ross and Ernest van den Haag, *The Fabric of Society: An Introduction to the Social Sciences* (New York: Harcourt, Brace, 1957), p. 165.

[63] Ernest van den Haag, *Passion and Social Constraint* (New York: Stein and Day, 1963), p. 280.

[64] See Newby, *Challenge to the Court.*

Haag begs the question that the Court should have ignored modern social science because its findings were not stated in mathematical terms. But it is apparent that Gregor and van den Haag did not actually accept this premise or really believe in the first place that social science was capable of great precision. For if they did, they would not have attempted to demonstrate that public school integration inflicts harm.[65]

It is obvious that the fundamental theoretical hypotheses of social science cannot be tested in as convincing a manner as those of natural science. It is also apparent that for the time being, most of the important findings of social science will be based on indirect data and will remain tentative, because it is impossible to submit critical social problems to laboratory observation. As van den Haag himself writes, "What is worse for the social sciences is that it is nearly impossible to *reproduce* any of the situations they are concerned with. Because of this, we cannot *actually* isolate variables from one another so as to ascertain which are necessary and sufficient to produce the effects of which we suspect them to be the cause; we can do so only in our analytical models." Thus social science explanation of large-scale social problems probably will always be based on indirect data and will rarely pinpoint independent variables. Van den Haag has observed that "the evidence for the theories of the social sciences is . . . unlikely ever to be as conclusive as the evidence for propositions in physics can be. The propositions of the social sciences are unlikely ever to be definitely tested."[66] However, these difficulties, which are characteristic of social science in general, have not prompted van den Haag to argue that the hypotheses of social science, even those as suggestive as the Freudian metaphor, should be ignored. That is, van den Haag has not argued in general that modern social science should be dismissed or ignored, the one exception, of course, being the social science findings used by the Supreme Court.

In short, the social science used by the Supreme Court was not above criticism. As one psychologist aptly stated, "At the purely descriptive level, these studies are clear and consistent.

---

[65] Gregor, "The Law, Social Science, and School Segregation," pp. 626–35.
[66] Van den Haag, *Passion and Social Constraint*, p. 344.

The fundamental question that they leave unanswered, is that of causation. To what extent are obtained differences in ability a result of the separate and unequal treatment received by whites and Negroes in educational facilities, vocational opportunities, and the more subtle psychological components of the cultural setting?"[67] But although the studies did not reveal the precise amount of harm inflicted by school segregation, or whether different kinds of segregated facilities caused more or less harm than segregated schools, these unanswered questions do not suggest that the social science findings were inadequate in terms of the immediate question of fact posed by the Court in the Brown case. The question of fact was whether segregated schools were equal. Insofar as the social science findings did confirm that segregated schools inflicted harm, albeit an incalculable measure of harm, questions about the precise kind and amount of harm, and whether school segregation was the only cause of harm, were not necessarily relevant to the Court's definition of the immediate fact situation. The social science findings documented adequately the fact that segregated schools were unequal. And southern whites undoubtedly knew all along, as Ambrose Caliver has pointed out, "how such a system would affect Negroes—their goals, values, aspirations, and attitudes, as well as their knowledge, habits, and spirits. Segregated schools have prevented Negroes from achieving those major desires found in every human being—a sense of security, a sense of belonging, a desire for appreciation, and a desire for self-expression."[68]

The Court probably realized, as Justice Frankfurter has noted, that psychology was a "subtle" science, and that a social science finding of fact on the effects of segregation could not be stated as precisely as a mathematical measurement on a bolt of cloth. Nevertheless, there can be no doubt that modern social science provided substantial and authoritative evidence that segregated schools were unequal. "Substantial evidence," Chief Justice Hughes once wrote, "is more than a mere scintilla. It means such

[67] Anne Anastasi, "Psychological Research and Educational Desegregation," 35 *Thought* 419, 431 (1960).
[68] Ambrose Caliver, "Segregation in American Education: An Overview," 303 *Annals of the American Academy of Political and Social Science* 17, 23 (1956).

relative evidence as a reasonable mind might accept as adequate to support a conclusion."[69]

It is not incidental that no significant element of the social science community has disagreed with the social science finding that racial segregation is harmful. Indeed, as Thomas Pettigrew has noted, only three psychologists (Garrett, McGurk, and Shuey) of the approximately 21,000 members of the American Psychological Association have disputed this finding.[70] More important, the Court's finding of harm remains compatible with subsequent psychological research.[71]

For the most part, criticism of the social science findings used by the Court has been coupled with the assumption or the explicit argument that the Negro is biologically inferior to the white man. As I. A. Newby has shown, such "popularizers of scientific racism" as Carleton Putnam, James Jackson Kilpatrick, Nathaniel Weyl, and Stefan Possony have mounted a concerted attempt to demonstrate the biological inferiority of the Negro. At the same time a few social scientists have sympathized with this literature. According to Newby, Ernest van den Haag is the "most prominent sociologist who has identified himself with segregationists and scientific racists. . . ."[72]

Modern social science, however, rejects conclusively the notion of racial inferiority. As Pettigrew has written, "The overwhelming opinion of modern psychology concludes that the mean differences often observed between Negro and white children are largely the result of enviromental, rather than genetic factors." Moreover, he adds, sociology and anthropology share in this conclusion.[73] More recently, the council of the Society for the Psychological Study of Social Issues issued a report:

[69] Edison Co. v. Labor Board, 305 U.S. 197, 229 (1938).

[70] Thomas F. Pettigrew, *A Profile of the Negro American* (Princeton, N.J.: D. Van Nostrand, 1964), p. 101.

[71] Mary E. Goodman, *Race Awareness in Young Children*, rev. ed. (New York: Collier Books, 1964), pp. 248–68. See also the statement by Kenneth B. Clark in *Hearings before the Select Committee on Equal Educational Opportunity of the United States Senate, Ninety-first Congress, Second Session, on Equal Educational Opportunity: An Introduction* (Washington, D.C.: U.S. Government Printing Office, 1970), pp. 71–86, and the statement by Thomas F. Pettigrew, Part 2, pp. 744–801.

[72] Newby, *Challenge to the Court*, p. 180.

[73] Pettigrew, *Profile of the Negro American*, p. 133.

The evidence of four decades of research on this problem can be readily summarized. There are marked differences in intelligence test scores when one compares a random sample of whites and Negroes. What is equally clear is that little definitive evidence exists that leads to the conclusion that such differences are innate. The evidence points overwhelmingly to the fact that when one compares Negroes and whites of comparable cultural and educational background, differences in intelligence test scores diminish markedly; the more comparable the background, the less the difference. There is no direct evidence that supports the view that there is an innate difference between members of different racial groups.

. . . We maintain that the racism and discrimination in our country impose an immeasurable burden upon the black person. Social inequalities deprive large numbers of black people of social, economic, and educational advantages available to a great majority of the white population.[74]

In conclusion, modern social science findings provided the Court with an adequate picture of empirical reality. The Court was therefore able to determine on an empirical basis whether segregated schools were actually equal. But not only did the high bench invalidate public school segregation; at the same time it rejected the underlying rationale of segregation—that the two races were biologically distinct and unequal. Although the Court had never stated explicitly that the black race was a lesser form of the human species, this sentiment was conveyed by dicta in the two most significant cases involving the American Negro before the Brown decision. In the Dred Scott case Chief Justice Roger Taney had remarked that "the unhappy black race were separated from the white by indelible marks."[75] And in the Plessy case Justice Henry Brown had affirmed that "legislation is powerless to eradicate racial instincts or to abolish distinctions based upon physical differences. . . ."[76]

However, the Brown case, unlike the Dred Scott and Plessy cases, was free from any facile intimation that the Negro was

[74] "SPSSI Council Statement on Race and Intelligence," 25 *Journal of Social Issues* 1–2 (1969).

[75] Dred Scott v. Sandford, 19 Howard 393, 410 (1857).

[76] Plessy v. Ferguson, 163 U.S. 537, 551 (1896).

biologically inferior to the white man. Modern social science had confirmed that the notion of biological inferiority was untenable. In using social science, the Supreme Court suggested that the long-standing inequality of the two races was not due to any biological traits of the Negro. On the contrary, the Court reasoned that public school segregation was one cause of inequality. In other words, the Court rejected the once-prevalent assumption that the two races were inherently unequal, finding instead that segregated schools were inherently unequal. Throughout history race has been an emotionally charged idea. Therefore, it is not surprising that the Court's finding of fact as well as its finding of law created much controversy.

CHAPTER NINE

Using Social Science: Reflections and Conclusions

The Perils of Social Science

The Supreme Court's use of modern social science in the Brown case[1] can be viewed as the grand realization of a fundamental tenet of sociological jurisprudence—"that statutes are to be viewed," as Benjamin Cardozo aptly put it, "not in isolation or *in vacuo*, as pronouncements of abstract principles for the guidance of an ideal community, but in the setting and the framework of present-day conditions, as revealed by the labors of economists and students of the social sciences in our country and abroad."[2] As we have seen, during the period of economic due-process adjudication, which began in the late nineteenth century and lasted until 1937, the high bench for the most part ignored the wisdom of this simple tenet. In turn, the proponents of sociological jurisprudence claimed that the Court had been blinded by a mechanical jurisprudence or was making constitutional law primarily in terms of arid and abstract legal syllogisms that failed to reflect empirical reality.

Whereas the Court had once been castigated for disregarding the teachings of social science, ironically enough the Brown case prompted several critics to speculate that the Court's continuous use of social science could have perilous effects on constitu-

---

[1] Brown v. Board of Education of Topeka, 347 U.S. 483 (1954).
[2] Benjamin N. Cardozo, *The Nature of the Judicial Process* (New Haven, Conn.: Yale University Press, 1961), p. 81.

tional law. One sociologist saw fit to remark that "we may reach a point where we shall be entitled to equality under law only when we can show that inequality has been or would be harmful."[3] A political scientist was moved to warn that "when science asserts itself in the law, there is always the danger, and the strong possibility, that it will become irresponsible."[4] These comments were undoubtedly symptomatic of the traditional tension between law and social science. This tension was expressed most cogently by Edmond Cahn, a well-known jurist. Although Cahn supported the Brown decision, he scored the Court's use of social science, arguing in general that social science was potentially inimical to law. In his view, fundamental constitutional rights could easily be preserved without the support of social science. But if the Court became too enamoured of social science, he suggested, this attraction might be at the expense of those rights.

The immediate problem, Cahn wrote, concerned the Brandeis brief, with its sociological and economic data. The brief may be a helpful device for a judge as long as it is used to support legislation, but it creates an "awkward logical predicament" when the purpose is to invalidate legislation. "If statistics, expert opinions, graphs, and similar data," Cahn stated, "are sufficient to establish that the legislative or administrative authorities have acted rationally, then is it ever possible to prove that they have acted otherwise?" Moreover, he pointed out that "shrewd resourceful lawyers can put a Brandeis brief together in support of almost any conceivable exercise of legislative judgment."[5] It therefore makes a great deal of difference whether the Court uses social science or not. Cahn charged that the social sciences are inconstant and undependable disciplines. Social psychology, in particular, is characteristically limited by "the recurrent lack of agreement on substantive premises" and "the recurrent lack of extrinsic, empirical means for checking and verifying inferred

[3] Morroe Berger, "Desegregation, Law, and Social Science," 23 *Commentary* 471, 476 (1957).

[4] Walter Berns, "Law and Behavioral Science," 28 *Law and Contemporary Problems* 185, 208 (1963).

[5] Edmond Cahn, "A Dangerous Myth in the School Segregation Cases," 30 *New York University Law Review* 150, 153–54 (1955).

results."[6] Given the tentative nature of social science findings, it is not reassuring that present-day social scientists are liberals, for the social scientists of tomorrow may very well turn out to be racists. Therefore, he concluded, just as the "sagacious Mr. Justice Holmes was to insist that the Constitution be not tied to the wheels of any economic system whatsoever, we ought to keep it similarly uncommitted in relation to the other social sciences."[7]

Cahn doubtless had a general point—the relationship between law and social science will not be fruitful unless social science is used with critical intelligence. However, as we shall see, Cahn's overall critique of the Court's use of social science was too simplistic and ultimately generated more heat than light. To begin with, he assumed erroneously that social science findings are synonymous with the personal values and biases of social scientists. Having confused modern social science with an economic system or an idiosyncratic set of values, it seemed logical to him that in using social science, the Court might superimpose on the Constitution the personal values of social scientists. However, as Arnold Rose has noted, Cahn can be "cited as an example of a lawyer unaware of the difference between social science and a social ideology."[8] Moreover, Cahn underestimated the significance of the Court's use of social science findings in the Brown case, probably because he believed that the commands of the Constitution are "absolute" and "fixed" and thus require relatively little interpretation.[9] Indeed, he has maintained that the fundamental constitutional principles that provide for liberty and equality are not worded ambiguously but, rather, are formulated in clear and precise terms. Accordingly Cahn has described the Constitution as an ideal vehicle for preserving individual rights because it provides a judge with "legitimate standards" for rendering decisions. The Constitution "is the criterion of his responsibility because it enables the parties before him and the general public

[6] *Ibid.*, p. 167.

[7] *Ibid.*

[8] Arnold M. Rose, "The Social Scientist as an Expert Witness in Court Cases," in Paul F. Lazarsfeld *et al.*, eds., *The Uses of Sociology* (New York: Basic Books, 1967), p. 113.

[9] Edmond Cahn, "The Parchment Barriers," 32 *American Scholar* 21 (1962–63).

to ascertain whether he has decided correctly, reasonably, rightfully. Thus the text is the beginning and also the end of his process of judging. As he judges by it, he knows he will be judged by it."[10] In the final analysis, Cahn has remarked, the Constitution offers a judge "textual authority," "personal valor," and even "moral salvation."[11]

The Constitution may indeed be an instrument of saving grace. Nor can Cahn be faulted for stating "that a solemn legal prohibition *can* mean literally and precisely what it says. . . ."[12] But if fundamental constitutional principles—"due process of law" and "equal protection of the laws"—do mean precisely what they say or if their meaning is self-evident, how can the Court rationally change its mind about the constitutionality of social welfare measures and racial segregation, especially when the public is equipped and stands ready to pass judgment on its decisions? While the plain meaning of broadly formulated constitutional principles may be obvious on some occasions, an overview of constitutional adjudication generally supports the assertion that "no words are so plain and unambiguous that they do not need interpretation in relation to a context of language or circumstances."[13] Indeed, as we have seen, the process of judicial interpretation can be regarded as a dialectical process in which the precise meaning of constitutional principles is worked out in the context of judicially defined facts that are frequently derived from extralegal sources. The Supreme Court does not have the option of choosing between a hypothetically pure interpretation of the Constitution that reflects the absolute and fixed meaning of the document and a comparatively tawdry and ignoble interpretation that reflects changing and imperfectly understood fact situations. The simple reason is, of course, that no such judicial option exists.

The Court interprets the Constitution differently not only because society changes but also because its understanding of society changes in the light of new knowledge. In other words, fact

---

[10] *Ibid.*, p. 35.
[11] *Ibid.*, p. 36.
[12] *Ibid.*, p. 38.
[13] Carleton Kemp Allen, *Law in the Making*, 7th ed. (Oxford: Clarendon Press, 1966), p. 506.

situations and the way in which the Court understands them lend color to the meaning of the Constitution. Thus, while the Court's use of social science in the Brown case underscored in a striking manner the critical nexus between law and fact, this nexus did not become problematic for the first time simply because the Court formally used modern social science. This is not to imply that the relationship between law and social science warrants no special concern. But it is necessary to emphasize that if the Court does not use social science findings to define problematic fact situations, then constitutional principles will probably be interpreted in the context of facts that are derived from sources far less reliable than social science.

Yet even though the Court must grapple frequently with factual questions that may be amenable to social science explanation, it still lacks a dependable channel of communication with the various disciplines of social science. Unfortunately the Brandeis brief still remains the primary legal vehicle through which the Court has been apprised of social science findings. But the utility of a Brandeis brief can be questioned because the Court has no guarantee that the brief will always contribute to the integrity of the fact-finding process. An enterprising lawyer probably can build a Brandeis brief to support or challenge any legislative act. Moreover, a Brandeis brief in itself is not proof that the data and hypotheses it contains are valid. Actually, no formal tests are prescribed for the materials that may be included in the brief. Any kind of extralegal material—from astrology to social science —can go into a Brandeis brief.[14] Surely, then, serious questions can be raised about the Brandeis brief, but its liabilities should not be automatically imputed to social science. The Brandeis brief is not a method of explanation; that is, the brief is not social science. It is simply a record of information or a vehicle that has been used to bring social science findings to the attention of the Court. Instead of depicting the liabilities of social science, the brief actually reflects the shortcomings of the adversary system, suggesting that the Court does require additional means for getting at the facts. The creation of a judicial research agency or

[14] Francis D. Wormuth, "The Impact of Economic Legislation upon the Supreme Court," 6 *Journal of Public Law* 296, 312 (1957).

a special liaison committee with the social science community would enhance the Court's fact-finding capabilities and might also deter some lawyers from attempting to misrepresent the data and hypotheses of social science.

The adversary system almost induces opposing counsel to misrepresent or manipulate facts before the Court. The primary goal of the advocate is, after all, to achieve a favorable legal decision even at the expense of empirical truth. For that matter, the courtroom setting, with its ringing tones of partisanship, is not the ideal place to examine social science findings. In finding facts, the Court cannot really afford to be wholly respectful of the criteria of scientific method. The Supreme Court justice, unlike the social scientist, may have to reach factual conclusions even though empirical data may not be available, for the simple reason that the decision-making process must be terminated at some point. The Court cannot always reserve decision until all the facts are in. As an agency of government, the Court must act invariably on the basis of the best available data.

Since the adversary system may actually impede the flow of objective social data, the proper conclusion to be drawn is that the Court requires more and not less exposure to the work of social scientists. At the same time it would be foolish to argue that because social science findings can be misrepresented, only social science should be used by the Court with special caution. The possibility of misrepresentation is not peculiar to social science. Any body of knowledge that seeks general explanations of the social world is open to misrepresentation, but social science findings are less likely to be misrepresented than many other kinds of knowledge. Since scientific knowledge is ideally intersubjectively transmissible or is testable by the general scientific community, there is less chance that a scientific hypothesis, as opposed to a historical hypothesis, will be declared proven when it actually remains tentative.

Needless to say, the Court cannot easily adjudicate contemporary constitutional issues in a rational way if its facts are drawn exclusively from history, common knowledge, or mere judicial intuition. Social science findings may be particularly useful to the Court in cases in which it abandons precedent and overtly makes constitutional law. On these occasions the Court will not only take into consideration the immediate fact situation of a case, but it will also evince a special concern for the probable consequences of its decisions.[15] Figuratively speaking, creative lawmaking cases seem to invite the use of social science findings. But although relevant social science findings may be in demand, there is no guarantee that they will always be available, and the Court may then have to run the risk of making constitutional law on the basis of factual assumptions that are not entirely credible in terms of the standards of empirical inquiry. Two important cases, Escobedo v. Illinois[16] and Miranda v. Arizona,[17] were part of the Warren Court's sustained effort to make the concept of criminal justice an ongoing issue of federal concern. They provide good examples of the Court's critical need for empirical data in creative lawmaking cases and also reveal the shadow of uncertainty that can envelope a judicial decision when such data are unavailable.

In the Escobedo case, decided in 1964, the Court infused further meaning into the Sixth Amendment guarantee of the assistance of counsel in all criminal proceedings.[18] It held that the amendment, made applicable to the states through the due-process clause of the Fourteenth Amendment, required the police to honor the petitioner's request for the assistance of a lawyer during an interrogation process following his arrest. The Court ruled specifically that the refusal of the police to honor this request was a violation of the constitutional right to counsel, and such a refusal thereby rendered any incriminating statements made to the police during the interrogation process inadmissible in a state trial.

Justice Arthur Goldberg, speaking for the Court, based his

[15] Edwin W. Patterson notes, "I suspect that a good many judicial opinions, even those purporting only to interpret or to apply the law, are influenced by unspoken assumptions as to the factual consequences of the law." See Patterson, *Law in a Scientific Age* (New York: Columbia University Press, 1963), p. 60.

[16] Escobedo v. Illinois, 378 U.S. 478 (1964).

[17] Miranda v. Arizona, 384 U.S. 436 (1966).

[18] In Gideon v. Wainwright, 372 U.S. 335 (1963), the Court had overturned established precedent when it ruled that the Sixth Amendment right to counsel was applicable to the states and that they were required to appoint counsel for indigent defendants in both capital and noncapital cases.

opinion on two critical factual assumptions. Goldberg pointed out first that unless a person suspected of committing a crime was guaranteed the right to counsel before indictment and any formal judicial proceeding, it could reasonably be assumed that the police might attempt to extract an involuntary confession. Second, with respect to the consequences of the Court's decision or its probable impact on law enforcement, Goldberg wrote that the Court's unprecedented restriction of the police forces of the states would not interfere seriously with their work. On the contrary, he reasoned, "we have learned the lesson of history, ancient and modern, that a system of criminal law enforcement which comes to depend on the 'confession' will, in the long run, be less reliable and more subject to abuses than a system which depends on extrinsic evidence independently secured through skillful investigation."[19] "If the exercise of constitutional rights will thwart the effectiveness of a system of law enforcement," he added, "then there is something very wrong with that system."[20]

However, the Court's factual assumptions were not documented adequately. Goldberg had referred loosely to historical and social science literature, but this literature was clearly too vague and general. The Court's documentation was not empirically convincing. It certainly failed to impress four dissenting justices, who took a very dim view of the probable factual consequences of the decision. Justice Harlan stated tersely, "The rule announced today is most ill-conceived and . . . it seriously and unjustifiably fetters perfectly legitimate methods of criminal law enforcement."[21] Justice Potter Stewart wrote that the Court was supported "by no stronger authority than its own rhetoric. . . ." The decision would "frustrate the vital interests of society in preserving the legitimate and proper function of honest and purposeful police investigation."[22] Justice White, in a dissenting opinion joined by Clark and Stewart, pointed out that the decision cast suspicion on the integrity of all police officers, although it was "unsupported by relevant data or current material based upon

[19] Escobedo v. Illinois, 378 U.S. 478, 488–89 (1964).
[20] *Ibid.*, p. 490.
[21] *Ibid.*, p. 493 (dissenting opinion).
[22] *Ibid.*, p. 494 (dissenting opinion).

our own experience."[23] The Court's action might not render the police wholly ineffective, but law enforcement "will be crippled and its task made a great deal more difficult. . . ."[24]

On the basis of factual assumptions unequivocally rejected by the four dissenting justices, the Court had interpreted the Sixth and Fourteenth Amendments and found it necessary to issue, in effect, an important policy directive to the nation's police forces. To be sure, the Escobedo decision hardly reflected the plain meaning of the Sixth Amendment, which clearly refers to the right to counsel during the trial procedure and not before it. Nor could the decision be simply deduced from the traditional idea of due process. As Judge Henry J. Friendly remarked, "That due process requires the aid of counsel before a suspect responds to every inquiry from the police is nothing like so clear. No legal procedures or rules are at play; the question put is, or ought to be, solely one of fact."[25] The Court's decision was clearly a dialectical product of constitutional principles interpreted in the context of extralegal factual assumptions regarding police behavior and the probable social consequences that would follow if such behavior was checked. The Escobedo ruling stirred up widespread uneasiness, not because the Court had pumped meaning into the Sixth and Fourteenth Amendments but because Goldberg's opinion gave rise the impression that the Court was acting on the basis of unsupportable factual assumptions or, worse, was making policy decisions in the dark.

Two years later, in the Miranda case, the Court spelled out the full import of the procedural guarantees announced in Escobedo. Chief Justice Warren, speaking for the majority of five, ruled in general that "basic rights that are enshrined in our Constitution—that 'No person . . . shall be compelled in any criminal case to be a witness against himself,' and that 'the accused shall . . . have the Assistance of Counsel,' "[26] are rights that operate in police stations as well as in federal and state courtrooms. More to the point, Warren affirmed that a criminal suspect "must be warned prior to any questioning that he has the right to remain

[23] *Ibid.*, pp. 498–99 (dissenting opinion).
[24] *Ibid.*, p. 499 (dissenting opinion).
[25] Henry J. Friendly, "The Bill of Rights as a Code of Criminal Procedure," 53 *California Law Review* 929, 946 (1965).
[26] Miranda v. Arizona, 384 U.S. 436, 442 (1966).

silent, that anything he says can be used against him in a court of law, that he has the right to the presence of an attorney, and that if he cannot afford an attorney one will be appointed for him prior to any questioning if he so desires."[27] Furthermore, Warren noted that while an individual could waive these rights, the prosecution would bear the burden of proof in demonstrating that a waiver was voluntary.

The chief justice's opinion was based on two critical factual assumptions analogous to those advanced in the Escobedo case. First, Warren stated that "the modern practice of in-custody interrogation is psychologically rather physically orientated" and that police usually attempt to elicit incriminating evidence from a criminal suspect through the art of psychological manipulation.[28] Second, he declared that experience showed that the termination of psychological methods of interrogation would not result in less efficient law enforcement. But these factual assumptions, unlike Goldberg's, were elaborately documented.

Warren conceded at first that full knowledge of what occurs in police interrogation rooms was not available. But "a valuable source of information about present police practices . . . may be found in various police manuals and texts which document procedures employed with success in the past, and which recommend various other effective tactics."[29] These manuals, he contended, are used extensively by police agencies and present a stark picture of the intimidating practices employed throughout the country. Citing numerous excerpts from police manuals, Warren described thoroughly the psychological techniques and milieu of the interrogation process. "It is obvious that such an interrogation environment is created for no purpose other than to subjugate the individual to the will of the examiner."[30] "Unless adequate protective devices are employed to dispel the compulsion inherent in custodial surroundings, no statement

[27] *Ibid.*, p. 479.
[28] *Ibid.*, p. 448.
[29] *Ibid.* Warren, it may be noted, had been a law enforcement official for many years. As a county district attorney and as the attorney general of California, he had a first-hand knowledge of police interrogation methods and needed no textbooks to know what went on in police stations.
[30] *Ibid.*, p. 457.

obtained from the defendant can truly be the product of his free choice."[31] On the other hand, Warren emphasized that a more scrupulous regard for the basic constitutional rights called into question by psychological interrogation practices would not only be in the interest of the dignity of the individual but would also enhance "the integrity of the fact finding processes in court."[32]

The chief justice explained that the Court's decision was not intended to interfere with the traditional function of the police: "The limits we have placed on the interrogation process should not constitute an undue interference with a proper system of law enforcement."[33] He noted that the record of the Federal Bureau of Investigation demonstrated that it was able to operate effectively under similar restrictions. He pointed out that the experience of police in England, Scotland, India, and Ceylon, as well as of the military police in the United States, suggested that there has been "no marked detrimental effect on criminal law enforcement in these jurisdictions as a result of these rules." In short, Warren insisted, "lawlessness will not result from warning an individual of his rights or allowing him to exercise them."[34]

Despite the Court's efforts at documentation, its factual assumptions were sharply challenged by four dissenting justices. The police manuals, which the Court had used as its chief source of extralegal data, were curtly dismissed by Justice Tom C. Clark as "merely writings in this field by professors and some police officers." "Not one," he observed, "is shown by the record here to be the official manual of any police department, much less in universal use in crime detection."[35] Clark also found the Court's appraisal of the probable consequences of its decision to be wanting. "Such a strict constitutional specific inserted at the nerve center of crime detection may well kill the patient." Therefore, he continued, "since there is at this time a paucity of information and an almost total lack of empirical knowledge on the practical operation of requirements truly comparable to those announced by the

---

[31] *Ibid.*, p. 458.
[32] *Ibid.*, p. 466.
[33] *Ibid.*, p. 481.
[34] *Ibid.*, p. 489.
[35] *Ibid.*, p. 499 (dissenting opinion).

majority, I would be more restrained lest we go too far too fast."[36]

Justice Harlan, joined by Stewart and White, also argued that the decision would have dangerous consequences. Harlan wrote that the Court had strained the meaning of both the Constitution and history without being able to "make the powerful showing that its new rules are plainly desirable in the context of our society, something which is surely demanded before those rules are engrafted onto the Constitution and imposed on every State and county in the land."[37] "What the Court largely ignores," Harlan contended, "is that its rules impair, if they will not eventually serve wholly to frustrate, an instrument of law enforcement that has long and quite reasonably been thought worth the price paid for it."[38] In the final analysis "the Court is taking a real risk with society's welfare in imposing its new regime on the country. The social costs of crime are too great to call the new rules anything but a hazardous experimentation."[39]

Justice White, in a dissenting opinion endorsed by Harlan and Stewart, protested most vigorously that the Court's factual assumptions were empirically inadequate. White noted first that the Court's action in extending the constitutional right against self-incrimination to police stations had "no significant support in the history of the privilege or in the language of the Fifth Amendment."[40] Nevertheless, he reasoned that while it was clear that the decision was "at odds" with history and a "departure" from precedent, this did not prove that the Court "has exceeded its powers or that the Court is wrong or unwise in its present interpretation of the Fifth Amendment." The decision did, however, underscore the obvious: "The Court has not discovered or found the law in making today's decision, nor has it derived it from some irrefutable sources; what it has done is to make new law and new public policy in much the same way that it has in the course of interpreting other great clauses of the Constitution.

---

[36] *Ibid.*, pp. 500–501 (dissenting opinion).
[37] *Ibid.*, p. 515 (dissenting opinion).
[38] *Ibid.*, p. 516 (dissenting opinion).
[39] *Ibid.*, p. 517 (dissenting opinion).
[40] *Ibid.*, p. 526 (dissenting opinion).

This is what the Court historically has done. Indeed, it is what it must do and will continue to do until and unless there is some fundamental change in the constitutional distribution of governmental powers."[41] Obviously White did not wish to quarrel with the lawmaking or policy-making functions of the Court. But it was necessary, he stated emphatically, to examine the factual basis of the Court's rulings and to evaluate their consequences in terms of the long-range interests of society. Policy-making decisions "cannot rest alone on syllogism, metaphysics or some ill-defined notions of natural justice, although each will perhaps play its part." Instead, he argued, such decisions confirm that it is the duty of the Court to consider all the interests and factors involved, "at least insofar as the relevant materials are available; and if the necessary considerations are not treated in the record or obtainable from some other reliable source, the Court should not proceed to formulate fundamental policies based on speculation alone."[42]

Most significantly, White argued that there was no new available knowledge to justify the Court's precedent-breaking decision. In his view police manuals were not reliable sources of data on which to form assumptions regarding police interrogation practices. "Judged by any of the standards for empirical investigation utilized in the social sciences the factual basis for the Court's premise is patently inadequate."[43] What made this such a serious matter, White suggested, was the debilitating effect the decision would have on law enforcement.

The *Escobedo* and *Miranda* cases demonstrate quite clearly that the Court does "make policy decisions by going outside established 'legal' criteria found in precedent, statute and constitution."[44] More important, each case suggests that whenever the Court abandons precedent and overtly makes constitutional law, the rationality of the new ruling may be open to question if the Court is unable to demonstrate that its decision was based on

[41] *Ibid.*, p. 531 (dissenting opinion).
[42] *Ibid.*, p. 532 (dissenting opinion).
[43] *Ibid.*, p. 533 (dissenting opinion).
[44] Robert Dahl, "Decision-Making in a Democracy: The Supreme Court as National Policy-Maker," 6 *Journal of Public Law* 279 (1957).

adequate empirical data. In other words, creative lawmaking cases not only invite the use of social science, but, as Justice White's dissenting opinion in the Miranda case intimates, they almost oblige the Court to use social science findings.

White's dissenting opinion in the Miranda case was particularly interesting. Not too long ago one might have expected a conservative justice like White to criticize the Court for overtly making constitutional law and for relying on empirical data instead of precedent. But White freely admitted what most conservative justices have been reluctant in the past to acknowledge —that, in general, the meaning of the Constitution cannot be deduced simply by way of syllogism from the exact wording of its provisions, and that the Court does not merely find law but often makes it. White also confirmed that the Court could not rationally interpret the Constitution in a legal vacuum. As a policy-making body, the Court had to consider not only the constitutional text but also the factual consequences of its decisions. Such evaluations, he emphasized, had to be made on the basis of all relevant material and data, which preferably should meet the empirical standards of social science.

In view of the traditional tension between law and social science, there was more than a note of irony in White's strenuous objection to the Court's use of police manuals. White was not disturbed because the Court had based its interpretation of the Constitution on extralegal facts. What bothered him was that the manuals did not provide the Court with an adequate empirical understanding of police interrogation practices. Whereas in the past a conservative justice would probably have been quick to rebuke his liberal brethren for using social science, in the Miranda case the liberal majority found itself in the anomalous position of being criticized by the conservative minority for not using social science. It is worth observing that what White did not say may be as instructive as what he did say. White did not infer that the Court should use social science only when it upheld legislation or when it was relying on a formal or informal principle of presumptive constitutionality. On the contrary, he effectively suggested that the Court could profitably use social science whenever it went beyond precedent and overtly made constitutional law. Finally, if it is granted that every decision either to apply or to abandon precedent actually constitutes a policy judgment, then implicit in White's argument is the suggestion that the Court should inform itself of social science findings even in cases in which it merely applies established law.

Social Science and Social Change

It is doubtlessly true, as Felix Frankfurter has remarked, that "the types of cases now calling for decision to a considerable extent require investigation of voluminous literature far beyond the law reports and other legal writings."[45] The question arises whether some justices are more inclined than others to resort to extralegal material in general and social science in particular. Obviously not all Supreme Court justices have been favorably predisposed toward social science. Yet others, such as the liberals Brandeis and Cardozo, staunchly advocated the use of social science. It is reasonable to assume that the liberal members of the Court are more likely to cite extralegal material (and, whenever possible, social science) in their opinions because they will be less hesitant than conservative members to render creative lawmaking decisions that cannot rationally be explained simply on the basis of established precedents.

Needless to say, there are several conceptions of the "liberal" justice. Traditionally, liberals and conservatives were thought to differ primarily on the basis of their conception of the nature of the judicial role or function, liberals believing in judicial activism and loose construction and conservatives believing in judicial restraint and strict construction. But Glendon Schubert has written that it is the "substantive policy differences of contemporary politics, and therefore of contemporary liberalism and conservatism, and not primarily differences in judicial role conceptions, that have divided the Court. The differences in role concepts have been important, but not as the cause of differences among the justices; rather the talk about role concepts . . . has

[45] Ferguson v. Moore-McCormack Lines, 352 U.S. 521, 547 (1957) (dissenting opinion).

served as a smokescreen to disguise and cover up the tracks of the underlying substantive ideological differences."[46] It follows from this view that the contemporary liberal justice will be receptive to change and strongly committed to political, economic, and social reform. More specifically, the ideal liberal justice will be firmly committed to the rights of all citizens regardless of race or class. When a choice has to be made between the civil rights of the individual and the power of government, he will tend to vote in favor of the individual. The liberal justice will support far-reaching legislative reforms and seek to preserve traditional civil rights; he will also attempt to expand the scope of the Bill of Rights to encompass new situations and to cover individuals previously left unprotected.[47] Most important, the liberal justice will not view law primarily as an abstract set of principles. He will be particularly concerned with the actual operation and effects of law. Thus he will shun abstract legal syllogisms and will endeavor to make constitutional law that reflects empirical reality. In short, the interests and knowledge of the ideal liberal justice will not be limited to formal legal materials. He will view man not simply as a legal animal but as a political, social, and economic animal as well. Believing that all knowledge is relevant to law, liberal justices will cite extralegal material more often than conservatives and will be favorably predisposed to social science.

During the past fifty years liberal justices have cited extralegal material more often than conservative justices. Chester Newland has pointed out that after Brandeis joined the Supreme Court in 1916, for a period of nine years he was "the only member of the Court . . . who cited extra-judicial writings."[48] From 1916 to 1957, Newland reports, six justices never cited learned journals, and seven justices did so in only one or two opinions.

---

[46] Glendon Schubert, *The Constitutional Polity* (Boston: Boston University Press, 1970), p. 79. While role concepts do not generally appear to be the crucial factor in determining whether a justice is liberal or conservative, it should be noted that Felix Frankfurter stands as an exception. Frankfurter was a conservative judge in the sense that he consistently preached the idea of judicial self-restraint.

[47] Harold J. Spaeth, *The Warren Court: Cases and Commentary* (San Francisco: Chandler Publishing Co., 1966), pp. 22–23.

[48] Chester A. Newland, "Innovation in Judicial Techniques: The Brandeis Opinion," 42 *Southwestern Social Science Quarterly* 22, 24 (1961).

The six justices who did not cite learned journals were Edward
D. White, Joseph McKenna, William R. Day, Willis Van Devanter, Mahlon Pitney, and John H. Clarke. The seven who rarely
cited learned journals were "Holmes (twice), Butler (twice),
Taft (once), Sutherland (once), Sanford (once), Roberts (once),
and McReynolds (once)." With the possible exception of
Holmes, none of these justices can be regarded as liberals. In fact,
all of the justices in this group of thirteen, who were on the
bench between 1932 and 1937, opposed the New Deal.[49] On the
other hand, Newland has found that, besides Brandeis and
Cardozo, the six justices who have cited learned journals most
frequently were "all Roosevelt appointees: Frankfurter, Douglas,
Black, Jackson, Rutledge, and Reed."[50]

Presently, as a result of President Nixon's conception of judicial fitness, the liberal contingent on the Court has been reduced to Justices William O. Douglas, William J. Brennan, and
Thurgood Marshall. Liberal justices are not equally liberal on
every issue,[51] and while it seems true that liberals in the past have
been more inclined than conservatives to cite extralegal material,
particularly social science findings, an important exception should
be noted. The liberal justice who feels competent to answer the
basic historical question, that is, one who prefers to apply the
"fixed" meaning of the Constitution derived from the precise
wording of the text or divined from the intentions of the framers,
may be less inclined to use social science than other liberal
justices. This is not to imply that the use of history necessarily
precludes the use of social science, but one should realize that
a liberal justice may favor a historical approach to judicial interpretation. Some justices, as Charles Miller notes, may simply be
"history-minded."[52]

Justice Black, for example, took the general position that the
meaning of the Constitution is plainly revealed by a literal reading of its provisions. Black suggested that not only is the meaning
of the Constitution invariably clear, but also its meaning does

[49] Van Devanter, McReynolds, Sutherland, Butler, and Roberts.
[50] Newland, "Innovation in Judicial Techniques," p. 26.
[51] See Spaeth, *The Warren Court*, p. 27.
[52] Charles A. Miller, *The Supreme Court and the Uses of History* (Cambridge,
Mass.: Belknap Press, 1969), p. 198.

not change. For Black, then, the equal-protection clause did not suddenly in 1954 mean that public school segregation was unconstitutional. As far as he was concerned, the equal-protection clause had always banned school segregation.[53] Although Black frequently emphasized the all-revealing character of the words of the Constitution, he did not deny the obvious simplicity of the historical approach to judicial interpretation. "While I realize that an argument based on the meaning of words lacks the scope, and no doubt the appeal, of broad policy discussions and philosophical discourses . . . for me the language of the Amendment is the crucial place to look in construing a written document such as our Constitution."[54] While Black probably would not have conceded that the meaning of broad constitutional principles like due process and equal protection is often dialectically related to the Court's finding of extralegal facts, he did suggest that "constitutional rights [can] turn on the resolution of a factual dispute." On such occasions the Court is "duty-bound to make an independent examination of the evidence in the record."[55]

Needless to say, Black's argument that the meaning of the Constitution remains constant is difficult to reconcile with the fact that the Court does not simply find or discover the meaning of the Constitution but often infuses meaning into the constitutional text. His simplistic and historically oriented conception of the process of judicial interpretation would encumber a creative lawmaking Court and cannot be reconciled with the fact that judicial decisions frequently do represent, as he has put it, the "Court's more enlightened theories of what is best for our society."[56] Whether the Court should infuse meaning into the Constitution is clearly a moot question. Obviously the Court has little choice in the matter when it seeks to apply a broad constitutional principle like equal protection to disparate fact situations. The meaning of the principle of equal protection, as

[53] Harper v. Virginia State Board of Elections, 383 U.S. 663, 677–78, n. 7 (1966) (dissenting opinion).
[54] Katz v. United States, 389 U.S. 347, 365 (1967) (dissenting opinion).
[55] Brookhart v. Janis, 384 U.S. 1, 4 (1966).
[56] Harper v. Virginia State Board of Elections, 383 U.S. 663, 677 (1966) (dissenting opinion).

is the case with other broad constitutional principles, is not fully known, nor is it unalterably fixed. The truth is, as Justice Douglas has written, that "notions of what constitutes equal treatment for the purpose of the Equal Protection Clause *do* change."[57]

Briefly, then, because liberal justices are fundamentally committed to change and reform, they favor a creative lawmaking role for the Court that is relatively unrestricted by the authority of precedent. Thus they will be inclined to resort generally to extralegal material and particularly to social science in order to make and explain their lawmaking decisions. As might be expected, the opinions of Justices Douglas and Brennan from 1960 to 1968 show numerous citations from extralegal material. Douglas has resorted to myriad extralegal materials, including social science and history as well as philosophy and literature. He has cited journals like the *Annals* of the American Academy of Political and Social Science[58] and such authors as John Hazard,[59] George Kennan,[60] Hannah Arendt,[61] George Orwell,[62] Alfred Kinsey,[63] and Jacques Barzun.[64] Needless to say, he has also referred to traditional academic works in political science[65] and economics.[66] Brennan has also cited the *Annals*[67] and traditional works in political science. He used Bentley's *The Process of Government* and Truman's *The Governmental Process* to document the extralegal fact that "groups which find themselves unable to achieve their objectives through the ballot frequently turn to the courts."[68]

[57] *Ibid.*, p. 669.

[58] Poe v. Ullman, 367 U.S. 497, 511 (1961) (dissenting opinion); Communist Party v. Control Board, 367 U.S. 1, 173 (1961) (dissenting opinion).

[59] McNeal v. Culver, 365 U.S. 109, 118 (1961) (concurring opinion).

[60] Bantam Books, Inc. v. Sullivan, 372 U.S. 58, 73 (1963) (concurring opinion).

[61] DuBois Clubs v. Clark, 389 U.S. 309, 314 (1967) (dissenting opinion).

[62] Gibson v. Florida Legislative Committee, 372 U.S. 539, 575 (1963) (dissenting opinion).

[63] Boutilier v. Immigration Service, 387 U.S. 118, 130 (1967) (dissenting opinion).

[64] Gideon v. Wainwright, 372 U.S. 335, 349 (1963) (concurring opinion).

[65] Wright v. Rockefeller, 376 U.S. 52, 66 (1964) (dissenting opinion).

[66] Baltimore and Ohio Railway Co. v. United States, 386 U.S. 372, 447 (1966) (dissenting opinion).

[67] Head v. New Mexico Board, 374 U.S. 424, 439 (1963) (concurring opinion).

[68] N.A.A.C.P. v. Button, 371 U.S. 415, 429–30, n. 12 (1963).

A good example of Brennan's use of extralegal materials, especially social science findings, is his long concurring opinion in the case of Abington School District v. Schempp,[69] decided in 1963. In this case the Court held that the First Amendment, "in the light of history," prohibited the state of Pennsylvania from prescribing an official prayer for use in public schools.[70] Brennan pointed out that "an awareness of history and an appreciation of the aims of the Founding Fathers do not always resolve concrete problems."[71] "A too literal quest for the advice of the Founding Fathers" was "futile and misdirected" because it is obvious that "the historical record is at best ambiguous, and statements can readily be found to support either side of the proposition."[72] Turning instead to the sociological question of the effects of prayer reading in schools, Brennan stated that even though children had the option of excusing themselves from prayer-reading sessions, such an option "subjects them to a cruel dilemma." Children are reluctant "to be stigmatized as atheists or nonconformists"; they are disinclined "to step out of line or to flout 'peer-group norms.'" This social science finding "is the widely held view of experts who have studied the behaviors and attitudes of children." Brennan documented this point with extensive citations from social science literature.[73]

It should be noted, however, that while liberals may be more favorably predisposed toward social science than conservatives, there is no necessary reason that conservative justices could not use social science findings—perhaps to document, for example, the adverse consequences a creative lawmaking decision might produce. Social science is not necessarily tied to liberalism. But although the methodology and findings of social science can be considered "value free," obviously social scientists as individuals are not free from biases nor are they uncommitted to values. The personal value preferences of social scientists will influence their selection of the kinds of problems or issues to be studied. Therefore, the social science findings that are available for judi-

[69] Abington School District v. Schempp, 374 U.S. 203 (1963).
[70] *Ibid.*, p. 205.
[71] *Ibid.*, p. 234 (concurring opinion).
[72] *Ibid.*, p. 237 (concurring opinion).
[73] *Ibid.*, p. 290 (concurring opinion).

cial use will reflect the problems that interest social scientists and not the needs of the Court. And since most social scientists are liberals,[74] the available findings of social science will probably be more useful to liberal than to conservative justices. In other words, since most social scientists are concerned in general with the problem of social change,[75] the particular studies they conduct usually deal with the social institutions and patterns of social interraction that such liberal justices as Douglas, Brennan, and Marshall are inclined to believe ought to be changed. Indeed, it was no coincidence that a relatively large body of social science literature dealing with the American Negro was available in 1954, thereby making it possible in the first place for the Court to use social science in the epoch-making Brown case.

It is reasonable to assume that the Court will discover social science findings to be most useful in cases that generally involve demands for social change.[76] An apparent exception are antitrust cases, where the Court will find economic data useful in deciding whether monopolistic practices have been established;[77] the idea is to restrict such practices for the express purpose of maintaining the economic status quo. In general, economic regulation cases involving the taxing and spending powers of government will lend themselves to the use of social science. The Court may use social science findings in the broad field of criminal law, from the stage of arrest to the point of punishment or rehabilitation. For example, studies have raised doubts about the deterrent effects of capital punishment. And if it is true, as Justice Clark has stated, that "our criminal law is to no small extent justified by the assumption of deterrence,"[78] then social science studies which clearly demonstrated that the death penalty was not an effective deterrent would throw new

---

[74] See Henry S. Kariel, *The Decline of American Pluralism* (Stanford, Calif.: Stanford University Press, 1961), pp. 113–37.

[75] See C. Wright Mills, *The Sociological Imagination* (New York: Oxford University Press, 1968).

[76] Cf. Abraham Kaplan, "Behavioral Science and the Law," 19 *Case Western Reserve Law Review* 57 (1967), and Stuart S. Nagel, "Law and the Social Sciences: What Can Social Science Contribute?" 51 *American Bar Association Journal* 356 (1965).

[77] See, for example, United States v. Von's Grocery Co., 384 U.S. 270 (1966).

[78] Breithaupt v. Abram, 352 U.S. 432, 439 (1957).

empirical light on commonly held factual assumptions regarding capital punishment. Social science could be indispensable to the Court if it decided to flesh out its 1972 *per curiam* decision in Furman v. Georgia. It held capital punishment to be a violation of the Eighth and Fourteenth Amendments but left open the real possibility that redrawn legislation uniformly imposing the death penalty might still meet the test of constitutionality.

It is not altogether inconceivable that social science findings could provide the Court with the factual grounds for effecting even more startling changes in the field of criminal law. For as Frankfurter once remarked, "The criminal law, not merely its notions of insanity, but the whole domain of criminology, derives from, or is based on, assumptions which one is again and again convinced are outmoded assumptions of fact."[79] Therefore, the very notions of criminal behavior and criminal responsibility are subject to change in the light of a systematic and firmly established body of social science findings.[80] The Wickersham Commission Reports, published in 1931, were perhaps the first step in this direction in that they represented the first systematic attempt to gain an empirical understanding of the whole criminal law process. For example, the commission surveyed the various political, economic, psychological, and sociological causes of crime but came to the indecisive conclusion that crime is a "complex phenomenon and its complexity must be taken into account both in searching for causes and also in suggesting methods of treatment."[81] Since then, however, fruitful research in criminology has been conducted that suggests the need for far-reaching changes in the whole field of criminal law.[82]

So far there have been no convincing indications that the Court is prepared to commit itself to a social science approach to

[79] Felix Frankfurter, *Of Law and Life and Other Things That Matter: Papers and Addresses of Felix Frankfurter, 1956–1963*, ed. Philip B. Kurland (Cambridge, Mass.: Belknap Press, 1965), p. 13.

[80] See Walter A. Rafalko, "Sociological Evidence as a Criminal Defense," 10 *Criminal Law Quarterly* 77 (1967–68).

[81] Wickersham Commission Reports, *Report on the Causes of Crime*, 1 (Washington, D.C.: U.S. Government Printing Office, 1931): 18.

[82] See Gerhard O. W. Mueller, *Crime, Law and the Scholars: A History of Scholarship in American Criminal Law* (London: Heinemann, 1969).

crime, in opposition to the country's traditional moral and punitive conception of criminal law. This is true though it has been argued that the biological and social sciences "have proved the free moral agent theory of human conduct preposterous in its assumptions and implications."[83] There are at least two cases or slight omens that suggest that the Court might at some point reassess, on the basis of social science findings, conventional factual assumptions regarding the twin concepts of criminal behavior and criminal responsibility. Such a reassessment could, of course, result in dramatic, judicially led changes in American criminal law. The first precursor of such change can be seen in the case of Robinson v. California,[84] decided in 1962, in which the Court invalidated a statute making it a misdemeanor for any person to be addicted to the use of narcotics. On behalf of the Court, Justice Stewart reasoned that because the statute made "the 'status' of narcotic addiction a criminal offense,"[85] it inflicted a cruel and unusual punishment in violation of the Eighth and Fourteenth Amendments. Although Stewart stopped far short of any sociological discussion of crime, he clearly indicated that the Court would not uphold any law that made "disease" a criminal offense. Whether the Court will in the near future come to view crime in general as a social disease is another matter. Yet Stewart's closing remark—"Even one day in prison would be a cruel and unusual punishment for the 'crime' of having a common cold"[86]—could be richly prophetic.

More than the faint outline of a social science approach to crime can be seen in the case of Powell v. Texas,[87] decided in 1968. Here the Court upheld the conviction of the appellant, who had been found guilty of being intoxicated in a public place. A county court had established the factual finding that chronic alcoholism was a disease that destroyed the afflicted person's will to resist drink, and that as a chronic alcoholic the appellant had involuntarily appeared in public "under a com-

---

[83] Geoffry Sawyer, *Law and Society* (Oxford: Clarendon Press, 1965), p. 194.
[84] Robinson v. California, 370 U.S. 660 (1962).
[85] *Ibid.*, p. 666.
[86] *Ibid.*, p. 667.
[87] Powell v. Texas, 392 U.S. 514 (1968).

pulsion symptomatic of the disease of chronic alcoholism." But the county court had ruled that chronic alcoholism was not a legal defense. Justice Marshall, speaking for the Court, rejected the county court's factual findings. He pointed out that only a primitive knowledge regarding alcoholism was available, and since there was little consensus on the concept of alcoholism as a disease, the Court was not in a position to announce "an important and wide-ranging new constitutional principle."[88] Marshall reasoned that the cruel-and-unusual-punishment clause as interpreted in the Robinson case could not be applied to the present circumstances, since "the appellant was convicted, not for being a chronic alcoholic, but for being in public while drunk on a particular occasion."[89] If the Court had been willing to view alcoholism as a disease, the striking result, in Marshall's words, "could only be a constitutional doctrine of criminal responsibility."[90]

Thus the majority soberly backed away from announcing a new doctrine of criminal responsibility, with all its momentous implications for change in the field of criminal law. But Justice Abe Fortas, in a dissenting opinion joined by Douglas, Brennan, and Stewart, argued that there were sufficient data to provide a context for analyzing the issues at hand. These data should not dictate a conclusion, Fortas wrote, because the Court would first have to determine whether the Constitution limits the circumstances under which punishment can be inflicted and whether those circumstances, if they exist, applied in the present case. The basic principle called into play in both the Robinson case and the present case is that "a person may not be punished if the condition essential to constitute the defined crime is part of the pattern of his disease and is occasioned by a compulsion symptomatic of the disease."[91] Therefore, Fortas concluded, "the findings in this case, read against the background of the medical and sociological data . . . compel the conclusion that the infliction upon the appellant of a criminal penalty for being in-

[88] *Ibid.*, p. 521.
[89] *Ibid.*, p. 532.
[90] *Ibid.*, p. 534.
[91] *Ibid.*, p. 569 (dissenting opinion).

toxicated in a public place would be 'cruel and inhuman punishment' within the prohibition of the Eighth Amendment."[92]

Social science findings may also be useful to the Court in cases
that deal with the religion and speech guarantees of the First
Amendment. As we have already noted, Justice Brennan has
used social science findings to document the fact that even
though children may be permitted to excuse themselves from
officially prescribed prayer sessions in school, they would still
be subject to a measure of coercion in violation of the establish-
ment-of-religion clause of the First Amendment.[93] Free-speech
cases, especially those involving the issue of obscenity, may
present occasions for the use of social science. For example,
when the Court first dealt directly with the issue of obscenity in
the case of Roth v. United States, decided in 1957,[94] Justice
Brennan reasoned on behalf of the Court that "implicit in the
history of the First Amendment is the rejection of obscenity as
utterly without redeeming social importance."[95] In short, the
Court ruled that obscenity was not within the area of constitutionally protected speech. Justice Douglas dissented, arguing
that the state could legislate against pornography only if it
could show that pornographic material induced antisocial behavior. And since there was no "dependable literature on the
effect of obscene literature on human conduct,"[96] he concluded
that the First Amendment prohibited both the federal and
state governments from blocking the flow of obscene material.
In subsequent obscenity cases Douglas pointed out that a causal
relationship between obscenity and antisocial behavior had not
been proven[97] and that exposure to obscene literature might
even "prevent anti-social conduct."[98]

In 1969 Douglas's empirical approach to the issue of obscenity
became majority doctrine in the case of Stanley v. Georgia.[99]

[92] *Ibid.*, pp. 569–70 (dissenting opinion).
[93] Abington School District v. Schempp, 374 U.S. 203 (1963) (concurring opinion).
[94] Roth v. United States, 354 U.S. 476 (1957).
[95] *Ibid.*, p. 484.
[96] *Ibid.*, p. 511 (dissenting opinion).
[97] Memoirs v. Massachusetts, 383 U.S. 413, 431 (1966) (dissenting opinion).
[98] Ginzburg v. United States, 383 U.S. 463, 491 (1966) (dissenting opinion).
[99] Stanley v. Georgia, 394 U.S. 557 (1969).

The Court took a decisive step away from its historically oriented position on obscenity as announced in the Roth case. Justice Thurgood Marshall, speaking for the Court, ruled that the First Amendment, as made applicable to the states through the due-process clause of the Fourteenth Amendment, prohibited a state from making the private possession of obscene material a crime. He reasoned that the Roth precedent did not apply to the present circumstances because it dealt with distribution, whereas the immediate constitutional question was one of possession. Although the factual problem of a causal relationship between exposure to obscene material and antisocial behavior had not been deemed relevant in the Roth case, Marshall emphasized in this instance that the Georgia statute assumed that "exposure to obscene materials may lead to deviant sexual behavior or crimes of sexual violence." Citing available social science findings, Marshall stated, "There appears to be little empirical basis for that assertion."[100] He continued, "Given the present state of knowledge, the State may no more prohibit mere possession of obscene matter on the ground that it may lead to antisocial conduct than it may prohibit possession of chemistry books on the ground that they may lead to the manufacture of home-made spirits."[101] It may very well be that on the basis of recent research, which suggests that exposure to obscene material does not induce antisocial behavior,[102] the Court may at some point completely abandon the Roth precedent.

Commonly held factual assumptions have generally been offered as reasons for excluding certain categories of people and kinds of social institutions from the procedural and substantive guarantees and restrictions of the Bill of Rights. When the Court is asked to extend the scope and substance of the Bill of Rights, it may wish to reconsider factual assumptions concerning patterns of social behavior and the functional needs of various social institutions. Women, children, soldiers, homosexuals, and

[100] *Ibid.*, p. 566.
[101] *Ibid.*, p. 567.
[102] See *The Report of the Commission on Obscenity and Pornography* (New York: Bantam Books, 1970).

mental patients form some categories of people who have never been fully protected by the Bill of Rights. Mental patients, for example, have long been incarcerated in private and state hospitals without benefit of adequate legal procedure and without ever being charged with indictable offenses.[103] Curiously enough, civil rights have not been fully operative in four of our basic social institutions—schools, hospitals, prisons, and the army—because it has generally been believed that these institutions could not operate effectively in terms of the sundry restrictions that flow from the Bill of Rights. Obviously these institutions must curtail some of the basic rights guaranteed by the Constitution. But there is no necessary reason that the Bill of Rights should pass completely into limbo, even in a prison. When constitutional issues arise involving such basic rights as free speech and press for the inmates of these total institutions, the Court could use social science to reassess the factual assumptions that have served as justifications for limiting these rights.

The United States is undoubtedly a litigious society. Tocqueville noted that "[s]carcely any political question arises in the United States that is not resolved sooner or later into a judicial question."[104] Needless to say, all sorts of pressing social problems —poverty, divorce, abortion, housing—can be translated into questions of due process or equal protection. And since "[d]ecisions on questions of equal protection and due process are based not on abstract logic but on empirical foundations,"[105] as Justice Harlan has remarked, the Court could look to social science for help in understanding fact situations that may suggest the need for new conceptions of what constitutes due process and equal protection. For that matter, insofar as social science is conterminous with the total scope of institutional law, and since law is ultimately concerned with social behavior, "there would seem to be almost no area in which the influence and the findings of the social and behavioral sciences might not be used to explain

[103] Justine Wise Polier, *The Rule of Law and the Role of Psychiatry* (Baltimore: Johns Hopkins Press, 1968), pp. 45–57.

[104] Alexis de Tocqueville, *Democracy in America*, ed. Phillips Bradley, 2 vols. (New York: Vintage Books, 1961), 1: 290.

[105] Katzenbach v. Morgan, 384 U.S. 641, 668 (1966) (dissenting opinion).

and improve the law in its daily operation upon the members of our society."[106]

Social Science and Political Prudence

Although social science findings can be useful in many of the penumbral areas of constitutional law involving such issues as obscenity, capital punishment, and criminal responsibility, the Court has not yet begun to use social science in a regular manner. The Court's casual use of social science presumably can be explained by the wide gaps in the general literature of social science. An even more critical consideration may be that many social science findings are still very tentative and consist of isolated conclusions rather than the firm explanations of a systematic body of research. Moreover, it is clear that the traditional tension between law and social science has just recently begun to diminish. Leonard Cottrell has observed that there still has not been "any general systematic exploitation of social science resources by the legal profession in theory, research, teaching, or practise."[107] Be that as it may, the Supreme Court has indicated that it considers social science to be an authoritative body of knowledge, and it is reasonable to expect social science to play an increasingly influential role in future constitutional adjudication. But since many social science findings are tentative and remain subject to revision, it may very well be asked how the Court should use social science in the making of constitutional law. If the Court began to use social science in an indiscriminate manner, the results could be disconcerting. If, for example, social science were to prove that children who do not pray in school tend to become neurotic, a Court that blindly followed social science would be inclined to rule that compulsory prayer sessions in public schools did not violate the First Amendment.

[106] Samuel M. Fahr and Ralph H. Ojemann, "The Use of Social and Behavioral Science Knowledge in Law," 48 *Iowa Law Review* 59 (1962–63). Cf. Michael Katz, "The Unmasking of Dishonest Pretensions: Toward an Interpretation of the Role of Social Science in Constitutional Litigation," 6 *American Sociologist* 54, 57–58 (1971).

[107] Leonard S. Cottrell, Jr., "The Interrelationships of Law and Social Science," in Harry W. Jones, ed., *Law and the Social Role of Science* (New York: Rockefeller University Press, 1966), p. 108.

Or if social science were to prove that integrated public schools were more harmful to Negroes than segregated schools, a Court that was wedded too closely to social science might rule that school segregation was constitutional. Of course, these are hypothetical situations, but they do illustrate the kinds of problems that could arise if the Court ever permitted social science to dictate its decisions.

However, there is no necessary reason to believe that the ultimate result of the Court's use of social science will be that social scientists rather than the Court makes constitutional law. Although the Court uses social science, it does not logically follow that social scientists will be able to use the Court. Needless to say, the Court alone selects, out of a range of alternative courses of legal action, the one that it thinks best serves the needs of the nation. Moreover, the Court alone determines the pattern of legal reasoning that goes into a given judicial opinion and thus the particular factual questions that are raised and that need to be answered. Therefore, it can hardly be doubted that the Court, and not the social scientist, retains absolute authority to determine the legal relevance of all social science findings and whether in any given instance a specific social science finding is to be used.

The underlying fear that social science could at some point replace the normative principles of the Constitution probably stems from a basic misunderstanding of what social science can and cannot do. In general, social science can provide the Court with empirical explanations of society. That is, social science can explain the etiology of social behavior, the effects of law on social behavior, the probable consequences of legal decisions, and how values or goals can best be realized. In the simplest of terms, social science can resolve factual problems. But while social science can be used to answer many of the factual questions that may engage the attention of the Court, it cannot be used to answer the ultimate questions a policy-making Court must ponder. The Court is an arbiter of facts. But, more important, it is also an arbiter of values. Therefore, the Court must be concerned primarily with the fundamental democratic ideals the Constitution was designed to serve.

The Constitution, as can readily be seen from its preamble, is not an end in itself. Instead the Constitution presupposes as an article of faith that fundamental democratic ideals are valid and should be implemented. As Justice Brennan has suggested, democratic ideals can generally be understood in terms of the belief in the inviolable dignity of man.[108] The highest task of the Court, then, is not simply to render decisions that are literally consistent with the letter and form of the Constitution; nor, for that matter, is it simply to stretch the wording of the Constitution in order to meet the functional prerequisites of a changing society. The latter may be the basic task of the Court, but its highest calling is to make constitutional law in the light of the natural law underlying the Constitution, to make law that affirms and serves the democratic belief in the dignity of man. Obviously this is no easy task, because the constitutional roads leading to this higher end are lined with alternative signposts that reflect competing values, diverse moral codes, and multiple social objections— all of which must be read and studied by the Court. To be sure, empirical considerations will color the Court's judgment about what particular route it should follow. But essentially the Court is always faced with the task of weighing and choosing values. Social science cannot tell the Court what values should be preferred—whether, for example, free speech is a more choice-worthy value than public order. That is, social science cannot be used to verify or falsify value commitments. As Arnold Brecht has put it, "Science does not enable us to state in *absolute terms,* whether the purposes pursued by us or by others is good or bad, right or wrong, just or unjust, nor which of several conflicting purposes is more valuable than the other."[109] In short, then, social science findings can be used in the making of law, but they cannot displace law.

Although social science cannot be used to test the validity of the principles of the Constitution, it can be used to preserve their

---

[108] William J. Brennan, Jr., "Law and Social Sciences," in Alan F. Westin, ed., *The Supreme Court: Views from Inside* (New York: W. W. Norton, 1961), p. 144.

[109] Arnold Brecht, *Political Theory: The Foundations of Twentieth-Century Political Thought* (Princeton, N.J.: Princeton University Press, 1959), p. 124.

vitality. The value of the Constitution depends in the final analysis on whether or not it actually provides effective and meaningful legal guidelines for a society constantly confronted by new problems and needs. Surely it is not enough for the Court to be committed to the Constitution as an abstract document. That commitment must be translated into decisions that actively promote the realization of democratic ideals. But if the Court deliberately ignores the empirical insights of social science, the effects could be similar to those of the period of economic due-process adjudication. Then constitutional law was made for a society more imagined than real, and it consequently served vested interests rather than the common interest. Therefore, the Court should use social science to determine whether there are situations in which law arbitrarily grants privileges to some categories of persons or imposes disabilities on others. In the constitutional adjudication that arises out of such situations, social science will then provide the Court with a factual basis for exercising its creative lawmaking power. In other words, the Court should use social science in accord with the Baconian ethic that science should contribute to the relief of man's estate. This means that the Court must not use social science findings that are statements *about* values as if they were actually statements *of* values. For if social science findings were used to subvert the dignity of man, constitutional law would fail in its purpose as a reasoned system of principles that directs the minds and actions of men toward overarching democratic ideals and values that are not and never have been expressions of empirical truth.

Needless to say, in view of the political character of the Court, it would not be a very fruitful exercise to speculate about legal criteria that might indicate how closely and under what specific circumstances the teachings of social science should be followed. For that matter, simply because the Court makes constitutional law on the basis of factual assumptions does not necessarily mean that "there should be a one-to-one linking and testing" of every extralegal fact and an "endless dropping of empirical footnotes to points of law." At the same time, however, it would be "nonsense to say that better documentation of fact cannot ever be relevant to law because the final business of law is not truth but political preference."[110] Clearly, then, in using social science, as in all other matters, the Court must be guided by the high art of political statesmanship. Precisely how social science should be used is a question that can only be resolved on the level of politics. A prudent Court will make use of the empirical insights of social science, knowing that social science cannot answer the ultimate questions of law and that its factual findings do not represent infallible knowledge. Political prudence will confirm that social science should not be used slavishly. In the final analysis prudence will also reveal that while, ideally, "anyone would prefer to found lawmaking upon clearly indisputable facts, the practical choice is often between proceeding in ignorance and following the uncertain, tentative, and far from indisputable teachings of social science such as they are, for the simple reason that clearly indisputable facts are unavailable."[111]

In conclusion, it should be apparent that the Court's use of social science poses an intractable problem. No matter how intimate or distant the formal relationship between law and social science becomes, the Court will always have to cope with the underlying tension that is bound to exist between a discipline that prescribes what society ought to be and one that explains what society is. Whatever else the Court does, it still must reconcile the legal "ought" with the social "is." This reconciliation is achieved as the dialectical fruit of the process of judicial interpretation, wherein the precise meaning of the Constitution is hammered out in the context of specific fact situations. Accordingly facts or events will necessarily influence the precise meaning given to the Constitution, but the Constitution will also reshape social facts. In making constitutional law, the Court cannot simply follow the exact wording of the Constitution, nor can it be guided by facts alone. Yet the Court must be faithful to the spirit of the Constitution, just as it must define facts that ac-

---

[110] Harry Kalvern, Jr., "The Quest for the Middle Range: Empirical Inquiry and Legal Policy," in Geoffrey C. Hazard, Jr., ed., *Law in a Changing America* (Englewood Cliffs, N.J.: Prentice-Hall, 1968), p. 67.

[111] Kenneth Culp Davis, "A System of Judicial Notice Based on Fairness and Convenience," in Roscoe Pound *et al.*, eds., *Perspectives of Law: Essays for Austin Wakeman Scott* (Boston: Little, Brown, 1964), p. 87.

curately reflect empirical reality. For if the Court interprets the Constitution capriciously, or if it defines fact situations in a way that contradicts a systematic and comprehensive body of social science findings, its moral authority will surely be jeopardized. Therefore, the Court's permanent dilemma is that it must be faithful to both the Constitution and the facts, knowing all the while that its fidelity will be transmuted into new meanings for the Constitution and new social facts.

Selected Bibliography

BOOKS

Ashmore, Harry S. *The Negro and the Schools.* 2nd ed. Chapel Hill: University of North Carolina Press, 1954.

Auerbach, Carl A. *The Legal Process: An Introduction to Decision-Making by Judicial, Legislative, Executive, and Administrative Agencies.* San Francisco: Chandler Publishing Co., 1961.

Baritz, Loren. *The Servants of Power: A History of the Use of Social Science in American Industry.* Middletown, Conn.: Wesleyan University Press, 1960.

Barksdale, Hiram C. *The Use of Survey Research Findings as Legal Evidence.* New York: Printer's Ink Books, 1957.

Barzun, Jacques. *Darwin, Marx, Wagner: Critique of a Heritage.* 2nd rev. ed. Garden City, N.Y.: Doubleday Anchor Books, 1958.

Beard, Charles, and Beard, Mary. *The Rise of American Civilization.* New York: Macmillan, 1946.

Becker, Theodore L. *Political Behavioralism and Modern Jurisprudence: A Working Theory and Study in Judicial Decision-Making.* Chicago: Rand McNally, 1964.

Berger, Peter. *Invitation to Sociology: A Humanistic Perspective.* Garden City, N.Y.: Doubleday Anchor Books, 1963.

Berman, Daniel M. *It Is So Ordered: The Supreme Court Rules on School Segregation.* New York: W. W. Norton, 1966.

Bickel, Alexander M. *The Least Dangerous Branch: The Supreme Court at the Bar of Politics.* Indianapolis: Bobbs-Merrill, 1962.

————. *Politics and the Warren Court.* New York: Harper and Row, 1965.

————. *The Supreme Court and the Idea of Progress.* New York: Harper and Row, 1970.

Black, Hugo L. *A Constitutional Faith.* New York: Alfred A. Knopf, 1968.

Blaustein, Albert P., and Ferguson, Clarence E. *Desegregation and the Law.* New Brunswick, N.J.: Rutgers University Press, 1957.

Block, Charles J. *States' Rights: The Law of the Land.* Atlanta: Harrison Co., 1958.

Bodenheimer, Edgar. *Jurisprudence: The Philosophy and Method of the Law.* Cambridge, Mass.: Harvard University Press, 1962.

Boulding, Kenneth E. *The Impact of the Social Sciences.* New Brunswick, N.J.: Rutgers University Press, 1966.

Braithwaite, Richard B. *Scientific Explanation: A Study of the Function of Theory, Probability and Law in Science.* Cambridge: Cambridge University Press, 1964.

Brandeis, Louis D. *The Curse of Bigness: Miscellaneous Papers.* Edited by Osmond K. Fraenkel. Port Washington, N.Y.: Kennikat Press, 1965.

Brecht, Arnold. *Political Theory: The Foundations of Twentieth-Century Political Thought.* Princeton, N.J.: Princeton University Press, 1959.

Bronowski, J. *Science and Human Values.* Harmondsworth: Penguin Books, 1964.

Bryce, James. *The American Commonwealth.* Edited by Louis Hacker. 2 vols. New York: G. P. Putnam's Sons, 1959.

Cahill, Fred V., Jr. *Judicial Legislation.* New York: Ronald Press, 1952.

Cahn, Edmond, ed. *Supreme Court and Supreme Law.* Bloomington: Indiana University Press, 1954.

Cairns, Huntington. *Law and the Social Sciences.* New York: Harcourt, Brace, 1935.

Cardozo, Benjamin N. *The Nature of the Judicial Process.* New Haven, Conn.: Yale University Press, 1961.

———. *The Growth of the Law.* New Haven, Conn.: Yale University Press, 1963.

Carmichael, Peter A. *The South and Segregation.* Washington, D.C.: Public Affairs Press, 1965.

Clark, Kenneth B. *Prejudice and Your Child.* 2nd ed. Boston: Beacon Press, 1966.

Cohen, Felix. *The Legal Conscience: Selected Papers of Felix S. Cohen.* Edited by Lucy K. Cohen. New Haven, Conn.: Yale University Press, 1960.

Cohen, Morris R. *American Thought: A Critical Sketch.* Edited by Felix Cohen. Glencoe, Ill.: Free Press, 1954.

———. *Reason and Nature: The Meaning of the Scientific Method.* New York: Free Press, 1964.

Commager, Henry Steele. *The American Mind: An Interpretation of American Thought and Character since the 1880's.* New Haven, Conn.: Yale University Press, 1950.

Cooley, Charles Horton. *Human Nature and the Social Order.* New York: Charles Scribner's Sons, 1902.

Corwin, Edward S. *The "Higher Law" Background of American Constitutional Law.* Ithaca, N.Y.: Great Seal Books, 1955.

————. *American Constitutional History: Essays by Edward S. Corwin.* Edited by Alpheus Thomas Mason and Gerald Garvey. New York: Harper Torchbooks, 1964.

Cox, Archibald. *The Warren Court: Constitutional Decision as an Instrument of Reform.* Cambridge, Mass.: Harvard University Press, 1968.

Crick, Bernard. *The American Science of Politics: Its Origins and Conditions.* Berkeley and Los Angeles: University of California Press, 1960.

Daly, John J. *The Use of History in the Decisions of the Supreme Court: 1900–1930.* Washington, D.C.: Catholic University of America Press, 1954.

Darwin, Charles. *The Origin of Species.* London: Dent & Sons, 1963.

Davis, James E., *et al. Society and the Law.* Glencoe, Ill.: Free Press, 1962.

Dewey, John. *Freedom and Culture.* New York: Capricorn Books, 1963.

————. *Liberalism and Social Action.* New York: Capricorn Books, 1963.

Dollard, John. *Caste and Class in a Southern Town.* Garden City, N.Y.: Doubleday Anchor Books, 1957.

Durkheim, Émile. *The Rules of Sociological Method.* Translated by S. Solovay and J. Mueller. 8th ed. New York: Free Press, 1966.

Evan, William M. *Law and Sociology: Exploratory Essays.* Glencoe, Ill.: Free Press, 1962.

Ewing, Cortez A. M. *The Judges of the Supreme Court: 1789–1937.* Minneapolis: University of Minnesota Press, 1938.

Fairman, Charles. *Mr. Justice Miller and the Supreme Court.* New York: Russell & Russell, 1966.

Faris, Robert E. L. *Chicago Sociology: 1920–1932.* San Francisco: Chandler Publishing Co., 1967.

Fine, Sidney. *Laissez Faire and the General-Welfare State: A Study of Conflict in American Thought 1865–1901.* Ann Arbor: University of Michigan Press, 1967.

Fletcher, John L., Jr. *The Segregation Case and the Supreme Court.* Boston University Studies in Political Science, no. 4. 1958.

Frank, Jerome. *Courts on Trial.* Princeton, N.J.: Princeton University Press, 1950.

———. *Law and the Modern Mind.* Garden City, N.Y.: Doubleday Anchor Books, 1963.

———. *A Man's Reach.* Edited by Barbara Frank Kristein. New York: Macmillan, 1965.

Frankfurter, Felix. *Mr. Justice Holmes and the Supreme Court.* Cambridge, Mass.: Belknap Press, 1961.

———. *Law and Politics: Occasional Papers of Felix Frankfurter, 1913–1938.* Edited by Archibald MacLeish and E. F. Prichard. New York: Capricorn Books, 1962.

———. *Of Law and Life and Other Things That Matter: Papers and Addresses of Felix Frankfurter, 1956–1963.* Edited by Philip B. Kurland. Cambridge, Mass.: Belknap Press, 1965.

———, ed. *Mr. Justice Brandeis.* New Haven, Conn.: Yale University Press, 1932.

Frankfurter, Felix, and Goldmark, Josephine. *The Case for the Shorter Work Day.* 2 vols. (Brief for defendant in error, Bunting v. Oregon.) New York: National Consumers' League, 1915.

Frankfurter, Felix, and Landis, James M. *The Business of the Supreme Court.* New York: Macmillan, 1927.

Frazier, E. Franklin. *The Negro in the United States.* Rev. ed. New York: Macmillan, 1957.

Freund, Ernst. *The Standards of American Legislation.* Chicago: University of Chicago Press, 1917.

Freund, Paul A. *The Supreme Court of the United States: Its Business, Purposes, and Performance.* Cleveland: World Publishing Co., 1963.

———. *On Law and Justice.* Cambridge, Mass.: Belknap Press, 1968.

Friedman, Leon, ed. *Argument: The Oral Argument before the Supreme Court in Brown v. Board of Education of Topeka, 1952–55.* New York: Chelsea House, 1969.

Garraty, John A., ed. *Quarrels That Have Shaped the Constitution.* New York: Harper and Row, 1964.

Goldmark, Josephine. *Introduction to the Case against Nightwork for Women.* New York: National Consumers' League, 1918.

Goodman, Mary E. *Race Awareness in Young Children.* Rev. ed. New York: Collier Books, 1964.

Greenberg, Jack, and Hill, Herbert. *Citizen's Guide to Desegregation.* Boston: Beacon Press, 1955.

Gurvitch, Georges. *Sociology of Law*. New York: Philosophical Library, 1942.

Handlin, Oscar. *Race and Nationality in American Life*. Garden City, N.Y.: Doubleday Anchor Books, 1957.

Hankin, Gregory, and Hankin, Charlotte A. *Progress of the Law in the United States Supreme Court: 1930–1931*. New York: Macmillan, 1931.

Hart, H. L. A. *The Concept of Law*. Oxford: Clarendon Press, 1963.

Hayek, Friedrich A. *The Counter-Revolution of Science: Studies on the Abuse of Reason*. Glencoe, Ill.: Free Press, 1952.

Hazard, Geoffrey C., Jr., ed. *Law in a Changing America*. Englewood Cliffs, N.J.: Prentice-Hall, 1968.

Hofstadter, Richard. *Social Darwinism in American Thought*. Rev. ed. Boston: Beacon Press, 1966.

Holmes, Oliver Wendell. *The Mind and Faith of Justice Holmes: His Speeches, Essays, Letters and Judicial Opinions*. Edited by Max Lerner. New York: Modern Library, 1943.

———. *Collected Legal Papers*. New York: Peter Smith, 1952.

Hook, Sidney, ed. *Law and Philosophy: A Symposium*. New York: New York University Press, 1964.

Howe, Mark De Wolfe, ed. *Holmes-Pollock Letters*. Cambridge, Mass.: Belknap Press, 1961.

Hughes, Charles Evans. *The Supreme Court of the United States: Its Foundation, Methods and Achievements: An Interpretation*. New York: Columbia University Press, 1928.

Hughes, Graham, ed. *Law, Reason, and Justice: Essays in Legal Philosophy*. New York: New York University Press, 1969.

Humphrey, Hubert H., ed. *School Desegregation: Documents and Commentaries*. New York: Thomas Y. Crowell, 1964.

Hyneman, Charles S. *The Supreme Court on Trial*. New York: Atherton Press, 1963.

Jackson, Robert H. *The Struggle for Judicial Supremacy: A Study of a Crisis in American Power Politics*. New York: Vintage Books, 1941.

———. *The Supreme Court in the American System of Government*. New York: Harper Torchbooks, 1963.

Jones, Harry W., ed. *Law and the Social Role of Science*. New York: Rockefeller University Press, 1966.

Kantorowicz, Herman. *The Definition of Law*. Edited by A. H. Campbell. Cambridge: Cambridge University Press, 1958.

Kaplan, Abraham. *The Conduct of Inquiry: Methodology for Behavioral Science*. San Francisco: Chandler Publishing Co., 1964.

Kellogg, Charles Flint. *NAACP: A History of the National Association for the Advancement of Colored People.* Baltimore: Johns Hopkins Press, 1967.

Kelsen, Hans. *General Theory of Law and State.* Translated by Anders Wedberg. New York: Russell & Russell, 1961.

Kilpatrick, James Jackson. *The Southern Case for School Segregation.* New York: Crowell-Collier Press, 1962.

Konefsky, Samuel J. *The Legacy of Holmes and Brandeis.* New York: Collier Books, 1961.

Konvitz, Milton R., and Rossiter, Clinton, eds. *Aspects of Liberty.* Ithaca, N.Y.: Cornell University Press, 1958.

Kurland, Philip B. *Politics, the Constitution and the Warren Court.* Chicago: University of Chicago Press, 1970.

Lazarsfeld, Paul F., *et al.*, eds. *The Uses of Sociology.* New York: Basic Books, 1967.

Levi, Edward H. *An Introduction to Legal Reasoning.* Chicago: University of Chicago Press, 1968.

Levy, Leonard W., ed. *American Constitutional Law: Historical Essays.* New York: Harper Torchbooks, 1966.

Lewis, Anthony. *Portrait of a Decade: The Second American Revolution.* New York: Random House, 1964.

Lincoln, Abraham. *The Life and Writings of Abraham Lincoln.* Edited by Philip Van Doren Stern. New York: Modern Library, 1940.

Llewellyn, Karl N. *The Bramble Bush.* New York: Oceana Publications, 1960.

———. *Jurisprudence: Realism in Theory and Practice.* Chicago: University of Chicago Press, 1962.

McCloskey, Robert G., ed. *Essays in Constitutional Law.* New York: Alfred A. Knopf, 1957.

MacIver, R. M., ed. *Discrimination and National Welfare.* New York: Harper and Bros., 1949.

Mannheim, Karl. *Ideology and Utopia: An Introduction to the Sociology of Knowledge.* New York: Harcourt, Brace and World, 1936.

Marcuse, Herbert. *One-Dimensional Man: Studies in the Ideology of Advanced Industrial Society.* Boston: Beacon Press, 1969.

Mason, Alpheus Thomas. *Brandeis: Lawyer and Judge in the Modern State.* Princeton, N.J.: Princeton University Press, 1933.

———. *Brandeis: A Free Man's Life.* New York: Viking Press, 1946.

———. *William Howard Taft: Chief Justice.* New York: Simon and Schuster, 1965.

Mason, Alpheus Thomas, and Beaney, William M. *The Supreme Court in a Free Society.* Englewood Cliffs, N.J.: Prentice-Hall, 1959.

Mead, George Herbert. *Mind, Self and Society.* Edited by C. W. Morris. Chicago: University of Chicago Press, 1934.

Miller, Arthur Selwyn. *The Supreme Court and American Capitalism.* New York: Free Press, 1968.

Miller, Charles A. *The Supreme Court and the Uses of History.* Cambridge, Mass.: Belknap Press, 1969.

Miller, Loren. *The Petitioners: The Story of the Supreme Court of the United States and the Negro.* New York: Pantheon Books, 1966.

Miller, Perry, ed. *The Legal Mind in America: From Independence to the Civil War.* Garden City, N.Y.: Doubleday Anchor Books, 1962.

Mills, C. Wright. *The Sociological Imagination.* New York: Oxford University Press, 1968.

Moore, Blaine F. *The Supreme Court and Unconstitutional Legislation.* (*Studies in History, Economics and Public Law,* vol. 54, no. 2.) New York: Longmans, Green, 1913.

Morgenbesser, Sidney, ed. *The Philosophy of Science Today.* New York: Basic Books, 1967.

Muse, Benjamin. *Ten Years of Prelude: The Story of Integration since the Supreme Court's 1954 Decision.* New York: Viking Press, 1964.

Myrdal, Gunnar. *An American Dilemma: The Negro Problem and Modern Democracy.* New York: Harper and Bros., 1944.

Nagel, Ernest. *The Structure of Science: Problems in the Logic of Scientific Explanation.* New York: Harcourt, Brace and World, 1961.

National Consumers' League. *The Supreme Court and Minimum Wage Legislation.* New York: New Republic, Inc., 1925.

Newby, I. A. *Jim Crow's Defense: Anti-Negro Thought in America, 1900–1930.* Baton Rouge: Louisiana State University Press, 1965.

———. *Challenge to the Court: Social Scientists and the Defense of Segregation, 1954–1966.* Baton Rouge: Louisiana State University Press, 1967.

Newcomb, Theodore M., *et al.,* eds. *Readings in Social Psychology.* New York: Henry Holt, 1947.

Nussbaum, Arthur. *Fact Research in Law: Essays on Jurisprudence from the Columbia Law Review.* New York: Columbia University Press, 1963.

Ogburn, William F., and Goldenweiser, Alexander, eds. *The Social Sciences and Their Interrelations.* Boston: Houghton Mifflin, 1927.

Patterson, Edwin W. *Law in a Scientific Age.* New York: Columbia University Press, 1963.

Peckelis, Alexander H. *Law and Social Action: Selected Essays.* Edited by Milton R. Konvitz. Ithaca, N.Y.: Cornell University Press, 1950.

Peltason, J. W. *Fifty-eight Lonely Men: Southern Federal Judges and*

School Desegregation. New York: Harcourt, Brace and World, 1961. Paperback edition, Urbana: University of Illinois Press, 1971.

Pettigrew, Thomas F. *A Profile of the Negro American.* Princeton, N.J.: D. Van Nostrand, 1964.

Post, Charles Gordon. *The Supreme Court and Political Questions.* Baltimore: Johns Hopkins Press, 1936.

Pound, Roscoe. *Justice according to Law.* New Haven, Conn.: Yale University Press, 1951.

———. *An Introduction to the Philosophy of Law.* New Haven, Conn.: Yale University Press, 1961.

Pound, Roscoe, *et al.*, eds. *Perspectives of Law: Essays for Austin Wakeman Scott.* Boston: Little, Brown, 1964.

Powell, Thomas Reed. *The Supreme Court and State Police Power, 1922–1930.* Charlottesville, Va.: Michie Co., 1932.

———. *Vagaries and Varieties in Constitutional Interpretation.* New York: Columbia University Press, 1956.

Ross, Ralph, and van den Haag, Ernest. *The Fabric of Society: An Introduction to the Social Sciences.* New York: Harcourt, Brace, 1957.

Schmidhauser, John R. *The Supreme Court as Final Arbiter in Federal-State Relations.* Chapel Hill: University of North Carolina Press, 1958.

Schwartz, Bernard. *A Commentary on the Constitution of the United States.* 3 vols. New York: Macmillan, 1965.

Scott, Alfred M. *The Supreme Court versus the Constitution.* New York: Exposition Press, 1963.

Shapiro, Martin. *Law and Politics in the Supreme Court.* New York: Free Press, 1964.

Sorel, Georges. *Reflections on Violence.* Translated by T. E. Hulme. New York: Collier Books, 1961.

Sorokin, Pitirim A. *The Crisis of Our Age: The Social and Cultural Outlook.* New York: E. P. Dutton, 1941.

Spencer, Herbert. *The Man versus the State.* Caldwell, Idaho: Caxton Printers, 1946.

Stanton, William. *The Leopard's Spots: Scientific Attitudes toward Race in America, 1815–1859.* Chicago: University of Chicago Press, 1960.

Stone, Julius. *Legal System and Lawyers' Reasonings.* Stanford, Calif.: Stanford University Press, 1964.

———. *Law and the Social Sciences: The Second Half Century.* Minneapolis: University of Minnesota Press, 1966.

———. *Social Dimensions of Law and Justice*. Stanford, Calif.: Stanford University Press, 1966.

Sumner, William Graham. *Essays*. Edited by Albert G. Keller and Maurice R. Davie. 2 vols. New Haven, Conn.: Yale University Press, 1934.

———. *Folkways*. Boston: Ginn and Co., 1940.

Sutherland, Arthur E. *Constitutionalism in America: Origin and Evolution of Its Fundamental Ideas*. New York: Blaisdell Publishing Co., 1965.

Swisher, Carl Brent. *American Constitutional Development*. 2nd rev. ed. Boston: Houghton Mifflin, 1954.

Talmadge, Herman E. *You and Segregation*. Birmingham, Ala.: Vulcan Press, 1955.

Teggert, Frederick J. *Theory and Processes of History*. Berkeley and Los Angeles: University of California Press, 1962.

Ten Broek, Jacobus. *Equal under Law*. New York: Collier Books, 1965.

———, et al. *Prejudice, War and the Constitution*. Berkeley and Los Angeles: University of California Press, 1968.

Tocqueville, Alexis de. *Democracy in America*. Edited by Phillips Bradley. 2 vols. New York: Vintage Books, 1961.

Tumin, Melvin M. *Segregation and Desegregation: A Digest of Recent Research*. New York: Anti-Defamation League of B'nai B'rith, 1957.

Twiss, Benjamin R. *Lawyers and the Constitution: How Laissez-Faire Came to the Supreme Court*. New York: Russell & Russell, 1962.

Van den Haag, Ernest. *Passion and Social Constraint*. New York: Stein and Day, 1963.

Vose, Clement E. *Caucasians Only: The Supreme Court, the NAACP, and the Restrictive Covenant Cases*. Berkeley and Los Angeles: University of California Press, 1959.

Ward, Lester F. *Dynamic Sociology: Or Applied Social Science*. Vol. 1. New York: D. Appleton & Co., 1913.

Warren, Charles. *The Supreme Court in United States History*. 2 vols. Boston: Little, Brown, 1926.

Warren, Earl. *The Public Papers of Chief Justice Earl Warren*. Edited by Henry M. Christman. New York: Capricorn Books, 1966.

Weber, Max. *From Max Weber: Essays in Sociology*. Edited and translated by H. H. Gerth and C. Wright Mills. New York: Oxford University Press, 1958.

Westin, Alan F., ed. *The Supreme Court: Views from Inside*. New York: W. W. Norton, 1961.

Wiener, Philip P. *Evolution and the Founders of Pragmatism.* New York: Harper Torchbooks, 1965.

Witmer, Helen Leland, and Kotinsky, Ruth, eds. *Personality in the Making: The Fact-Finding Report of the Midcentury White House Conference on Children and Youth.* Palo Alto, Calif.: Science and Behavior Books, 1952.

Woodward, C. Vann. *The Strange Career of Jim Crow.* 2nd rev. ed. New York: Oxford University Press, 1966.

Workman, William D. *The Case for the South.* New York: Devin-Adair Co., 1960.

ARTICLES AND ESSAYS

Albertsworth, E. F. "Program of Sociological Jurisprudence." 8 *American Bar Association Journal* 393 (1922).

Anastasi, Anne. "Psychological Research and Educational Desegregation." 35 *Thought* 419 (1960).

Anderson, William. "The Intentions of the Framers: A Note on Constitutional Interpretation." 49 *American Political Science Review* 340 (1955).

Angell, Robert C. "The Value of Sociology to Law." 31 *Michigan Law Review* 512 (1933).

"Appendix to Appellants' Briefs: Statements by Social Scientists (Filed in School Segregation Cases, October Term, 1952)—The Effects of Segregation and the Consequences of Desegregation: A Social Science Statement." 2 *Social Problems* 227 (1955).

Aronson, M. "Tendencies in American Jurisprudence." 4 *Toronto Law Review* 103 (1941).

Barnett, James D. "External Evidence of the Constitutionality of Statutes." 58 *American Law Review* 88 (1924).

Berger, Morroe. "Desegregation, Law, and Social Science." 23 *Commentary* 471 (1957).

Berns, Walter. "Law and Behavioral Science." 28 *Law and Contemporary Problems* 185 (1963).

Bernstein, Barton J. "Plessy v. Ferguson: Conservative Sociological Jurisprudence." 48 *Journal of Negro History* 196 (1963).

Beutel, Frederick K. "Some Implications of Experimental Jurisprudence." 48 *Harvard Law Review* 169 (1934).

Bickel, Alexander M. "The Original Understanding and the Segregation Decision." 69 *Harvard Law Review* 1 (1955).

Bickle, H. W. "Judicial Determination of Questions of Fact Affecting the Constitutional Validity of Legislative Action." 38 *Harvard Law Review* 6 (1924–25).

Bischoff, Ralph F. "One Hundred Years of Court Decisions: Dred Scott after a Century." 6 *Journal of Public Law* 411 (1957).

Black, Charles L. "The Lawfulness of the Segregation Decisions." 64 *Yale Law Journal* 421 (1959–60).

Borinski, Ernst. "A Legal and Sociological Analysis of the Segregation Decision of May 17, 1954." 15 *University of Pittsburgh Law Review* 622 (1954).

Brandeis, Louis D. "The Living Law." 10 *Illinois Law Review* 461 (1916).

Brown, Ray A. "Fact and Law in Judicial Review." 56 *Harvard Law Review* 899 (1943).

Byrnes, James F. "Guns and Bayonets Cannot Promote Education." 41 *U.S. News and World Report* 100 (1956).

———. "The Supreme Court Must Be Curbed." 40 *U.S. News and World Report* 50 (1956).

Cahn, Edmond. "A Dangerous Myth in the School Segregation Cases." 30 *New York University Law Review* 150 (1955).

———. "Jurisprudence." 31 *New York University Law Review* 182 (1956).

———. "The Parchment Barriers." 32 *American Scholar* 21 (1962–63).

Cantor, Nathaniel. "Law and the Social Sciences." 16 *American Bar Association Journal* 385 (1930).

Cardozo, Benjamin N. "A Ministry of Justice." 35 *Harvard Law Review* 113 (1921).

Carter, Robert L. "Legal Background and Significance of the May 17th Decision." 2 *Social Problems* 215 (1955).

Chein, Isidor. "What Are the Psychological Effects of Segregation under Conditions of Equal Facilities?" 3 *International Journal of Opinion and Attitude Resolution* 229 (1949).

Clark, Kenneth B. "Desegregation: An Appraisal of the Evidence." 9 *Journal of Social Issues* 1 (1953).

———. "The Social Scientist as an Expert Witness in Civil Rights Litigation." 1 *Social Problems* 5 (1953).

———. "The Desegregation Cases: Criticism of the Social Scientist's Role." 5 *Villanova Law Review* 224 (1960).

Cohen, Julius. "Factors of Resistance to the Resources of the Behavioral Sciences." 12 *Journal of Legal Education* 67 (1959).

Cook, William W. "Scientific Method and the Law." 13 *American Bar Association Journal* 281 (1927).

Corwin, Edward S. "Reports of the National Conference on the Science of Politics." 18 *American Political Science Review* 148 (1924).

Cowan, Thomas A. "The Relation of Law to Experimental Social Science." 96 *University of Pennsylvania Law Review* 484 (1948).

———. "Law, Morality and Scientific Method: A Review Article." 38 *Nebraska Law Review* 1039 (1959).

Davis, Kenneth Culp. "Judicial Notice." 55 *Columbia Law Review* 945 (1955).

"Declaration of Constitutional Principles." 1 *Race Relations Law Reporter* 435 (1956).

De Lacy, G. L. " 'Segregation Cases' Supreme Court." 38 *Nebraska Law Review* 1017 (1959).

Denman, William. "Comment on Trials of Fact in Constitutional Cases." 21 *American Bar Association Journal* 805 (1935).

Derber, Milton. "What the Lawyer Can Learn from Social Science." 16 *Journal of Legal Education* 145 (1963).

Deutscher, Max, and Chein, Isidor. "The Psychological Effects of Enforced Segregation: A Survey of Social Science Opinion." 26 *Journal of Psychology* 259 (1948).

Doro, Marion E. "The Brandeis Brief." 11 *Vanderbilt Law Review* 783 (1958).

Drake, Joseph H. "The Sociological Interpretation of Law." 16 *Michigan Law Review* 599 (1918).

Ernst, Morris, *et al.* "The Lawyer's Role in Modern Society: A Round Table." 4 *Journal of Public Law* 1 (1955).

Fahr, Samuel M. "Why Lawyers Are Dissatisfied with the Social Sciences." 1 *Washburn Law Journal* 161 (1961).

Fahr, Samuel M., and Ojemann, Ralph H. "The Use of Social and Behavioral Science Knowledge in Law." 48 *Iowa Law Review* 59 (1962–63).

Finkelstein, Michael O. "The Application of Statistical Decision Theory to the Jury Discrimination Cases." 80 *Harvard Law Review* 338 (1966).

Frankfurter, Felix. "Mr. Justice Brandeis and the Constitution." 45 *Harvard Law Review* 68 (1934).

Friendly, Henry J. "The Bill of Rights as a Code of Criminal Procedure." 53 *California Law Review* 929 (1965).

Fuller, Lon L. "An Afterword: Science and the Judicial Process." 79 *Harvard Law Review* 1604 (1965–66).

Garfinkel, Herbert. "Social Science Evidence and the School Segregation Cases." 21 *Journal of Politics* 37 (1959).

Geis, Gilbert. "The Social Sciences and the Law." 1 *Washington Law Journal* 569 (1962).

Gibbs, Jack P. "The Sociology of Law and Normative Phenomena." 31 *American Sociological Review* 315 (1966).

Glueck, Sheldon. "The Social Sciences and Scientific Method in the Administration of Justice." 167 *Annals of the American Academy of Political and Social Science* 106 (1933).

Graham, Howard J. "The 'Conspiracy Theory' of the Fourteenth Amendment." 47 *Yale Law Journal* 371 (1937) and 48 *Yale Law Journal* 171 (1938).

———. "Procedure to Substance: Extra-Judicial Rise of Due Process, 1830–1860." 40 *California Law Review* 483 (1952–53).

Greenbaum, Edward S. "Need for Continuous Study of Law in Action." 287 *Annals of the American Academy of Political and Social Science* 174 (1953).

Greenberg, Jack. "Social Scientists Take the Stand: A Review and Appraisal of Their Testimony in Litigation." 54 *Michigan Law Review* 953 (1956).

Gregor, A. James. "The Law, Social Science, and School Segregation: An Assessment." 14 *Case Western Reserve Law Review* 621 (1963).

Haines, Charles G. "Judicial Review of Acts of Congress." 45 *Yale Law Journal* 816 (1936).

Hamilton, Walton H. "The Path of Due Process of Law." 48 *Ethics* 269 (1938).

Harris, Robert J. "The Constitution, Education, and Segregation." 29 *Temple Law Quarterly* 409 (1956).

Heyman, Ira Michael. "The Chief Justice, Racial Segregation, and the Friendly Critics." 49 *California Law Review* 104 (1961).

Holland, Henry M., Jr. "Cardozo on Legal Method: A Reconsideration." 15 *Journal of Public Law* 122 (1966).

Jaffe, Louis L. "Judicial Review: Question of Fact." 69 *Harvard Law Review* 1020 (1956).

———. "Was Brandeis an Activist? The Search for Intermediate Premises." 80 *Harvard Law Review* 986 (1967).

Jones, Harry W. "The Plain Meaning Rule and Extrinsic Aids in the Interpretation of Federal Statutes." 25 *Washington University Law Quarterly* 2 (1939).

Kadish, Sanford H. "Methodology and Criteria in Due Process Adjudication: A Survey and Criticism." 66 *Yale Law Journal* 319 (1957).

Kales, Albert M. " 'Due Process,' the Articulate Major Premise and the Adamson Act." 26 *Yale Law Journal* 519 (1917).

———. "New Methods in Due Process Cases." 12 *American Political Science Review* 241 (1918).

Kaplan, Abraham. "Behavioral Science and the Law." 19 *Case Western Reserve Law Review* 57 (1967).

Karst, Kenneth L. "Legislative Facts in Constitutional Litigation." In Philip B. Kurland, ed., *The Supreme Court Review*. Chicago: University of Chicago Press, 1960.

Katz, Michael. "The Unmasking of Dishonest Pretensions: Toward an Interpretation of the Role of Social Science in Constitutional Litigation." 6 *American Sociologist* 54 (1971).

Kauper, Paul G. "Segregation in Public Education: The Decline of Plessy v. Ferguson." 52 *Michigan Law Review* 1137 (1954).

Kelly, Alfred H. "Clio and the Court: An Illicit Love Affair." In Philip B. Kurland, ed., *The Supreme Court Review*. Chicago: University of Chicago Press, 1965.

Kendler, Tracy S. "Contributions of the Psychologist to Constitutional Law." 5 *American Psychologist* 505 (1950).

Kohn, Janet G. "Social Psychological Data, Legislative Fact, and Constitutional Law." 29 *George Washington Law Review* 136 (1960).

Korn, Howard L. "Law, Fact, and Science in the Courts." 66 *Columbia Law Review* 1080 (1966).

Kort, Fred. "Quantitative Analysis of Fact-Patterns in Cases and Their Impact on Judicial Decisions." 79 *Harvard Law Review* 1595 (1965–66).

Leflar, Robert A., and Davis, Wylie H. "Segregation in the Public Schools—1953." 67 *Harvard Law Review* 377 (1954).

Lewis, Ovid C. "Parry and Riposte to Gregor's 'The Law, Social Science, and School Segregation': An Assessment." 14 *Western Law Review* 637 (1963).

Linder, Leo J. "Social Responsibility of the Social Scientist and Lawyer." 7 *Lawyer's Law Guild Review* 54 (1957).

Llewellyn, Karl N. "Law and the Social Sciences: Especially Sociology." 62 *Harvard Law Review* 1286 (1955).

Loevinger, Lee. "Law and Science as Rival Systems." 19 *University of Florida Law Review* 530 (1966–67).

Louisell, David W. "The Psychologist in Today's Legal World." 39 *Minnesota Law Review* 235 (1955).

McCary, J. L. "The Psychologist in Court." 33 *Chicago-Kent Law Review* 230 (1955).

McGurk, Frank C. J. " 'Psychological Tests': A Scientist's Report on Race Differences." 49 *U.S. News and World Report* 92 (1956).

——. "The Law, Social Science and Academic Freedom: A Psychologist's View." 5 *Villanova Law Review* 247 (1959–60).

McKay, Robert B. "Social Science, Segregation and the Law." 89 *School and Society* 172 (1961).

McLaughlin, Andrew C. "The Court, the Corporation, and Conkling." 46 *American Historical Review* 45 (1940–41).

McWhinney, Edward. "An End to Racial Discrimination in the United States? The School-Segregation Decisions." 32 *Canadian Bar Review* 545 (1954).

Maguire, John M., and Hahesy, Jefferson E. "Requisite Proof of Basis for Expert Opinion." 5 *Vanderbilt Law Review* 432 (1952).

Malan, G. H. T. "The Behavioristic Basis of the Science of Law." 8 *American Bar Association Journal* 737 (1922).

Marshall, Thurgood. "An Evaluation of Recent Efforts to Achieve Racial Integration in Education through Resort to the Courts." 21 *Journal of Negro Education* 316 (1952).

Maslow, Will. "How Social Scientists Can Shape Legal Process." 5 *Villanova Law Review* 241 (1960).

Morris, Clarence. "Law, Reason and Sociology." 107 *University of Pennsylvania Law Review* 147 (1958).

Murphy, Paul L. "Time to Reclaim: The Current Challenge of American Constitutional History." 69 *American Historical Review* 64 (1963).

Nagel, Stuart S. "Law and the Social Sciences: What Can Social Science Contribute?" 51 *American Bar Association Journal* 356 (1965).

Newland, Chester A. "Innovation in Judicial Techniques: The Brandeis Opinion." 42 *Southwestern Social Science Quarterly* 22 (1961).

Patterson, Edwin W. "Some Reflections on Sociological Jurisprudence." 44 *Virginia Law Review* 395 (1958).

Peckelis, Alexander. "The Case for a Jurisprudence of Welfare." 11 *Social Research* 312 (1944).

Pollack, Louis H. "The Supreme Court under Fire." 6 *Journal of Public Law* 428 (1957).

Pope, Jack. "The Presentation of Scientific Evidence." 31 *Texas Law Review* 794 (1953).

Pound, Roscoe. "Liberty of Contract." 18 *Yale Law Journal* 454 (1909).

―――. "The Call for a Realistic Jurisprudence." 44 *Harvard Law Review* 697 (1930).

―――. "Jurisprudence." In Edwin R. A. Seligman, ed., *The Encyclopaedia of the Social Sciences*. Vol. 7. New York: Macmillan, 1957.

Rafalko, Walter A. "Sociological Evidence as a Criminal Defense." 10 *Criminal Law Quarterly* 77 (1967–68).

Reuter, E. B. "Racial Theory." 50 *American Journal of Sociology* 452 (1945).

Riesman, David. "Some Observations on Law and Psychology." 19 *University of Chicago Law Review* 30 (1951).

Rose, Arnold M. "Sociological Factors in the Effectiveness of Projected Legislative Remedies." 11 *Journal of Legal Education* 470 (1959).

Sanborn, F. B. "Social Science in the Nineteenth Century." 30 *Journal of Social Science* 1 (1892–95).

Schulman, Robert E. "The Psychologist as an Expert Witness." 15 *Kansas Law Review* 88 (1966).

Selznick, Philip. "The Sociology of Law." 12 *Journal of Legal Education* 521 (1960).

―――. "Sociology and Natural Law." 6 *Natural Law Forum* 84 (1961).

Simpson, G. E. "Re-examination of William Graham Sumner on Law and Social Change." 14 *Journal of Legal Education* 299 (1962).

Simpson, Sidney P., and Field, Ruth. "Law and the Social Sciences." 32 *Virginia Law Review* 855 (1946).

Sorenson, Robert C., and Sorenson, Theodore C. "The Admissibility of Opinion Research Evidence." 28 *New York University Law Review* 1213 (1953).

Sutherland, Arthur E., Jr. "The American Judiciary and Racial Segregation." 20 *Modern Law Review* 201 (1957).

"Symposium: Law and Social Science." 5 *Villanova Law Review* 215 (1960).

Ten Broek, Jacobus. "Admissibility and Use by the United States Supreme Court of Extrinsic Aids in Constitutional Construction." 26 *California Law Review* 287 (1938).

Touster, Saul. "Law and Psychology." 5 *American Behavioral Scientist* 3 (1961–62).

Ulmer, S. Sidney. "Earl Warren and the Brown Decision." 33 *Journal of Politics* 689 (1971).

Van den Haag, Ernest. "Social Science Testimony in the Desegregation Cases: A Reply to Professor Kenneth Clark." 6 *Villanova Law Review* 69 (1960).

Vose, Clement E. "The National Consumers' League and the Brandeis Brief." 1 *Midwest Journal of Political Science* 267 (1957).

Waite, Edward F. "Race Segregation in the Public Schools: Jim Crow at the Judgment Seat." 38 *Minnesota Law Review* 612 (1954).

Warren, Charles. "The Progressiveness of the United States Supreme Court." 13 *Columbia Law Review* 294 (1913).

Warren, Earl. "Science and the Law: Change and the Constitution." 12 *Journal of Public Law* 3 (1963).

Weiler, Paul. "Two Models of Judicial Decision-Making." 46 *Canadian Bar Review* 406 (1968).

Wilson, Woodrow. "The Law and the Facts." 5 *American Political Science Review* 1 (1911).

Wofford, John G. "The Blinding Light: The Uses of History in Constitutional Interpretation." 31 *University of Chicago Law Review* 502 (1963–64).

Woodard, Calvin. "Reality and Social Reform: The Transition from Laissez-Faire to the Welfare State." 72 *Yale Law Journal* 286 (1962).

Woodward, Julian L. "A Scientific Attempt to Provide Evidence for a Decision on Change of Venue." 17 *American Sociological Review* 447 (1952).

Wormuth, Francis D. "Learned Legerdemain: A Grave but Implausible Hand." 6 *Western Political Quarterly* 543 (1953).

———. "The Impact of Economic Legislation upon the Supreme Court." 6 *Journal of Public Law* 296 (1957).

Wyzanski, Charles E., Jr. "A Trial Judge's Freedom and Responsibility." 65 *Harvard Law Review* 1281 (1952).

———. "History and Law." 26 *University of Chicago Law Review* 237 (1958–59).

Ziskind, David. "The Use of Economic Data in Labor Cases." 6 *University of Chicago Law Review* 607 (1939).

LAW REVIEW NOTES AND COMMENTS

"The Consideration of Facts in 'Due Process' Cases." 30 *Columbia Law Review* 360 (1930).

"Grade School Segregation: The Latest Attack on Racial Discrimination." 61 *Yale Law Journal* 730 (1952).

"The Presumption of Constitutionality Reconsidered." 36 *Columbia Law Review* 283 (1936).

"The Presentation of Facts Underlying the Constitutionality of Statutes." 49 *Harvard Law Review* 631 (1936).

"Public Opinion Surveys as Evidence: The Pollsters Go to Court." 66 *Harvard Law Review* 498 (1953).

" 'Separate-but-Equal': A Study of the Career of a Constitutional Concept." 1 *Race Relations Law Reporter* 283 (1956).

"Social and Economic Facts: Appraisal of Suggested Techniques for Presenting Them to the Courts." 61 *Harvard Law Review* 692 (1948).

PUBLIC DOCUMENTS

Brandeis, Louis D. Brief for defendant in error, submitted in Muller v. Oregon, 208 U.S. 412 (1908).

Eastland, James O. "Remarks on School Integration Cases in the United States Supreme Court." 101 *Congressional Record—Senate* 7119 (1955).

Kelly, Alfred H. "An Inside View of Brown v. Board." 108 *Congressional Record—Senate* 17931 (1962).

Thurmond, Strom. "Remarks." 108 *Congressional Record—Senate* 17930 (1962).

Table of Cases

Chicago, Milwaukee & St. Paul R.R. v. Minn., 134 U.S. 418 (1890).
Civil Rights Cases, 109 U.S. 3 (1883).
Colegrove v. Green, 328 U.S. 549 (1946).
Coleman v. Miller, 307 U.S. 433 (1939).
Communist Party v. Control Board, 367 U.S. 1 (1961).
Connecticut General Life Insurance Co. v. Johnson, 303 U.S. 77 (1938).
Consolidated Edison Co. v. N.L.R.B., 304 U.S. 555 (1939).
Coppage v. Kansas, 236 U.S. 1 (1915).
Coronado Coal Co. v. United Mine Workers, 268 U.S. 295 (1925).
Cumming v. Board of Education, 175 U.S. 528 (1899).
Davis v. County School Board of Prince Edward County, 103 F. Supp. 337 (1952).
Dennis v. United States, 341 U.S. 494 (1951).
Dick v. New York Life Insurance Co., 359 U.S. 437 (1959).
Dred Scott v. Sandford, 19 Howard 393 (1857).
DuBois Clubs v. Clark, 389 U.S. 309 (1967).
Edison Co. v. Labor Board, 305 U.S. 197 (1938).
Elwell v. Fosdick, 134 U.S. 500 (1890).
Escobedo v. Illinois, 378 U.S. 478 (1964).
Federal Power Commission v. Hope Natural Gas Co., 320 U.S. 591 (1944).
Ferguson v. Moore-McCormack Lines, 352 U.S. 521 (1957).
Ferguson v. Skrupa, 372 U.S. 726 (1963).
Fisher v. Hurst, 333 U.S. 147 (1948).
Gebhart v. Belton, 91 A. 2d 137 (1952).
Gibson v. Florida Legislative Committee, 372 U.S. 539 (1963).
Gideon v. Wainwright, 372 U.S. 335 (1963).
Ginzburg v. United States, 383 U.S. 463 (1966).
Gong Lum v. Rice, 275 U.S. 78 (1927).
Gorham Co. v. White, 14 Wallace 511 (1872).
Hairston v. Danville & Western Railway Co., 208 U.S. 598 (1908).
Haley v. Ohio, 332 U.S. 596 (1948).
Hammond v. Schappi Bus Line, 275 U.S. 164 (1927).
Harper v. Virginia State Board of Elections, 383 U.S. 663 (1966).
Hawley v. Walker, 232 U.S. 718 (1914).
Head v. New Mexico Board, 374 U.S. 424 (1963).
Holcombe v. Beal, 347 U.S. 974 (1954).
Holden v. Hardy, 169 U.S. 366 (1898).
Home Building & Loan Association v. Blaisdell, 290 U.S. 398 (1934).
Housing Authority v. Banks, 347 U.S. 974 (1954).
Jacobson v. Massachusetts, 197 U.S. 11 (1905).

Robinson v. California, 370 U.S. 660 (1962).

Roth v. United States, 354 U.S. 476 (1957).

St. Joseph Stock Yards Co. v. United States, 298 U.S. 38 (1936).

San Mateo v. Southern Pacific Railway Co., 116 U.S. 138 (1885).

Santa Clara County v. Southern Pacific Railroad Co., 118 U.S. 394 (1886).

Santa Cruz Fruit Packing Co. v. N.L.R.B., 303 U.S. 453 (1938).

Schechter Corp. v. United States, 295 U.S. 495 (1935).

Schollenberger v. Pennsylvania, 171 U.S. 1 (1898).

Senn v. Tile Layers Protective Union, 301 U.S. 468 (1937).

Shelley v. Kraemer, 334 U.S. 1 (1948).

Sipuel v. Oklahoma, 332 U.S. 631 (1948).

Slaughterhouse Cases, 16 Wallace 36 (1873).

Smyth v. Ames, 169 U.S. 466 (1898).

South Carolina v. United States, 199 U.S. 437 (1905).

Stainback v. Mo Hock Ke Lok Po, 336 U.S. 368 (1949).

Stanley v. Georgia, 394 U.S. 557 (1969).

Stettler v. O'Hara, 243 U.S. 629 (1917).

Steward Machine Co. v. Davis, 301 U.S. 548 (1937).

Stewart Dry Goods Co. v. Lewis, 294 U.S. 550 (1935).

Strauder v. West Virginia, 100 U.S. 303 (1880).

Sturges v. Crowninshield, 4 Wheaton 122 (1819).

Sweatt v. Painter, 339 U.S. 629 (1950).

Tanner v. Little, 240 U.S. 369 (1916).

Thomas v. Collins, 323 U.S. 516 (1945).

Truax v. Corrigan, 257 U.S. 312 (1921).

United States v. Butler, 297 U.S. 1 (1936).

United States v. Carolene Products Co., 304 U.S. 144 (1938).

United States v. Sprague, 282 U.S. 716 (1931).

Virginia, Ex Parte, 100 U.S. 339 (1880).

Ware v. Hylton, 3 Dallas 199 (1796).

Washington Va. and Maryland Coach Co. v. N.L.R.B., 301 U.S. 142 (1937).

West Coast Hotel Co. v. Parrish, 300 U.S. 379 (1937).

Wickard v. Filburn, 317 U.S. 111 (1942).

Wilson v. Standefer, 184 U.S. 399 (1902).

Wolff Packing House Co. v. Court of Industrial Relations, 262 U.S. 522 (1923).

Wright v. Rockefeller, 376 U.S. 52 (1964).

Wynehamer v. New York, 13 N.Y. 378 (1856).

Index